O9-BHI-668

THE HAPPY COOK

125 RECIPES FOR EATING EVERY DAY LIKE IT'S THE WEEKEND

DAPHNE OZ

PHOTOGRAPHS BY AMY NEUNSINGER

wm.

WILLIAM MORROW

An Imprint of HarperCollins*Publishers*

ALSO BY DAPHNE OZ

Relish: An Adventure in Food, Style, and Everyday Fun

The Dorm Room Diet

HarperCollins books may be purchased for educational, business, or sales promotional use. For information please e-mail the Special Markets Department at SPsales@harpercollins.com.

FIRST EDITION

Designed by Suet Yee Chong
Photographs by Amy Neunsinger

Library of Congress Cataloging-in-Publication Data has been applied for.

ISBN 978-0-06-242690-1

16 17 18 19 20 INDD/QGT 10 9 8 7 6 5 4 3 2 1

for mommy and grandmommy,

the original happy cooks, around whose dinner tables
I will always be in paradise

CONTENTS

INTRODUCTION

becoming a happy cook

For me, cooking has always been a celebration, from start to glorious, edible finish. I'm the girl who *loves* to grocery shop. Euphoria is the bounty of a late summer farmers' market. I see nothing wrong with planning vacations around meals I want to eat, plotting lunch at breakfast and dinner at lunch. The level of joy I get from something as simple as the perfect slice of pizza is right up there with the way "normal" people feel when their team wins the Super Bowl. I'm as excited by Michelin stars as I am by locals-only dives, because this mouth of mine will never tire of talking about and tasting and chasing and exploring and loving wonderful food.

I grew up around a dinner table that at the holidays included nearly thirty immediate family members, a perpetually hungry and boisterous crowd who rarely left the kitchen. It was our therapy center, the rec room, the stage, the ring, and the only place I ever wanted to be.

When I brought my husband, John, home to meet everyone a few months into dating, he may have had a moment of pause when he saw there was no limit to the amount of excitement we could generate over a humble but impeccably balanced egg sandwich. But he came to appreciate that celebrating with food was not an occasional thing for our clan—it was a daily necessity, a way of life. And luckily, he decided he wanted in.

Now, we get to slurp ramen together at our favorite neighborhood haunt, picnic with a hodgepodge assortment of edible loot, have date night with our version of a memorable pasta from an Italian adventure, and nosh on leftovers for a midnight snack—and teach our kids to do the same!

This is all to say that a bad meal depresses me. Every meal is a chance to bond with the people I love over plates worth remembering. And with so many delicious things to try, I refuse to waste even one bite on food that is only fuel and no fun.

I've been to culinary school and studied integrative nutrition, but my approach to food is as a jubilant eater, first and forever. My culinary education began at my mother's elbow at the stove. Both she and my grandmother are wild cooks, throwing a splash of this and a dash of that into pots and pans, turning out delicious dishes full of heart and flavor. Yes, they had to feed a crowd, but they made cooking exciting and personal, a liberty rather than a chore.

They taught me that a happy cook is casual and confident. Her meals are flavorful, unfussy, and often improvised. If she gets lost in conversation and the pasta sauce is forgotten and burns, she's at the ready with a simple blend of garlic, olive oil, and chile flakes. The happy cook recognizes that necessity is the mother of invention, and that the best meals may rise from the ashes of a few memorable mishaps.

And that's still how I think about the best home cooking—there's no point in creating a meal whose process is so rigid that it robs the cook of all the fun and freedom this time should represent. To be a happy cook is to make your kitchen your own.

That's where this book comes in. When I wrote my last book, *Relish: An Adventure in Food, Style, and Everyday Fun,* my focus was on finding easy ways to do little things a little bit better across my entire life, from my home to my wardrobe, from my relationships to my career, and beyond. Of course, this journey started with food. Life had gotten cluttered and busy, and I found the easiest place to start to take it back and elevate it was by making simple improvements to my meals in ways that made them everyday celebrations. With the goal of maximizing every moment on the path to happiness, food paved the way for the rest of the process to flow.

After *Relish* came out, I discovered my readers felt the same way. I heard from newly minted hostesses who scrapped overwrought, stressful meals in favor of sangria and a bowl of chili for easy gatherings; gents who had never cooked before who now had a signature dish; moms who had been relying on the same menu plan week after week and were spicing it up with great results; even grandmas who thought they wouldn't like a new recipe they saw, gave it a spin anyway, and now get requests for it from family and friends. The thing I heard most often from these readers? "Cooking makes me happy." I couldn't agree more.

That simple sentence got me thinking: Cooking at home can feel overwhelming, or obligatory, or routine, or make us nervous when the kitchen should be the place we feel most empowered to make the choices we want, experiment, and live on the edge—what's the worst that can happen? I think our problem is all in the framing—we see cooking as a duty to be mastered, rather than seeing it as something to be enjoyed

JASMINE TEA
VIKING

along the way, with a delicious reward at the end. *The Happy Cook* is as much about sharing my favorite everyday celebration meals with you as it is about giving you license to personalize and discover your own.

Part of this personalization involves taking the time to develop a way of eating and cooking that makes us feel good, inside and out. People constantly ask me, "But what do you *really* eat?" They know I have this connection to health—Dr. Oz for a dad will do that to you!—and that I care passionately about the quality of what goes into my body, especially now that I'm also feeding little mouths. I used practical healthy eating strategies to lose forty pounds in college, and have kept it off for the last decade (two fifty-pound weight-gain pregnancies notwithstanding). But they also know that I categorically refuse to eat food that isn't delicious. I'm not looking to outlaw every last drizzle of oil, pat of butter, sprinkle of salt, or spoon of sugar. I don't count calories or grams or ounces with my food. But I still want to feel strong in my skin and look good in my clothes—so how does that work?

The compromise for me has always been to take the healthy essentials—fresh fruits and veggies, lean proteins, a selection of grains and beans and seeds—and flavor them with just enough of the decadent indulgences we all crave to make them crave-worthy in themselves. This is how I eat healthy—but even more, it's how I eat happy.

These days, I cook in a wild, wonderful kitchen. I have visions of slinking around the kitchen in a silky dress, licking spatulas of frosting and swooning over the perfect crown roast, doing my ultimate domestic goddess act. But most days, I'm cooking in an old T-shirt and sweatpants with *maybe* an apron to catch some of the spills, tripping over toys, and rushing to get something on the table. It's the domestic godd*ish* version, and it is sometimes chaos, but it is always fun! And the food is just as delicious.

My taste buds crave new flavors, so I mix up classics, tweak one thing, and change a whole dish. I try to keep things uncomplicated. More often than not, my meals are simple, fast, and impromptu—as in, let me see what's in the fridge and make something that tastes good to use all the stuff I forgot I'd bought that's about to turn. Like the breakfast I made this past weekend because everyone was hungry and all we had were eggs, goat cheese on the verge of expiration, half an onion, and my daughter's frozen broccoli and spinach. Sauté the onions, quickly defrost the veggies in the microwave, then chop them up and toss them into the pan with the onions and some herbs and salt. Beat a few eggs and pour over your vegetable mix, before finishing with a few dollops of goat cheese and some tapenade I just found in the pantry. Into a 350°F oven until set, and suddenly you have a fancy frittata!

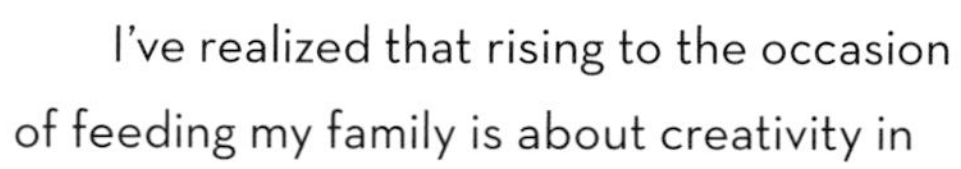

I've realized that rising to the occasion of feeding my family is about creativity in

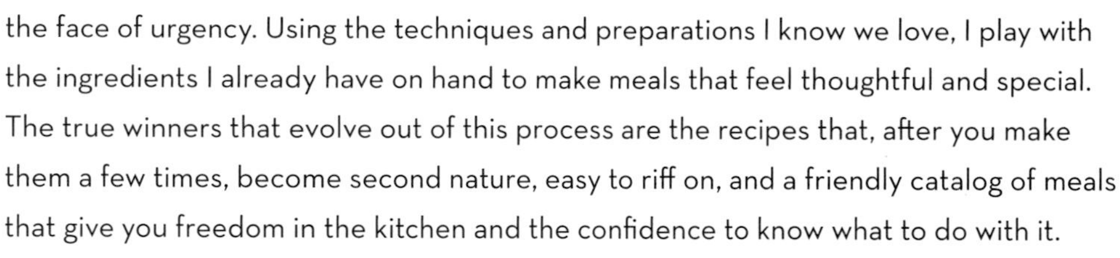

the face of urgency. Using the techniques and preparations I know we love, I play with the ingredients I already have on hand to make meals that feel thoughtful and special. The true winners that evolve out of this process are the recipes that, after you make them a few times, become second nature, easy to riff on, and a friendly catalog of meals that give you freedom in the kitchen and the confidence to know what to do with it.

This book is a compendium of the real-life balancing act that goes on in my home, and the recipes that I make and eat with my husband and kids on a daily basis. It's not all healthy, and it's not all bad. This is the food I crave, the food I thrive on, and the food that's the most fun for me to make. You'll see it's a mix of some healthy favorites, some recipes I've adjusted to make a little healthier or easier (or ideally both!) than they normally would be, and then some straight-up, go-for-gold indulgences that are worth every bite . . . and every little crumb on the plate, too.

I've included a variety of dishes for the variety of lives I lead throughout the week—and I imagine you do, too. There are weeknight wonders that get dinner on the table fast when you've got bath times and bedtimes to get to (or a quiet night in with Netflix and wine, the dream!). There are comfort classics worth waiting a little longer for on the weekends, and maybe inviting a few friends over to share the fruits of your labor. Some recipes may be totally new to you—things that I grew up making that play with my Turkish or Italian heritage, or a favorite restaurant meal I've tried to re-create at home.

These are the dishes I love to eat and love to make, which is why I return to them over and over again.

There are some things I do to make it a little easier on myself. I make an effort to keep healthy ingredients on hand so that even in my desperate moments when I've got zero brainpower to devote to creating a magnificent meal, the "easy" choice is also a healthy one. I'm a lot more likely to entertain if it doesn't require five hours in the kitchen, and you'll see that most of my "fancier" dishes remain relatively simple, or at least require only small amounts of active cooking. I've also tried to limit the ingredients to mainly the items that you'll already have in your fridge and pantry or can be found at your local supermarket, and I've included tons of substitution suggestions and variations so that, if you don't have a particular item, you can just swap it out for something you do have. The few specialty items I like to use are easy to find online, but I'm a big fan of making my own easy flavor boosters—compound butters, pestos, gremolatas, herbed or spiced oils—and I'll share these with you, too, so a star meal is always only a spoonful or drizzle away.

Being happy in the kitchen is more than anything about being easy on yourself. My goal for you is that your kitchen will become your kingdom. I want you to celebrate every meal, with food that's artfully simple, inviting, comforting, memorable, and more than the sum of its parts. I want you to entertain brilliantly, with confidence and casualness and a healthy dose of whimsy. When you're cooking with and feeding your family and friends, I want them to see your joy and pleasure in the process. I want you to be the happiest cook, and I think that's something well worth toasting.

Cheers!

xx D

THE NEW YORK TIMES BOOK REVIEW 15

breakfast and brunch

Whether you're rushing out the door to a morning meeting or coaxing the most out of a lazy weekend lie-in, breakfast and brunch should be a bright spot on the agenda. And there's no better place than the first meal of the day to prove that healthy does not have to be hard.

A sprinkle of indulgence that takes an otherwise healthy meal to next-level deliciousness is always a good choice in my book. Why? Because nothing sends me running back to the kitchen to graze my way through a whole second meal faster than eating a first one that is bland and unsatisfying.

The way to make consistently good choices is to make them ones I actually *want* to make. In this chapter, you'll find quick recipes for easy weekday wonders, so you can finally put away the fiber cereal and skim milk for good in favor of Warrior Waffles packed with protein, Chocolate-Almond Breakfast Bars loaded with chia and flax seeds, or 10-Minute Breakfast Tacos with lean beans, avocado, and fresh salsa.

And if sticky-sweet carbs or smoky-salty bacon are in order, savor a stack of Coconut-Mango Pancakes, indulge in Shirred Eggs with Bacon and Kale, or relish the simple pleasure of a warm slice of Oatmeal Banana Nut Bread with a pat of salted butter melting on top. It's the most important meal of the day, so let's make it a great one.

OATMEAL BANANA NUT BREAD

I'll admit to a total fascination with banana bread. I grew up making many different versions with my mom—with yogurt or sour cream, with or without chocolate chips, with pecans instead of walnuts, using different flours and different fats—because we always had overripe bananas around. With all our experimenting, we reached the happy conclusion that there's no such thing as "bad" banana bread (unless you put artificial banana flavor in it, and then *nothing* can save you).

To me, a warm slice slathered with soft butter and sprinkled with sea salt is just about as comforting as it gets. This recipe was my chance to get what I love without feeling guilty about it. My version is a truly decadent feat of caramelized-banana-and-brown-sugar goodness. But it just also happens to be packed with rolled oats and whole wheat flour, which I find makes it slightly more dense, moist, and cake-like . . . not exactly a bad thing.

MAKES 1 LOAF

1 cup plus 2 tablespoons walnut or pecan pieces (toasted, optional)

2/3 cup rolled oats

6 tablespoons (3/4 stick) unsalted butter, melted, plus 1/2 tablespoon at room temperature for greasing the pan

1 cup whole wheat flour

1 1/4 teaspoons baking powder

1/2 teaspoon baking soda

1 teaspoon kosher salt

3 very ripe (preferably black) bananas

1/2 cup packed light brown sugar

2 large eggs

1/2 cup Greek yogurt

1 teaspoon pure vanilla extract

If toasting the nuts, preheat the oven to 350°F. Place the nuts on a rimmed baking sheet and toast for 8 to 10 minutes, shaking the pan at the halfway point. Leave the oven on and reduce the oven temperature to 325°F.

Transfer half the nuts to a cutting board to cool, then chop them into small pieces. If not toasting, simply chop half of the nuts into small pieces.

Place the remaining nuts in a food processor, add the oats, and pulverize until very fine. Empty into a medium bowl and reassemble the food processor.

Lightly coat an 8 1/2- to 9-inch loaf pan with half of the softened butter. Line the loaf pan lengthwise with a strip of parchment paper and another one crosswise to create a sling. Leave yourself a few inches of overhang on all sides. Use the remaining softened butter to grease the parchment. It might seem like overkill, but this will make removing a perfectly formed loaf a breeze.

Add the whole wheat flour, baking powder, baking soda, and salt to the oat mixture and whisk together.

In the food processor, combine the bananas, brown sugar, eggs, Greek yogurt, vanilla, and melted butter until smooth. Add the wet mix to the flour mixture and stir gently until just incorporated. Fold in the chopped nuts.

Transfer the batter to the prepared loaf pan and spread it out evenly. Bake the loaf until a cake tester inserted into the center comes out lightly damp and flecked with crumbs, 55 to 65 minutes.

Remove the bread from the oven and let cool completely in the pan, then use the parchment overhang to lift the loaf out of the pan. Remove the parchment, then slice and serve.

TOASTING NUTS

Toasting nuts is rarely essential to a recipe, but it is one of those moments when a small investment of extra time at the beginning yields majorly delicious results. That said, the difference between sweet, delicately roasted nuts and burned, bitter pellets of doom is roughly 15 seconds, so watch them closely!

I like to roast whole nuts in the oven, because this method gets more evenly roasted results as opposed to the scorching that happens so easily in a skillet. Pine nuts are the exception: put them in a cold, dry skillet and warm over medium heat until they are faintly golden brown, shaking the pan regularly to redistribute. Otherwise, the following guide will get you great results.

Preheat the oven to 350°F for all nuts, except hazelnuts, which should roast at 275°F. Place the nuts on a rimmed baking sheet and toast until sweetly fragrant, shaking the pan every 5 minutes (suggested times are below). If desired, toss with some olive oil (or specific nut oil) and a sprinkle of salt before roasting. See toasting times below:

PECANS/WALNUTS: 8 to 10 minutes
CASHEWS: 10 to 12 minutes
ALMONDS: 12 to 15 minutes
PEANUTS: 15 to 20 minutes
HAZELNUTS: 15 to 20 minutes at 275°F

Remove the baking sheet from the oven and let cool slightly before chopping nuts, if desired. For skin-on hazelnuts, remove the skins by wrapping them in a kitchen towel after toasting and rubbing them between your fingers.

COCOA GRAIN-NO-LA

One thing I totally embraced from the Paleo craze was the idea of grainless granola. Instead of being about crispy, crunchy oats, this blend is all about the substance and flavor of a variety of nuts and coconut. I love having a little bag with me in my purse for easy travel snacking, and it's an incredible dose of protein and healthy fat—both great for lasting energy. My favorite version at the moment is this chocolatey confection—it tastes kind of like healthier Almond Joys.

MAKES ABOUT 5½ CUPS

¾ cup unsweetened shredded coconut

1 cup sliced almonds

¾ cup roughly chopped walnuts

¾ cup roughly chopped cashews or pecans (or a combination)

½ cup pumpkin seeds (pepitas)

¼ cup chia seeds

1 tablespoon unsweetened cocoa powder

½ cup pure maple syrup

¼ cup grapeseed, coconut, or extra-virgin olive oil

1½ cups mixed dried fruit (optional), such as pitted and chopped dates, chopped dried apples, chopped dried apricots, cherries, cranberries, currants, or raisins

Flaky sea salt

Preheat the oven to 300°F. Line a rimmed baking sheet with parchment paper.

In a large bowl, combine the coconut, almonds, cashews, walnuts and/or pecans, pumpkin seeds, chia seeds, cocoa, maple syrup, and oil and stir until well combined and evenly coated. Turn the mixture out onto the prepared baking sheet, spreading it out evenly.

Bake for 30 minutes, stirring halfway through. Stir in the dried fruit (if using) and bake until the mixture looks dry, 6 to 10 minutes longer. Sprinkle with a few pinches of flaky salt, let cool completely, and pack it into a mason jar or airtight container. It will keep for several weeks if stored in a cool, dry spot.

VARIATION: *Use 1 teaspoon ground ginger and a pinch of chile flakes in place of the cocoa, then add the grated zest of 2 limes when the baking is done for a crazy Thai flavor explosion.*

CRISPY-CRUNCHY HONEY-THYME GRANOLA

I was blown away the first time I tried granola that was a bit savory. Most granola is so predictable with its dried fruit and cloying sweetness that it can be, well, kind of granola. But the vibrant flavor of fresh thyme massaged all over rolled oats, nuts, and seeds, coated with butter and honey and a generous pinch of flaky sea salt to finish, totally changed the way my family does breakfast. Sprinkled over yogurt with whatever cut-up fresh or stewed fruit we have on hand, this granola makes weekday mornings feel anything but ordinary.

MAKES ABOUT 6 CUPS

2½ cups rolled oats

½ cup salted roasted sunflower seeds

2 cups mixed chopped raw nuts: walnuts, cashews, almonds, hazelnuts, pecans, or pistachios

½ cup sesame seeds

Scant ½ cup extra-virgin olive oil

¼ cup fresh thyme leaves

½ cup honey

1 teaspoon pure vanilla extract

1 teaspoon kosher salt

Flaky sea salt

Preheat the oven to 300°F. Line a rimmed baking sheet with parchment paper.

In a large bowl, mix together the oats, sunflower seeds, nuts, and sesame seeds. Set aside.

In a medium skillet, combine the olive oil and thyme and cook over medium-high heat, swirling often, until the thyme is fragrant, about 3 minutes. The thyme may fry and spit a little, which is fine. Remove from the heat and let the thyme oil cool and infuse, at least 10 minutes. Swirl the honey, vanilla, and kosher salt into the thyme oil.

Pour the honey-thyme oil over the oat mixture and stir to combine. Turn the mixture out onto the prepared baking sheet, spreading it out as evenly as possible.

Bake the granola, stirring every 10 minutes, until it is crisp and golden brown, about 45 minutes. Sprinkle it with a few pinches of flaky salt and let it cool completely, then pack into mason jars or other airtight containers. The granola will keep for several weeks if stored in a cool, dry spot.

SHIRRED EGGS WITH BACON AND KALE

Shirred eggs are essentially the easiest fancy eggs around. Forget frying or scrambling: These babies are bathed in a splash of cream and a sprinkle of cheese as they bake to perfection. The result is gently cooked, never-dry whites surrounding a golden yolk that should be left slightly molten and oozy, all the better for mopping up with buttered toast.

This particular recipe is one of my favorite examples of the trade-offs we make to be able to eat happy and healthy. On the one hand, each serving gets the lactic love mentioned above—and some bacon. (Yes, real bacon.) On the other, we'll also be cramming in 6 cups of kale. The delicious result begs the question: Why choose?

Last thing: this recipe can be made in individual portion 4-inch ramekins, skillets, or just about any oven-safe dish. If you want to make it family style (a great brunch option), try a 2-quart baking dish. No need to overcrowd the eggs—it's nice to give them a little room to spread out and see lacy pieces of kale peeking out underneath. Also, the recipe is portioned for 1 egg per person, but you could just as easily make it 2 (or more) if you're in the mood.

MAKES 4 SERVINGS

3 bacon strips

1/4 teaspoon smoked paprika

2 tablespoons extra-virgin olive oil

1 medium shallot, finely chopped

1 teaspoon finely chopped fresh thyme

1 teaspoon finely chopped fresh oregano

2 bunches Tuscan (lacinato) kale, washed, dried, ribs removed, and leaves thinly sliced (about 6 cups)

1 teaspoon kosher salt

4 large eggs

1/4 cup heavy cream

1/4 cup finely grated Parmigiano-Reggiano cheese

3 slices sourdough or whole wheat bread

Flaky sea salt

Preheat the oven to 350°F.

Heat a large skillet over medium heat. Add the bacon and cook, stirring often, until the bacon is crisp and browned, 4 to 5 minutes. Add the smoked paprika, cook 15 seconds longer, then remove from the heat. Use a slotted spoon to transfer the bacon to a plate and set aside (don't line the plate with a paper towel—you want to save all that delicious bacon fat!).

Return the skillet to the stove. If there isn't much fat in the skillet, add 1 tablespoon of the olive oil along with any drippings you've collected on the plate with the cooling bacon. Add the shallot and fresh herbs and cook, stirring often, until the shallot is soft, 3 to 4 minutes. Add the kale and kosher salt and cook, stirring often, until the kale wilts and is tender, 2 to 3 minutes. Remove from the heat.

Set four 4-inch ramekins on a rimmed baking sheet. Use the remaining olive oil to grease the ramekins, rubbing it all over the insides. Divide the kale among the ramekins. Crack an egg into each ramekin, then pour 1 tablespoon of cream over each serving and sprinkle with 1 tablespoon of the Parmigiano. Bake until the whites are nearly set and the yolks are cooked to your desired degree of doneness, 10 to 12 minutes.

Meanwhile, roughly chop the bacon and toast the bread. Slice the bread in half or into 1-inch-wide strips, often called "soldiers," which are even better than halves for dunking into swimming pools of creamy eggs.

When the eggs are finished, remove from the oven and sprinkle the bacon and some flaky sea salt over the top. Serve immediately with the toast.

TIP: *The eggs will continue cooking even after you remove them from the oven, so make sure you don't overcook and dig in right away!*

CITRUS-BROWN SUGAR BUTTER

When it comes to easy, at-home cooking, a lot of keeping my active cook time to a minimum comes down to relying on a set of delicious flavor boosters I always have on hand. I'm a big fan of making my own infused oils, tapenades, pestos, chimichurris, and gremolatas because they quickly add a ton of flavor to everything from fish and meat to rice, lentils, and even salad dressings. And compound butter is my flavor genie because it happily goes sweet or savory. I love this version packed with thyme, a little citrus, and just a hint of brown sugar on top of breakfast pastries or waffles, or massaged under chicken skin for an incredibly decadent bird.

MAKES 8 OUNCES

- 2 sticks (8 ounces) unsalted butter, at room temperature
- 3 tablespoons light brown sugar
- 1 teaspoon kosher salt
- Zest of 2 lemons
- Zest of 1 orange
- 1 teaspoon crushed red chile flakes (optional)
- Leaves from 3 fresh thyme sprigs

In a stand mixer fitted with the paddle attachment (or a large bowl if using a hand mixer), blend the butter, brown sugar, salt, lemon zest, orange zest, chile flakes (if using), and thyme, scraping down the sides of the bowl occasionally, until the butter mixture is well combined and smooth.

Use immediately (though making it a day in advance will give the flavors time to marry) or transfer to a sheet of parchment paper and roll into a 12-inch log. Store in the fridge for up to 3 days or freeze in a resealable freezer bag for up to 3 months. You can slice off rounds from the frozen logs as needed for recipes—a knife soaked in hot water works great for this. Simply cover the exposed end with more parchment paper before returning to the freezer bag.

TIP: *You can portion the butter into a couple of smaller logs wrapped in parchment paper, wax paper, or plastic wrap. Leave one in the fridge for easier everyday use and throw the others in the freezer for later.*

CHOCOLATE-ALMOND BREAKFAST BARS

I first discovered the beauty of blending chia seeds and chocolate on a trip out to LA to see family. My aunt Sonya had baked "cookies" for her kids for a weekend breakfast treat—she has four boys under eight—and they were gobbling the things up. I tried one and immediately understood why. Imagine: warm, gooey cookie dough, chocolate melting through the center. This is what you get from the insanely easy combination of just four ingredients: almond butter, coconut oil, chocolate chips, and chia seeds. I ate five. Fine, ten. And then I immediately went home and started working on the adult version. Slightly more filling, a touch salty to mellow the sweet, these can be eaten like a protein bar, with no guilt or artificial anything. Behold...

MAKES 12 BARS

Flaky sea salt
1/4 cup chia seeds
1/4 cup flaxmeal
1/2 cup chocolate chips (preferably bittersweet)
1/2 cup almond flour
1 1/4 cups quick-cooking oats (not instant)
1/4 cup sesame seeds
1/2 cup almond butter
1/4 cup honey
1/4 cup coconut oil
1/2 teaspoon kosher salt

Preheat the oven to 350°F. Line an 8- or 9-inch square pan with 2 sheets of parchment paper to make a sling, leaving a couple of inches of overhang on all sides so you can easily lift out the cooled bars. Sprinkle a pinch of flaky sea salt over the parchment paper (trust me).

In a large bowl, combine the chia seeds and flaxmeal and whisk in 1/2 cup room-temperature water. Set aside until the mixture creates a gel, about 4 minutes. Stir in the chocolate chips and almond flour.

In a large skillet, toast the oats over medium heat, shaking the pan often, until fragrant, 4 to 5 minutes. Add to the chia mixture. Add the sesame seeds to the skillet and shake pan to toast until evenly golden, 1 to 2 minutes. Add them to the bowl with the chia mixture and stir to combine.

Add the almond butter, honey, coconut oil, and kosher salt to the skillet and cook, stirring often, until the mixture comes to a simmer, about 2 minutes. Pour over the oat mixture and stir and mash to combine.

Transfer the mixture to the prepared baking pan and use the bottom of a cup to press the mixture into the pan, making a firm, even layer.

Bake for 20 to 25 minutes, until the bars are fudgy but firm enough to handle. Remove from the oven and immediately score the dough; leave in the pan to cool. Lift the bars out of the pan, break them apart, and enjoy, or store in an airtight container for up to 3 days.

TIP: *Make your own flaxmeal by grinding flaxseeds to a fine powder in a spice mill or coffee grinder.*

VEGAN VEGGIE LOVE MUFFINS

Go with me here. These little gems came in especially handy when I was pregnant with my son and had a rough time looking sideways at a vegetable throughout my first trimester. The delicious carrots and yellow beets in this mix could easily be swapped with other naturally sweet veggies like grated sweet potatoes, regular beets, even butternut squash or pumpkin.

MAKES 12 MUFFINS

- **1/4 cup coconut oil, melted, plus extra for greasing the pan**
- **1 medium Granny Smith apple, peeled, cored, and roughly chopped**
- **2 medium carrots, peeled and roughly chopped**
- **1 medium yellow beet (about 4 ounces), peeled and roughly chopped**
- **Zest of 1 lemon plus 2 tablespoons lemon juice**
- **3/4 cup coconut milk**
- **1/3 cup pure maple syrup**
- **2 tablespoons grated fresh ginger**
- **1/2 cup flaxmeal (see Tip, page 23)**
- **1 1/2 cups white whole wheat flour**
- **1/2 cup coconut flour**
- **1/4 cup chia seeds**
- **2 teaspoons baking powder**
- **1/2 teaspoon baking soda**
- **1 teaspoon kosher salt**
- **3/4 cup golden raisins**
- **1/2 cup unsweetened coconut flakes**

Preheat the oven to 375°F. Lightly coat 12 cups of a muffin tin with the softened coconut oil.

Place the apple chunks in a microwave-safe bowl, cover the bowl with plastic wrap, and use the tip of a paring knife to poke a few holes in the plastic. Microwave until the apple is soft, about 1 1/2 minutes. (If you're not a fan of the microwave, you can steam or sauté the apples instead.) Carefully remove the plastic wrap and transfer the apple chunks to a large bowl, then mash them with a fork.

In a food processor, combine the carrots, beet chunks, and lemon zest and process until the vegetables are shredded into small pieces, about 15 seconds.

To the mashed apples, add the lemon juice, coconut milk, maple syrup, ginger, 1/4 cup coconut oil, and flaxmeal and whisk to combine. Set aside for 5 minutes.

In a medium bowl, whisk together the flour, coconut flour, chia seeds, baking powder, baking soda, and salt.

Add the carrot mixture to the apple mixture and whisk to combine, then stir in the dry ingredients until just incorporated. Fold in the raisins.

Divide the batter among the muffin cups, filling each one completely. Sprinkle the coconut on top of the muffins.

Bake until the center of a muffin springs back to light pressure, 16 to 18 minutes. Let cool for 5 minutes, then remove from the pan to eat or store in an airtight container for up to 3 days.

SUNSHINE CITRUS MUFFINS

Good morning, sunshine! When I was growing up, my mom would make tons of muffins and freeze them to reheat on rushed mornings. These are a particularly bright bunch, golden yellow with cornmeal and spiked with the bright citrus scents of grapefruit, orange, and lime. The ricotta keeps them light and moist, so they're not quite like cornbread, though they do have that familiar flavor. The compound Citrus-Brown Sugar Butter on page 21 goes amazingly well with these! If you like, you can skip the glaze and just go straight for a slather of this butter when the muffins are still warm out of the pan.

MAKES 12 MUFFINS

- **2 sticks unsalted butter, at room temperature, 1/4 stick reserved for greasing pan**
- **1 1/2 cups all-purpose flour**
- **1/3 cup fine cornmeal**
- **2 1/2 teaspoons baking powder**
- **3/4 teaspoon baking soda**
- **1 teaspoon kosher salt**
- **2/3 cup plus 2 tablespoons granulated sugar**
- **Zest of 1 grapefruit (preferably a ruby red grapefruit) plus 1 1/2 tablespoons grapefruit juice**
- **Zest of 1 lime**
- **Zest of 1 orange or tangerine**
- **1 teaspoon pure vanilla extract**
- **2 large eggs**
- **1 cup ricotta cheese**
- **1 cup powdered sugar**

Preheat the oven to 350°F. Lightly coat 12 cups of a muffin tin with the softened butter.

In a medium bowl, whisk together the flour, cornmeal, baking powder, baking soda, and salt.

In a small bowl, combine the granulated sugar and grapefruit, lime, and orange zests. Work the sugar into the zest with your fingertips. When the mixture looks like wet sand and smells amazing, it's done. Measure out 2 tablespoons of the citrus sugar and set aside in a small bowl.

Add the remaining citrus sugar to a stand mixer fitted with the paddle attachment. Add the remaining softened butter and beat on medium-high to cream the mixture until light and airy, 1 to 2 minutes. Reduce the speed to medium, add the vanilla and beat in the eggs one at a time, using a rubber spatula to scrape down the sides and bottom of the bowl as needed.

Reduce the speed to medium-low. Add half the flour mixture, mixing until just combined, then the ricotta, then the rest of the flour mixture until just combined. Avoid overmixing.

Divide the batter among the prepared muffin cups. Bake until the center of a muffin springs back to light pressure and a cake tester inserted into the center of a muffin comes out clean, 18 to 22 minutes. Let the muffins cool for 5 minutes in the pan, then run a paring knife around each one and turn it out onto a rimmed baking sheet.

Add the powdered sugar and grapefruit juice to the bowl with the remaining citrus sugar and whisk until smooth. Spoon a little over each slightly warm muffin. Let set at least 15 minutes before serving. The muffins will keep for up to 3 days if stored in an airtight container.

TIP: *If you want to make a few batches all at once while you have your equipment out and dirty, skip the glaze and freeze the baked muffins until ready to eat. Reheat on a baking sheet at 350°F before serving and make the glaze to drizzle on the warmed muffins if desired.*

SEGMENTING CITRUS

To segment citrus, start by cutting away the citrus peel and all the pith. Then, using a paring knife, hold the fruit firmly in one hand and carefully cut along the edge of one segment, staying as close to the white divider membrane as possible. Repeat along the edge of each divider membrane, levering the knife to pull each segment of fruit out as it is released. Save the segments in a bowl. Squeeze the remaining citrus to extract all the juice into the segment bowl before discarding the membranes.

MUSHROOM AND FIG CRÊPES

Sadly, I don't speak French. The only phrase I can remember perfectly is one that I asked a French friend to write out phonetically in my phone so I could say it properly: *"pa tro quee see voo play,"* which (hopefully) means "don't overcook it, please." Whenever I travel to France, I say this boldly to every crêpe vendor I visit. It seems to work, though I get a lot of eye rolls. And every perfectly light golden brown, delicate, melt-in-your-mouth crêpe is so worth being the most obvious tourist in town.

Once you get the handle of using an everyday skillet to achieve almost-Paris-like results, you'll be making crêpes at home regularly because they are basically skinny, skinny delicious pancakes that can be used to envelope anything sweet or savory. I like to crank out a stack and then set down either a huge tub of Nutella (live a little—if you can resist Nutella, you are magical and/or not human), some soft salted butter and granulated sugar (my personal favorite), or a delightful array of savory fillings as in this recipe, so people can mix and match their own creations. If you feel like going for something simpler, a few lovely slices of ham and Gruyère cheese (and a little hot pepper jelly if you have it) are always a crowd-pleasing combination. Savory crepes make a great meal with a frisée or mixed greens side salad dressed simply in olive oil and lemon juice with a little salt and pepper (add some minced shallots, a little Dijon mustard, and a pinch of sugar to the vinaigrette if you have them)! Très chic, you little culinary queen.

MAKES 8 FILLED CRÊPES (4 SERVINGS)

CRÊPES

2 large eggs

5 tablespoons (1/2 stick plus 1 tablespoon) unsalted butter, 3 tablespoons melted

1 1/2 cups whole milk, warmed

1 tablespoon sugar

1 cup white whole wheat flour

1/2 teaspoon kosher salt

MUSHROOM FILLING

2 tablespoons unsalted butter

1/2 medium sweet onion, thinly sliced

1 teaspoon kosher salt

1 tablespoon finely chopped fresh thyme leaves

(Ingredients continue on the next page.)

To make the crêpe batter, in a medium bowl, whisk together the eggs, 3 tablespoons melted butter, warm milk, and sugar. Whisk in the flour and 1/2 teaspoon salt until smooth. Transfer the batter to a large measuring cup, cover with plastic wrap, and refrigerate for at least 30 minutes or overnight.

Remove the batter from the refrigerator and let it come to room temperature while you make the mushroom filling.

To make the filling, in a large nonstick skillet, melt the butter over medium-high heat. Add the onion and 1/2 teaspoon of the salt and cook for 2 minutes, stirring regularly. Add the thyme and cook until fragrant, about 1 minute, then add the mushrooms. Cook until the mushrooms are golden brown and tender, being careful not to let them steam (try to keep them in a single layer in the pan) and stirring just to prevent them from burning, 7 to 8 minutes. Add the remaining salt and the arugula (if using) to the pan, tossing to wilt. Transfer the mixture to a medium bowl.

- **1 pound cremini (baby bella) or button mushrooms, ends trimmed, mushrooms thinly sliced**
- **1 cup arugula or other spicy green (optional)**
- **1 cup (4 ounces) coarsely grated Gruyère or aged cheddar cheese**
- **12 fresh figs (about 1 pint), quartered**

To make the crêpes, wipe out the skillet. Set it over medium heat and rub it with a bit of the remaining butter to lightly grease the pan. When the butter sizzles, add 2 to 3 tablespoons crêpe batter and, holding the skillet by the handle, rotate it to spread the batter into a thin sheet across the entire surface of the skillet. Cook until golden brown, 1 to 2 minutes. Use a silicone spatula to flip if desired and cook 20 seconds more on the opposite side. (I like mine a little blond and underdone, so I'll often just slip them out onto a plate after the first side is done cooking. You can always reheat in the pan when you're assembling the crêpes.)

Repeat to make the rest of the crêpes, wiping the pan every other crêpe or so and greasing the pan with butter each time. As you cook them, transfer the crêpes to a large plate and cover it with an upturned mixing bowl to keep them warm.

To assemble fill each crêpe with 2 to 3 tablespoons of mushrooms, a sprinkle of grated cheese, and a few fig slices. Fold as you like—like an envelope, or a burrito, or into thirds; all that matters is that the filling stays inside. Serve warm.

TIP: *If you are feeding a crowd and want to keep assembled crêpes warm, preheat the oven to 250F°. As you work, set the filled crêpes on a baking sheet and keep warm in the oven while assembling the remaining crêpes. Serve warm.*

10-MINUTE BREAKFAST TACOS

So you should know this about me: If I could have only one snack for the rest of my life, it would most definitely be chips, salsa, and fresh guacamole. And my drink of choice would be a tequila soda with lots of lime and a splash of pineapple juice. And when I retire, you just might find me and my husband and (hopefully) a brood of kids and grandkids basking on a beach in Tulum, Mexico, snacking from a picnic spread, overcrowding the hammock, and listening to live music at night under bright stars.

In the meantime, I'll settle for a divinely simple breakfast taco. These guys take 10 minutes, and offer layer upon layer of flavor—and they happen to be protein- and fiber-packed to keep you full all morning. They also travel well, if you leave the salsa off and roll them up tight in foil. (And shh, they're also vegan and can easily go gluten-free if you choose the right tortilla.)

MAKES 4 TACOS

SWEET ONION SALSA

1/2 jalapeño pepper (more if you like it spicy)

1 small sweet onion, minced

Juice of 1 orange

1/2 teaspoon sugar

1 teaspoon kosher salt

TACOS

1 tablespoon extra-virgin olive oil

1 small sweet onion, minced

1/2 teaspoon kosher salt

1/2 small jalapeño pepper, minced (optional)

1 medium garlic clove, minced or grated

1/4 teaspoon ground cumin

1/2 teaspoon dried oregano

One 15-ounce can cooked black beans (drained and rinsed if canned)

4 small corn tortillas, warmed (see Tip)

1/2 avocado, pitted, peeled, and diced

1 lime, cut into wedges

To make the salsa, in a blender, combine the jalapeño, onion, orange juice, sugar, and salt and blend on high until smooth and frothy, about 30 seconds. Reserve until ready to use.

To make the tacos, in a medium skillet, heat the olive oil over medium heat. Add the onion and salt and cook, stirring often, until the onion starts to soften and darken, about 4 minutes. Stir in the jalapeño, garlic, cumin, and oregano and cook until the garlic is fragrant, stirring often, about 1 minute. Stir in the black beans and cook until heated through, about 3 minutes. Set aside until ready to use.

Place the warmed tortillas on a platter or individual plates and divide the bean mixture among them. Top with the avocado and a spoonful of salsa. Serve with the lime wedges.

TIP: *Heat the tortillas in the microwave for 10 seconds, or by giving them a quick toss in a dry skillet over medium heat. If you're serving a crowd, spread the tortillas on a baking sheet and pop in a 350°F oven for a few minutes to heat.*

FRITTATA WITH SPINACH, OLIVES, AND CHICKEN SAUSAGE

I'm a big fan of frittatas because they're so fast and filling, and they're a great crowd-pleaser for breakfast, brunch, lunch, or even dinner. They're essentially the Italian version of a quiche (sans crust, which makes them even easier—sexy!). This particular combination happens to be my husband John's favorite. You get plenty of healthy bits with the garlic-spinach sauté and eggs, plus superflavorful chicken sausage and a smattering of olives and feta on top.

MAKES 4 SERVINGS

6 large eggs

1/4 cup whole milk

2 tablespoons plus 2 teaspoons extra-virgin olive oil

2 fully precooked chicken sausages, sliced into thin rounds

1/2 small red onion, thinly sliced

1 teaspoon kosher salt

2 garlic cloves, thinly sliced

3 cups baby spinach

1/3 cup pitted, roughly chopped Kalamata or salt and oil-cured olives (Turkish *gemlik* olives are my favorite)

1/3 cup crumbled feta cheese (preferably French or Bulgarian)

Flaky sea salt and freshly cracked black pepper

Preheat the oven to 350°F.

In a medium bowl, whisk the eggs and milk until frothy.

In a large ovenproof skillet, heat 2 teaspoons of the olive oil over medium-high heat. Add the chicken sausage coins and brown them on all sides, 4 to 6 minutes, turning often. Transfer the sausage to a plate until ready to use.

Add 1 tablespoon of the olive oil to the skillet and heat it over medium-high heat until shimmering. Add the onion and 1/2 teaspoon of the salt. Cook, stirring often, until the onion is soft but not browned (if the onion starts to brown, reduce the heat to medium). Add the garlic and cook, stirring often, until fragrant, about 1 minute. Add 1 tablespoon room temperature water to the pan to stop the garlic browning, and the remaining tablespoon of olive oil, then stir in the spinach and the remaining 1/2 teaspoon of the salt. Cook, stirring often, until the spinach is wilted and the water in the pan evaporates, about 2 minutes. Spread this frittata filling evenly in the skillet and layer with the chicken sausage.

Pour the egg-milk mixture over the frittata filling and use a silicone spatula to scrape the sides of the pan and gently pull eggs from the edges toward the middle so that soft curds form and the frittata begins to firm up.

Give the pan a couple of good shakes to release the frittata from the pan bottom (the top of the frittata will still be raw). Sprinkle the olives and feta over the eggs. Transfer the skillet to the oven and cook until the frittata is mostly dry (the feta will release some liquid—this is fine—but just be sure the egg is completely cooked) and lightly browned on top, 5 to 7 minutes.

Let rest 5 minutes, then slide the frittata onto a large plate and sprinkle with flaky sea salt and pepper to taste. Slice into wedges and serve warm or room temperature.

TIP: *Have leftover pasta or quinoa? Stir it into your frittata egg blend! Both add bulk and great texture to any frittata.*

OATMEAL FRITTATA WITH CINNAMON-APPLE COMPOTE

I first had a version of this at Hugo's Restaurant in LA. When my aunt Samantha told me to order it off the menu, I took one look at the description of a variety of soaked grains, baked with egg whites and served with cottage cheese and fruit and thought, *Why?* I didn't order it that day, but she did. And as soon as it came to the table, I could see why it was a favorite with the locals.

Imagine a more filling pancake, packed with nutty, chewy grains of all kinds. The egg white is just a binder to hold everything together, and you don't even remember it's there when you bite into what smells like baked cinnamon apple pie. Dipping bites of frittata back and forth between creamy, slightly salty cottage cheese and maple syrup with fresh fruit makes for an incredibly satisfying breakfast for people like me who can never choose if they want sweet or savory (and generally choose both).

I immediately went to work trying to re-create this masterpiece at home. The trick is to soak the grains the night before—just assemble before bed and they will be ready in the morning. The soaking helps make the grains more digestible, and also more chewy and sweet in the frittata rather than dry and oddly crunchy (trust someone who tried to skip this step a few times).

MAKES 4 SERVINGS

½ cup sliced almonds

¼ cup steel-cut oats

¼ cup kamut and/or spelt flakes

1 teaspoon plus a pinch of kosher salt

2 tablespoons unsalted butter

2 Granny Smith apples, halved, cored, and thinly sliced

1 tablespoon light or dark brown sugar

1 teaspoon ground cinnamon

⅛ teaspoon freshly grated nutmeg

¾ cup apple cider

6 large egg whites

4 tablespoons yogurt, sour cream, or cottage cheese

Pure maple syrup, for serving

In a small saucepan, combine the almonds, oats, kamut flakes, and ½ teaspoon of the salt. Cover with 1¼ cups water and bring to a boil over high heat. Remove from the heat, cover the pan, and leave to soak for 8 hours or overnight.

Preheat the oven to 350°F.

In a large ovenproof nonstick skillet, melt 1 tablespoon of the butter over medium heat. In a medium bowl, toss the apples with the brown sugar, cinnamon, nutmeg, and ¼ teaspoon of the salt. Pour the mixture into the skillet and cook until the apples are softened, stirring often, for about 4 minutes. Add the apple cider and simmer until the cider glazes the apples and the apples are very tender, 2 to 3 minutes. Transfer the apples to a bowl. Wipe out the skillet with a paper towel.

In a large bowl, whisk the egg whites and a pinch of salt until they hold medium peaks (a hand blender works very fast here, but a regular whisk gets the job done). Gently fold in the oat mixture and the remaining ¼ teaspoon salt.

Melt the remaining 1 tablespoon butter in the skillet over medium heat. Add the oat-egg white mixture and gently spread it out evenly in the pan. Cook until the frittata starts to set around the edges, 3 to 4 minutes. Transfer the frittata to the oven and bake until puffed and golden and the center bounces back to light pressure, about 8 minutes.

Invert the frittata onto a large platter and cut it into slices. Serve with the apples; yogurt, sour cream, or cottage cheese; and maple syrup.

TIP: *Make the oat mixture ahead of time—it keeps in the fridge for up to 1 week. You can make mini frittatas by folding 1/2 cup of the oat mixture into 2 egg whites to make one hearty portion. It's great with a simple pour of maple syrup, too.*

VARIATION: *You can also try adding a tablespoon or two of flaxmeal or chia seeds right before you combine the soaked grains with the beaten egg whites for an extra fiber- and omega-3-packed blend.*

SAVORY FRIED ONION OAT FRITTATA

Omit the apple mixture and in step 3, fry 1 diced large yellow onion in 1 tablespoon butter and 1 tablespoon olive oil over medium heat until softened, about 3 minutes. Stir in 1/2 teaspoon kosher salt, reduce the heat to medium-low, and cook, stirring often, until it starts to brown, about 6 minutes. Continue with steps 4 and 5 as directed. Serve with 2 tablespoons of chopped fresh dill stirred into 1/2 cup plain yogurt.

BUTTERNUT SQUASH AND GOAT CHEESE QUICHE

I think every home cook needs at least one quiche recipe in her repertoire. It's the perfect brunch food with a bright, crisp salad, and an equally perfect leftover lunch or dinner. It's also a technique that, once mastered, gives you endless leeway to play around with the flavors and ingredients you like—or the things you need to get rid of in your fridge. This particular quiche gets a little sweetness from the butternut squash, and since my daughter loves spinach everything, I put that in here for her. The herb and black pepper crust gives a crisp, buttery bite to offset the creamy filling. Perfect for grown-ups and grown-ups in training!

MAKES ONE 10-INCH QUICHE

HERB AND BLACK PEPPER CRUST

- 2 cups white whole wheat flour
- 1/2 cup finely grated Parmigiano-Reggiano cheese
- 1 tablespoon fresh thyme, finely chopped
- Freshly cracked black pepper
- 1/2 teaspoon kosher salt
- 10 tablespoons (1 stick plus 2 tablespoons) cold unsalted butter, cut into 1/2-inch pieces
- 5 tablespoons ice water

QUICHE FILLING

- 1 1/2 teaspoons kosher salt
- 1 shallot, very finely chopped
- 1 3/4 cups peeled and grated butternut squash (1 small to medium squash; use the medium holes of a box grater)
- 1 tablespoon finely chopped fresh thyme
- 2 teaspoons extra-virgin olive oil
- 1 1/2 cups roughly chopped baby spinach
- 2 large eggs

To make the herb and black pepper crust, in a food processor, mix the flour, Parmigiano, thyme, pepper, and salt. Add the butter and pulse until the mixture looks like cornmeal. While pulsing, drizzle in the ice water until the dough just sticks together, then turn the dough onto a large sheet of plastic wrap. Cover with another sheet of plastic wrap and press and shape the dough into a 1/2-inch-thick disc before sealing. Refrigerate for at least 30 minutes or up to 3 days.

Unwrap the dough and set it on a large sheet of parchment paper. Cover with another sheet of parchment and roll the dough into a 12-inch round. Peel off the top parchment layer and invert the dough into a 10-inch tart pan. Press the dough into the corners and up the sides of the pan, pinching off the excess at the top (save 1 parchment sheet). Refrigerate the dough for 20 minutes.

Meanwhile, adjust one oven rack to the bottom position and another to the middle position and preheat the oven to 375°F.

Place the saved parchment over the dough and fill the tart pan with pie weights or dried beans. Set the tart pan on a baking sheet, slide onto the bottom rack, and parbake the crust until the edges don't look raw anymore, 20 to 22 minutes. Carefully remove the parchment and pie weights from the crust, leaving the tart pan on the baking sheet.

To make the quiche filling, in a medium bowl, use your fingers to rub 1/2 teaspoon of the salt into the shallot and set aside for 5 minutes. Add the squash, thyme, oil, and 1/2 teaspoon of the salt and toss to combine. Add the spinach and toss to combine.

1 large egg yolk
3/4 cup whole milk
3/4 cup crème fraîche, Greek yogurt, or sour cream
One 4-ounce log fresh goat cheese, broken into small pieces

In another medium bowl, whisk together the whole eggs, egg yolk, milk, crème fraîche, and remaining 1/2 teaspoon salt.

Spread the squash mixture over the bottom of the parbaked crust. Pour the egg mixture over the squash mixture. Sprinkle the goat cheese over the top and bake until the filling is golden brown and set, 45 to 55 minutes. Cool for at least 20 minutes, then slice and serve. It's excellent served warm or at room temperature.

STORE-BOUGHT CRUST

The cheese in this crust helps make it extra crisp and adds an extra dimension of umami flavor. For a shortcut, unroll a sheet of store-bought pie dough and place it on a sheet of parchment paper, then sprinkle the thyme, pepper, and a few tablespoons of Parmigiano-Reggiano over the top and use a rolling pin to lightly roll them into the dough. Transfer the dough to the tart pan herbed-side up and proceed with the recipe.

WARRIOR WAFFLES

By now, most people know that gluten-free does not necessarily mean healthy or light. While it's true that many (most?) of us could benefit from having a little less gluten in our diets, the alternative of noshing on hyperprocessed food that traditionally has gluten and now doesn't is not much better.

Whenever I can, I choose foods that never had gluten to begin with. But the convenience of having frozen waffles on hand for fast breakfasts cannot be denied. I came up with this gluten-free recipe since I wasn't in love with the options in my freezer section that tasted fine but left me famished an hour later. I add protein powder and chia and/or flaxseeds for fiber and healthy fats to keep these as filling as they are delicious. You can make a bunch and freeze them—just pop one in the toaster when you're ready to eat. And one quick note: Sweet rice flour has a higher starch content than standard rice flour; it gives amazing results in the recipe, so don't substitute!

MAKES 6 WAFFLES

- **1 cup sweet white rice flour (see Note)**
- **3/4 cup almond flour**
- **1/3 cup cornstarch**
- **1/3 cup ground chia seeds or flaxmeal**
- **1/3 cup protein powder (I like unflavored or vanilla pea- or whey-based options)**
- **2 teaspoons baking powder**
- **1/2 teaspoon kosher salt**
- **4 large eggs, separated**
- **1 1/2 cups buttermilk, plus more to loosen the batter**
- **2 teaspoons pure vanilla extract**
- **2 tablespoons granulated sugar**
- **4 tablespoons (1/2 stick) unsalted butter, melted, plus more for the pan**

Preheat the oven to 250°F. Heat a waffle iron to high heat.

In a medium bowl, whisk together the rice flour, almond flour, cornstarch, ground chia seeds or flaxmeal, protein powder, baking powder, and salt.

In a separate medium bowl, beat all 4 egg yolks, the buttermilk, and the vanilla. Stir the buttermilk mixture into the dry ingredients, mixing just until combined. Batter should look like traditional pancake batter, so add a little bit more buttermilk or water if it is too thick a paste.

In a stand mixer fitted with the whisk attachment (or a large bowl if using a hand mixer), beat 2 egg whites on medium speed until they are frothy, 30 seconds to 1 minute. Reserve the remaining egg whites covered in the refrigerator for up to 2 days. Slowly start to sprinkle in the sugar and increase the speed to medium-high until the whites hold stiff peaks.

Whisk one-fourth of the beaten whites into the batter, then fold in the remaining beaten whites. Continuing to slowly fold the batter, drizzle in the melted butter.

Using a dishtowel or brush dipped in melted butter, lightly coat the waffle iron and, following the manufacturer's instructions, fill the mold without overflowing. Cook until browned, then transfer to a baking sheet to keep warm in the oven while you make the remaining waffles.

PARSNIP PECAN LOAF

So clearly I like to play with ways to sneak veggies and other healthy things into "breakfast breads" that are basically cakes, let's be honest. I'm all about finding that crossroads of happy and healthy, and I feel a little less guilty about eating cake for breakfast when there are vegetables involved.

This one is loaded up with whole wheat flour and rolled oats, and the parsnips add a very slight malted flavor, but mostly just a ton of moisture so that this bread stays decadent and moist—think zucchini bread. The little sprinkle of pecans and sugar that coat the top and crisp while the loaf bakes replace any need for fancy glazes. It's worth finding out which of those gnarly-looking root vegetables is actually a parsnip to make this (just wait until you smell it baking!), but you can easily substitute grated carrots, beets, or rutabaga.

MAKES 1 LOAF

- **1 1/2 cups pecans**
- **1 tablespoon unsalted butter, at room temperature**
- **1 cup all-purpose flour**
- **1/2 cup whole wheat flour**
- **1/2 cup rolled oats**
- **1 1/2 teaspoons baking powder**
- **1 1/2 teaspoons ground cardamom**
- **1 teaspoon ground cinnamon**
- **1 teaspoon kosher salt**
- **2 tablespoons granulated sugar**
- **2 medium parsnips, peeled and roughly chopped**
- **3/4 cup packed light brown sugar**
- **2 large eggs**
- **3/4 cup Greek yogurt**
- **1/3 cup grapeseed oil**
- **1 teaspoon pure vanilla extract**

Preheat the oven to 350°F.

Place the pecans on a rimmed baking sheet and toast until fragrant, 7 to 9 minutes. Transfer the pecans to a large plate to cool. Leave the oven on.

Lightly coat an 8 1/2 x 4 1/2-inch loaf pan with about 1/2 tablespoon of the butter. Line the loaf pan with a long strip of parchment paper lengthwise and another one crosswise to create a sling, making sure at least a couple of inches of parchment hang over the edges. Grease the parchment with the remaining butter.

In a food processor, combine the flours, oats, baking powder, cardamom, cinnamon, and salt and process until the oats are fine, about 30 seconds. Add 1/2 cup of the pecans and process until they are semifine, about 10 seconds. Transfer the mixture to a medium bowl.

Add the remaining 1 cup pecans and the granulated sugar to the food processor and pulse until the mixture looks semifine and sandy with a few larger bits of pecans remaining, about five 1-second pulses. Transfer the mixture to a small bowl.

Add the parsnips to the food processor and process until there aren't any large bits remaining, about 20 seconds. Add the brown sugar and pulse until the mixture looks like wet sand, about five 1-second pulses.

Transfer the parsnip mixture to a large bowl and whisk in the eggs. When they are well incorporated, whisk in the yogurt, oil, and vanilla. Add the flour-oat mixture to the parsnip mixture and use a wooden spoon to combine.

Transfer the batter to the prepared loaf pan. Sprinkle the pecan-sugar mixture over the top and loosely tent with foil. Bake until a cake tester inserted into the center of the loaf comes out clean, 55 to 65 minutes. Remove the foil with 10 minutes remaining to let the loaf top get golden brown.

Set the loaf aside to cool for at least 15 minutes in the pan, then use the parchment overhang to lift the loaf out of the pan. Remove the parchment, slice, and serve.

GUAVA-CHEESE HAND PIES

Whenever I am in LA, I make a beeline for Café Tropical in Silver Lake, an incredible little hole-in-the-wall Cuban coffeeshop and bakery. They make strong, creamy café con leche, and always have a few guava-cheese pies warm and wafting at checkout to make sure you can't resist the urge. The lure of tart, sweet guava paste and melting cream cheese enveloped in a fantastic crust is undeniable.

They serve a "slice" that is roughly the size of my head, but I started making little hand-pie versions for brunch parties and found that I can easily satisfy my craving with just a few bites, rather than eating my weight in cream cheese and jam, as fun as that sounds . . .

MAKE 8 HAND PIES

1 large egg

1/2 cup (4 ounces) guava paste (see Tip, page 46)

2 sheets prepared puff pastry (thawed if frozen)

1/2 cup (4 ounces) cream cheese

Flaky sea salt

Preheat the oven to 375°F. Line a rimmed baking sheet with parchment paper.

In a small bowl, beat the egg with 1 teaspoon water. Set aside.

Place the 4-ounce hunk of guava paste on a cutting board and cut into 8 thin slices. A thin slice is best so it will heat all the way through without burning.

Place the puff pastry on a cutting board and roll out slightly. Cut each sheet into quarters, for a total of 8 squares. Use a fork to prick each piece of dough all over about 6 times.

Place 1 tablespoon of the cream cheese at the center of the lower half of each piece of dough. Top each with a piece of guava paste. Use a pastry brush to lightly coat the perimeter of each puff pastry square with the egg wash, then fold the top over to the bottom and press to seal. Use a fork to crimp the edges, then place the hand pies on the prepared baking sheet.

If, at this point, the dough is sticky or soft, refrigerate the hand pies for 20 minutes.

Just before baking, brush the top of each hand pie with the egg wash and a sprinkle of sea salt. Bake the hand pies until golden brown, 18 to 20 minutes. I'm obliged to tell you to let them cool completely before serving, though I have never done this and the burned roof of my mouth is worth the perfectly melting combination of fruit and cream cheese. The hand pies are best eaten within a few hours of baking.

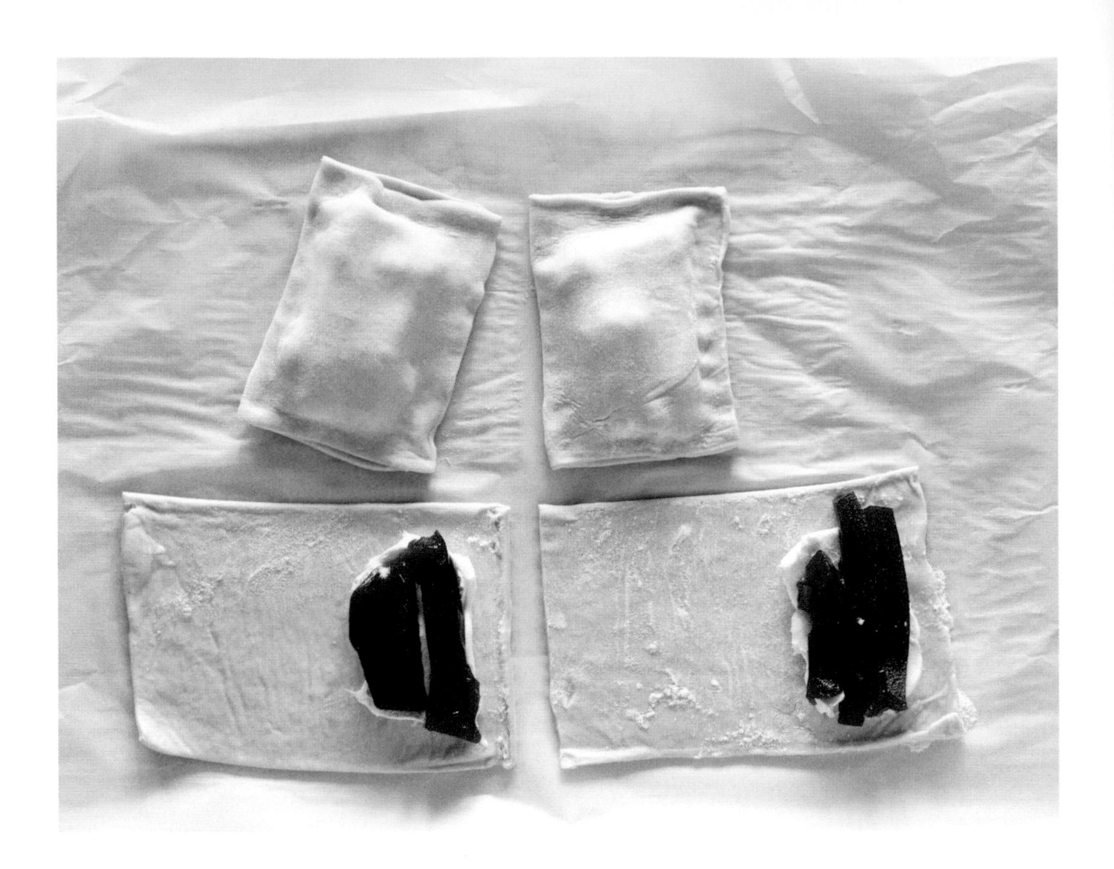

TIP: *If you buy guava paste in a tub or can rather than a brick, scoop out 1 tablespoon guava for each hand pie and spread it 1/4 inch thick, leaving enough pastry rim to seal the pie.*

MORE THINGS TO DO WITH PUFF PASTRY

Generally found in the freezer section of your grocery store, puff pastry is a versatile ally that I keep in my freezer at all times. Aside from these tasty hand pies, it makes a great topping for savory or sweet pie filling to spare you from having to make homemade crust. You can also use it to make easy hors d'oeuvres of all kinds. For instance, to make Cinnamon-Sugar or Cheesy Twists, simply brush 1-inch-wide strips of dough with egg wash, then sprinkle them with cinnamon sugar or grated Parmigiano-Reggiano cheese rubbed together with chopped fresh oregano and chile flakes. Give the strips a quick twist, then bake at 375°F to golden-brown, flaky perfection.

COCONUT-MANGO PANCAKES

I was craving my favorite Thai dessert—coconut sticky rice with fresh mango—for breakfast one day and thought a light and fluffy coconut pancake (made with coconut milk and coconut flour) with a ladle of fresh homemade mango-ginger syrup would do just fine. And it did.

MAKES 4 SERVINGS

MANGO SYRUP

1/4 cup sugar

Four 1/2-inch-thick rounds fresh ginger

1 vanilla bean (optional), split lengthwise (see Vanilla Bean 101, page 48)

1 teaspoon pure vanilla extract

1 1/2 cups bite-size mango chunks (from about 2 mangoes)

PANCAKES

1/2 cup coconut flour

1 teaspoon baking soda

1/2 teaspoon kosher salt

1/2 cup coconut or almond milk

1/2 cup ricotta cheese

1 teaspoon pure vanilla extract

4 large eggs

1/4 cup sugar

2 tablespoons coconut oil

To make the mango syrup, combine the sugar and 1/2 cup water in a small saucepan. Bring the water to simmer over medium-high heat and stir until the sugar is dissolved, 30 seconds to 1 minute. Add the ginger and simmer until the syrup is slightly reduced, about 3 minutes. Scrape in the seeds from the vanilla bean (if using), then whisk in the vanilla. Add the mangoes and remove from the heat. Set aside.

To make the pancakes, in a medium bowl, whisk together the coconut flour, baking soda, and salt. In a separate medium bowl, whisk together the coconut milk, ricotta, and vanilla.

In a stand mixer fitted with the whisk attachment (or a large bowl if using a hand mixer), beat the eggs on medium-high speed until they start to get frothy, about 30 seconds. Continue to whip, slowly sprinkling in the sugar, until the mixture is thick and creamy, another 1 to 2 minutes. Turn off the mixer. Use a rubber spatula to fold in the ricotta-coconut milk mixture, then add the dry mixture and fold it in until just incorporated. Set aside for 5 minutes.

Preheat the oven to 250°F.

In a large nonstick skillet or a flat-top griddle, heat a little bit of the coconut oil over medium-low heat. Dollop the batter onto the skillet 1/4 cup at a time, leaving space for the pancakes to spread. Cook until the pancakes are golden brown on the bottom and a little darker around the edges, about 6 minutes. Flip the pancakes over and cook on the other side until golden brown and the center of the pancake resists light pressure, about 4 minutes longer. Transfer the pancakes to an ovenproof platter or a parchment-lined rimmed baking sheet and place in the oven to remain warm. Repeat to make the rest of the pancakes.

Remove the ginger pieces from the mango syrup. Serve the pancakes with warm mango syrup.

TIP: *These pancakes have to cook low and slow because the coconut flour is heavy with lots of fiber, so don't rush them or they won't have time to rise properly. They won't bubble the way pancakes made with all-purpose flour do, so better to check and make sure the underside is golden brown and the edges slightly darker before flipping.*

VANILLA BEAN 101

To extract the seeds from the vanilla pod, split it in half lengthwise with a paring knife, then use the blunt side of the knife to run along the inside of each half and remove the dark brown paste of vanilla seeds inside. Reserve the vanilla pod to infuse a bowl of sugar or a bottle of vodka (or other alcohol). The longer it sits, the stronger the vanilla flavor will get.

EVERYTHING-BAGEL BISCUITS

I'm a Jersey girl, and weekend mornings growing up were reserved for piping hot bagels, made fresh at the local shop near our house. Bad bagels taste pretty much like bad bread—no need to waste calories on that. Good bagels are properly yeasted and boiled before being baked, so that their insides are both dense and fluffy, perfectly chewy, and just a tiny bit sweet. The next time you're in the tri-state area, make the pilgrimage to get a New Jersey bagel—you won't be disappointed.

Biscuits are the next best thing in the bread category for me, and so I've decided to meld my two favorites into one, delectable item: the everything-bagel biscuit. I make mine with whole wheat flour, and I started using whole wheat pastry flour in the blend because it makes the biscuits ever so slightly more tender and flaky. If you don't have both, you can just use all of one or the other (2 cups whole wheat flour since it is denser and will absorb more liquid or 2 1/2 cups whole wheat pastry flour, plus more for rolling).

This recipe is a little involved but not difficult, and you'll be a total biscuit boss—just work your way through a couple of quick steps and meditate through a few periods of rest and refrigeration. All these steps are annoying because they delay getting these tasty devils into your mouth . . . but after you've had your first bite of warm, pull-apart layers flecked with seeds and chives and pats of cream cheese, I can officially welcome you to my little corner of Jersey heaven.

MAKES 8 BISCUITS

MULTISEED MIXTURE

1/2 cup sesame seeds

2 tablespoons poppyseeds

1 1/2 teaspoons nigella seeds (optional)

2 tablespoons dried onion flakes

2 teaspoons garlic powder

1 1/2 teaspoons kosher salt

BISCUITS

1 1/4 cups whole wheat flour, plus extra for shaping

1 cup unbleached whole wheat pastry flour

3/4 cup minced chives (or cut with scissors)

2 teaspoons baking powder

2 tablespoons sugar

(Ingredients continue on the next page.)

To make the multiseed mixture, in a dry skillet over low heat, toast the sesame seeds until sweetly aromatic and lightly golden, about 2 minutes. Let them cool, then combine them in a small bowl with the poppyseeds, nigella seeds (if using), onion flakes, garlic powder, and salt.

To make the biscuits, in a medium bowl, whisk together the flours, chives, baking powder, sugar, salt, and 6 heaping tablespoons of the multiseed mixture. Add the butter and use a pastry cutter or your fingers to cut or pinch the butter into the dry ingredients until there aren't any butter pieces larger than a small pea.

In a small bowl, whisk the buttermilk and 1 of the eggs. Pour the mixture over the dry ingredients and use a fork to combine until the liquid is mostly absorbed.

Generously flour a work surface and set the dough on top. Sprinkle the top with more flour (the dough is pretty rich, so don't be afraid to use enough flour so that it doesn't stick when handling it). Use your hands to press and shape it into an 8 x 12-inch rectangle about 3/4 inch thick.

- 1/2 teaspoon plus a pinch of kosher salt
- 2 sticks (8 ounces) unsalted butter, cut into 1/2-inch pieces
- 1 cup buttermilk
- 2 large eggs
- One 8-ounce package cream cheese, at room temperature

Cut the cream cheese in half lengthwise and use your fingers to spread and push half the cream cheese onto the center third of the dough. Fold one side of the dough over the cream cheese layer, then the other side (like a business letter).

Roll the dough out again until it is a 1/2-inch-thick rectangle and repeat the business letter fold with the remaining cream cheese. Wrap in plastic wrap and refrigerate for 1 hour.

Line a rimmed baking sheet with parchment paper. Generously flour the work surface and the top of the dough. Roll the dough out to a 1-inch thickness.

Use a 3-inch biscuit cutter to stamp out as many rounds from the dough as possible. Don't twist the cutter when pressing out the biscuits—make one firm motion to press the cutter straight through the dough, dipping the cutter into flour if needed to prevent the biscuit from sticking to it.

Flip the biscuits and place them bottoms up on a baking sheet lined with parchment paper, then gently press the scraps together and cut out as many biscuits as you can (discard the remaining dough scraps). Chill the biscuits for at least 30 minutes or up to 3 hours.

Preheat the oven to 400°F.

Lightly beat the remaining egg with a pinch of salt and dip the top of each biscuit into the egg wash. Try not to let the egg wash drip down the sides of the biscuit—this will seal the edges and prevent the biscuit from rising properly. Dip the egg-washed side of each biscuit into the remaining multiseed mixture and place on the baking sheet, leaving 2 inches in between the biscuits.

Bake the biscuits until golden brown, about 18 minutes, turning the pan midway through cooking. Serve warm or at room temperature.

SPICY FRIED EGGS AND HAM

This dish is an homage to the breakfast John ate every morning we were on our honeymoon in Paris—a sizzling cast-iron skillet brought to the table with layers of ham, sunny side up eggs, and shredded Gruyère melting and gooey on top, the ham just crisping at the edges. He loved it so much that I tried to make it for him the first weekend we were home. I ended up riffing on the original to play with the flavors I love, adding chiles, shallots, and avocado. It remains one of our favorite breakfasts for hungry days.

MAKES 1 OR 2 SERVINGS

1/2 tablespoon extra-virgin olive oil

1 small shallot, halved and thinly sliced

1/4 teaspoon kosher salt

1/2 serrano chile, thinly sliced (optional)

2 large eggs

2 tablespoons shredded Monterey Jack cheese

1 slice deli ham

1/4 avocado, pitted, peeled, and finely diced, for garnish

Hot sauce, for serving (optional)

In a small nonstick skillet, heat the olive oil over medium-high heat. Add the shallot and salt and cook, stirring often, until it is translucent, about 2 minutes. Add the chile (if using) and cook 1 minute more.

Crack the eggs over the top and cover the skillet. Reduce the heat to medium-low and cook the eggs until the yolks are still jiggly but mostly opaque, about 2 minutes. (Reduce the time to 1 minute if you prefer a runnier yolk.) Uncover and sprinkle the Monterey Jack over the top. Cover and cook until the cheese melts, about 1 minute.

Uncover and lay the ham on top of the cheese. Flip the whole egg situation over so the ham is on the bottom, and continue to cook until the ham is crisp, 1 to 2 minutes. Slide out of the pan onto a plate and garnish with the avocado. If desired, serve with hot sauce.

drinks

For the most part, I tend to drink water when I'm thirsty. But these are the drinks I turn to when it's not thirst I'm looking to slake. Whether it's the easy-access vegetable bounty of Greens on Fleek that I rely on for smooth, glowing skin; the sweet-tart liquid gold of Sunbeam Juice or the peppery punch of Homemade Ginger Beer that help me beat common colds and upset tummies; or the cold-brew caffeine hit of Vegan Vietnamese-Style Iced Coffee and the easiest of homemade Fruit Sodas that take your everyday coffee or pop and make them just a little bit healthier, these are a few of my favorites!

HOMEMADE FRUIT SODAS

For good reason, I'm not a huge fan of soda. But I love flavorful, bubbly beverages, and I find that with these around, most people gladly go for the natural stuff rather than hitting the two-liter bottle. These are *awesome* for kids because the flavors are familiar, the sugars are natural, and they can totally mix and match. But they're equally perfect for adult refreshment as an easy "mocktail"—or you could of course add a splash of your favorite alcohol if the mood strikes.

EACH MAKES 1 TO 2 CUPS CONCENTRATE (FOR 4 TO 6 SERVINGS)

STRAWBERRY-WATERMELON

2 cups strawberries, hulled

2 cups cubed seedless watermelon

RASPBERRY-LIME

2 cups raspberries

1/2 cup fresh lime juice (about 4 limes)

2 tablespoons honey or maple syrup (more or less, to taste)

LEMON-PEACH

2 cups cubed peaches

1/2 cup fresh lemon juice (about 3 lemons)

2 tablespoons honey or maple syrup (more or less, to taste)

ORANGE-BLACKBERRY

2 cups blackberries (blueberries and/or raspberries work well too!)

1 cup fresh orange juice (2 to 4 oranges)

PINEAPPLE-MANGO-CHILE

1 1/2 cups cubed fresh pineapple

1 1/2 cups cubed mango

1/4 teaspoon chile powder

CHERRY-GINGER

2 cups pitted cherries

2 inches fresh ginger, peeled and chopped

For each recipe, blend the ingredients until smooth. Using a fine-mesh strainer, strain the puree to remove any seeds or pulp. Store the puree in an airtight container up to 1 week. When ready to use, combine with sparkling water to desired sweetness and to give your soda plenty of "pop."

TIP: *You can definitely use frozen fruit instead of fresh (but not canned!). Just thaw before pureeing.*

SUNBEAM JUICE

I'm a huge fan of tart orange juice, and I wait all year for the winter months when citrus season hits and my grocery overflows with my favorite Valencia oranges. They're not a great orange for eating because of all their seeds, but their juice runs like liquid gold—intoxicatingly sweet, with a burst of tartness that perfectly balances it. A glass of this freshly squeezed juice throws a little magic happy spell over the rest of my day.

When Valencias aren't around, this is how I get that perfect sweet-and-sour combo, no matter the juicing orange. I leave a bit of pith on (if you're not sure what pith is, see the box below) and juice the entire citrus in an electric juicer (like what you might use to make a green juice from vegetables), which yields a rich, frothy juice that is loaded with bioflavonoids—powerful antioxidants and immune boosters—concentrated in that white covering. There's a tender balance to how much pith to leave on—too much and it gets bitter; too little and you miss out on all that delectable, frothy cream. Try peeling the orange by hand, which will naturally leave just a bit of pith, or peeling with a knife and leaving on a few nice strips. Then cut in quarters, juice, and enjoy the creamiest OJ ever.

MAKES TWO 8-OUNCE SERVINGS

- **4 juice oranges, peeled (leave as much pith as possible) and quartered**
- **1 to 2 lemons (depending on how tart you like your orange juice), quartered**

Juice the orange quarters, then 1 lemon. Taste the juice and add more lemon segments if you like it more tart. You can easily change this recipe up with peeled grapefruit or lime in place of the lemon.

WHAT THE HECK IS PITH?

What we typically think of as citrus peel is made up of two parts: the vibrantly colored zest on the outside and the creamier white pith on the inside. The zest contains tons of natural essential oils, which is why it's a great citrus flavor boost for everything from butters to marinades; the pith tends to be a bit bitter, but it contains lots of the antioxidants and other healthy nutrients found in citrus.

HOMEMADE GINGER BEER

I actually love being pregnant (until I have to lose the baby weight), but one of the few downsides is the morning sickness I battle for the first trimester. I used to keep ginger ale on standby, but there's so little actual ginger and so much sugar in most of the commercially available options that they really don't do me much good.

I was looking for something with a real kick of ginger, so I started searching around online and came across a couple traditional recipes for Jamaican ginger beer. Once I gave it a try (so easy!) and a taste (so delicious!) I haven't been able to go back. I experimented with a few and came up with the blend I love best. If you're ready to get out of the ginger ale kiddie pool, this version is a rich, biting, gingery blend that warms your whole body, with a little hit of lime that makes it feel distinctly tropical. I love to keep a jar of the concentrate in the fridge. You can either pour it over ice and top with sparkling water to keep it cold, or combine 4 ounces concentrate with enough boiling water to dilute to your taste for a hot tea that is perfect in winter. The rum is obviously something I experimented with postpregnancy...

MAKES 36 OUNCES GINGER CONCENTRATE

1/2 cup granulated sugar

1/2 pound fresh ginger, peeled and roughly chopped (about 1 1/2 cups)

1/4 cup fresh lime juice (3 to 4 limes; optional)

Sparkling water or seltzer for serving

Lime wedges for serving

Rum (optional)

In a large pot, bring 5 cups water to a boil over high heat.

Stir in the sugar and ginger and cook, stirring occasionally, until the water returns to a boil. Boil for 2 minutes, then remove from the heat and set aside to cool to room temperature, about 2 hours.

Transfer the ginger and cooking liquid to a blender and puree in batches until smooth. Refrigerate the mixture overnight or for up to 12 hours, then strain through a fine-mesh sieve lined with cheesecloth, pressing down on the ginger with a rubber spatula to extract all the liquid.

Pour the strained ginger liquid into an airtight container and add lime juice (if using). Refrigerate until ready to use, up to 1 week.

To serve, pour 4 ounces (1/2 cup) of the concentrate over ice in a tall glass and top with sparkling water to taste. Serve with a lime wedge and a splash of rum if you like!

GREENS ON FLEEK

Juicing has been all the craze for a while now. Fruit-based combinations are pure sugar shots, but veggie combos may actually live up to their hype as antioxidant-boosting, anti-inflammatory elixirs of youth. Anecdotally, I've never had better skin than when I take essential fatty acid supplements and a probiotic and drink green juice at least once a day. You can get a similar combination of hydrating fats, immune-boosting probiotics, and rich nutrient infusion by adding a little bit of coconut oil (or olive oil) and yogurt to your daily juice. That little bit of fat may actually help your body absorb the vitamins and minerals better, and it will keep you full longer, which has always been my biggest problem with juicing.

When it comes to choosing your equipment, sadly, even a high-powered blender doesn't really deliver the same results as a juicer because the fiber isn't removed and the result is not very drinkable. You want to get a juicer with a slow extraction system that doesn't heat the fruits or vegetables being pushed through (heat destroys some of the more delicate enzymes). I really like The Tribest Slowstar (about $300). It's pricey, but it works well, and if you plan on drinking juice a few times a week, it's well worth the investment versus spending $8 or more per bottled juice.

This "recipe" is meant only as an inspiration for you to play with—try whatever greens you like, or whatever water-rich veggies you have in your fridge that you don't feel like cooking. There's no wrong way!

MAKES ABOUT 44 OUNCES JUICE

2 English (seedless) cucumbers, halved lengthwise and cut into quarters

1/2 bunch of mint

2 cups spinach (or any dark greens, such as beet greens, Swiss chard, dandelion greens, or kale)

4 celery stalks, halved

2 pears or apples, quartered

1/2 bunch of fresh flat-leaf parsley

1 lime, peeled and fruit quartered

1 lemon, peeled and fruit quartered

1 1/2 tablespoons coconut oil (optional), at room temperature or melted

1/2 cup whole-milk yogurt (optional)

Begin adding the vegetables, fruits, and herbs to the juicer, alternating tender and softer items with the more fibrous ones (as in the order at left).

Drink the juice right away or chill it in a glass jar or airtight container. It can be refrigerated for up to 3 days.

If using coconut oil and yogurt, you'll need to add them separately and it's best to add them right before drinking your juice, since the coconut oil will solidify when it gets cold. I find it's best to shake the juice together with them in a jar, or throw them quickly into a blender to emulsify. A good ratio to keep in mind is 2 tablespoons yogurt and 1 teaspoon of coconut oil per 10 ounces of juice.

VEGAN VIETNAMESE-STYLE ICED COFFEE

There are few things I enjoy more than a spoon of condensed milk stirred into espresso. Of course, opening cans of condensed milk is a dangerous proposition for me, because then I'm tempted to drizzle it on my oatmeal, slather it on toast, eat it by the spoonful like a sticky Pooh Bear in the honey pot, getting it all over my fingers and face . . . and soon the jar is gone and the consequences to my wardrobe are dire.

This is my vegan take on the drink I love. I've taken out the condensed milk and made a sweet coconut milk infusion with vanilla, dates, and cardamom to build out the Vietnamese spice profile. I love it iced, but it works great warmed as well.

MAKES FOUR 6-OUNCE SERVINGS

- **1 cup light coconut milk**
- **4 Medjool dates, pitted**
- **1/4 teaspoon ground cardamom**
- **Pinch of kosher salt**
- **1 vanilla bean, split lengthwise (see Vanilla Bean 101, page 48)**
- **2 cups strong cold-brewed coffee (see Tip)**
- **2 tablespoons maple syrup (optional)**
- **Ice**

In a small saucepan, combine the coconut milk, dates, cardamom, and salt and bring to a simmer over medium-high heat. Scrape in the vanilla seeds and add the pod, cover, and bring the entire blend to a simmer again, then remove from the heat, uncover, and cool for 20 minutes.

Remove and discard the vanilla pod, then pour the mixture into a blender and blend until well combined and smooth.

Fill 4 glasses with ice. Divide the date milk among the glasses, roughly 1/4 cup per glass, then pour 1/2 cup of the coffee over each. If you like a sweeter drink, add a little maple syrup to the glass. Serve with a straw and a smile.

TIP: *Fill an ice cube tray with coffee and freeze for coffee ice cubes that won't dilute your iced coffee. Once frozen, pop them out of the ice cube tray and store them in a resealable quart-size freezer bag for up to 2 months.*

WHY GO COLD BREW?

With cold brew coffee, no hot water ever touches the coffee grounds, so the acidity level is lower—meaning it's less bitter and easier on your tummy. Simply put 4 parts cool, filtered water to 1 part very coarsely ground coffee (fine ground will yield a cloudy cup) in a large container, stir to combine, and let sit on your countertop for 12 hours or overnight. In the morning, strain the coffee through a fine-mesh sieve lined with cheesecloth and you have a cold-brew coffee concentrate. For a standard cup of coffee, mix 2 parts water to 1 part of the concentrate and heat or enjoy cold.

soups

Soup, glorious soup. It's there to cure what ails you, fill your belly with hearty richness, or lavish you with flavorful broth when you want a lighter option. This chapter is a smattering of some of my favorites, from the herbiest Matzo Ball Soup you've ever tasted to a spring pea awakening in my totally originally titled Warm Spring Pea Soup. If you want your soup to transport you (don't we all?), try the Chilled Cucumber Yogurt Soup and settle into summer afternoon life on the Turkish coast, or maybe you're craving a taste-bud rodeo in Mexico with zesty Posole Verde. And don't skip the Homemade Vegetable Broth Concentrate recipe—it's going to change your soup *and* sauce game!

HOMEMADE VEGETABLE BROTH CONCENTRATE

You can finally stop playing warehouse to boxes of broth and dehydrated bouillon cubes—and all the toxic extra sodium and MSG packed into most commercial varieties—with this veggie-loaded, flavor-packed concentrate. Make a big batch and tuck it away in your freezer to boost any soup or sauce, add to your braises, boil grains, or just enjoy as a simple and savory broth on its own.

Also, I want to take this moment to pay homage to the humble leek. When it comes to building soups, the basic mirepoix mix of carrots, celery, and onion are good. Garlic is of course welcome—plus all those nice, fresh herbs—but leeks, with their delicate sweetness, their winsome ability to dissolve into oniony oblivion and be both faint and powerful, are the game changer. Leek love forever. OK, now go make this bouillon!

MAKES ABOUT 1¾ CUPS CONCENTRATE (TO MAKE 14 QUARTS BROTH)

- 1 medium yellow onion, roughly chopped
- 2 medium carrots, peeled and roughly chopped
- 1 medium celery stalk, roughly chopped
- 1 small leek, white and light-green parts only, cleaned and roughly chopped (see How to Clean Leeks)
- 2 garlic cloves, roughly chopped
- 1½ tablespoons tomato paste
- ½ bunch of fresh parsley with stems (about 2 cups)
- 2 tablespoons fresh thyme leaves
- Freshly cracked black pepper
- 1 ¾ cups kosher salt (remember, you're diluting this into 14 quarts of broth, so it's not that much per serving)

In a food processor, combine the onion, carrots, celery, leek, and garlic. Process until the mixture is finely chopped and completely combined. Add the tomato paste, parsley, thyme, and pepper to taste, and process until well combined but flecks of herbs are still visible. Pulse in the salt.

Place concentrate into an airtight container or resealable plastic bag in the freezer. Because of the salt, it will not freeze completely, and you will be able to scoop some out as needed (or you can individually portion smaller amounts into plastic bags). To use, dissolve 2 tablespoons of concentrate in 4 cups of boiling water and let steep for 5 minutes. If you need a clear broth, let steep for 5 to 10 minutes, then strain through a fine-mesh sieve.

HOW TO CLEAN LEEKS

To ensure your leeks won't carry any dirt or grit into your recipes, fill a medium bowl with cold water. Cut off the gnarly, dark green upper leaves, peel the outer layer or two off each leek, and slice the remaining stalk in half lengthwise. Place both halves in the bowl with water. Swish gently and do a leek peek, checking between the layers to make sure any dirt is removed. Dry on paper towels, then use as desired.

CHILLED CUCUMBER-YOGURT SOUP

Sometimes all you want to eat for lunch is a cool but filling soup. I have you covered. Beaten, frothy yogurt, crisp cucumbers, fresh dill and mint, and a generous drizzle of olive oil make this soup as flavorful as it is fast to make. On the coasts of Greece and southern Turkey, some version of chilled yogurt is just the thing to cool down in the sweltering summer heat, which basically makes this soup the next best thing to a dive in Mediterranean depths.

MAKES 6 SERVINGS

4 cups whole-milk yogurt
1 cup filtered water
2 tablespoons extra-virgin olive oil
2 teaspoons kosher salt
2 English (seedless) cucumbers, peeled and finely chopped
1/2 cup finely chopped fresh dill
2 tablespoons fresh mint, finely chopped
1/2 tablespoon dried oregano
1 small garlic clove, grated on a Microplane-style rasp
Freshly cracked black pepper

In a stand mixer fitted with the whisk attachment (or a large bowl if using a hand mixer), whip the yogurt and water on medium speed until the mixture is frothy, 3 to 5 minutes.

Add the olive oil and salt and continue to whip on medium speed for 1 minute. By hand, stir in the cucumbers, dill, mint, oregano, and garlic and pepper to taste. Taste and season with more salt and pepper if needed.

Cover the bowl with plastic wrap and refrigerate until you're ready to serve (the soup is best eaten within 24 hours of making).

HERBY MATZO BALL SOUP

This is far and away my favorite soup anytime I'm feeling under the weather or just in need of some comfort from the cold, wet winters we get here in New York City. It's hearty enough for a meal—especially if you tear in some of the chicken from the homemade broth, or from a rotisserie chicken. Boxed broth will work just fine, but homemade broth feels extra curative, and all that delicious collagen from the bones thickens the soup to a luxurious, velvety texture.

The matzo balls are where this dish really cranks up. I love them the size of golf balls, fluffy, and soaked through with golden elixir broth. You'll find that mine are a little different from typical Jewish deli fare because they're positively exploding with vibrant, fresh herbs, which I find gilds the lily in the most wonderful of ways.

MAKES 6 SERVINGS

CHICKEN BROTH

1 tablespoon grapeseed oil

1 whole chicken (roughly 4 pounds), cut into parts

1 yellow onion, roughly chopped

4 medium carrots—2 roughly chopped, 2 sliced into thin coins

1 celery stalk, roughly chopped

1/2 teaspoon whole black peppercorns

3 fresh thyme sprigs

2 fresh parsley sprigs

1 bay leaf

Kosher salt and freshly cracked black pepper

Chopped fresh dill for serving

Grated fresh horseradish or ginger (optional)

MATZO BALLS

3/4 cup matzo meal

1 teaspoon kosher salt

1/2 teaspoon garlic powder

1/2 teaspoon onion powder

3 tablespoons finely chopped fresh dill

(Ingredients continue on the next page.)

To make the chicken broth, in a large soup pot, heat the oil over medium-high heat. Add the chicken pieces and brown on both sides, about 8 minutes total. Drain off 3 tablespoons of fat and set it aside for the matzo balls (melted butter can be substituted).

Add the onion, chopped carrots, celery, peppercorns, thyme, parsley, and bay leaf to the pot with the chicken. Cover with 4 quarts (16 cups) cold water and bring to a boil over medium-high heat. Reduce the heat to medium-low, partially cover, and simmer gently until the broth is very rich and fragrant, about 1 1/2 hours. Remove from the heat, let the soup cool for 1 hour, and strain it through a fine-mesh sieve, reserving the carrots and slicing them into thin coins. Discard all the other vegetables. Return the broth to a clean soup pot. Pull the chicken from the bones and save for sandwiches or salads, or for returning to the soup.

While the broth is cooking, make the matzo balls. In a large bowl, combine the matzo meal, salt, garlic powder, onion powder, and herbs. Whisk to combine. In a medium bowl, whisk together the eggs, reserved chicken fat (or melted butter), and 3 tablespoons of chicken broth. Add the wet mix to the dry mix and stir to combine. The mixture will be quite loose until the matzo meal absorbs the liquid. Cover the bowl with plastic wrap and refrigerate for 30 minutes.

Remove the matzo ball mixture from the refrigerator, wet your hands, and roll into roundish balls the size of golf balls. Place the balls on a plastic-wrap-lined plate and refrigerate for at least 30 minutes.

3 tablespoons finely chopped fresh chives

3 tablespoons finely chopped fresh parsley

3 large eggs, lightly beaten

Bring a large pot of salted water to a boil over high heat. (If you made a double batch of broth or have some boxed on hand, you can certainly make this poaching liquid all or partially broth—the matzo balls will drink up the extra flavor!) Reduce the heat to medium, add the matzo balls, and simmer until light and fluffy, for 45 minutes. (You can cut into one—the inside should be fully cooked and soaked with liquid, not hard, dense, or darker colored than the rest of the ball.) Remove from the heat.

While the matzo balls cook, bring the broth to a simmer and season with salt and pepper as needed.

Use a slotted spoon to transfer the cooked matzo balls to the broth. Cook for 5 minutes more, then remove from the heat. Add the carrot slices to heat through.

To serve, place some soup and 2 matzo balls in each bowl. Sprinkle with fresh dill and horseradish (if using).

TIP: *After roasting a chicken, save the chicken bones to make soup. Keep the bones in a resealable gallon-size freezer bag in the freezer and keep adding to the bag. When you have 3 or 4 chicken frames, make the Chicken Broth as directed on page 73 and add the frames to the pot along with the vegetables, herbs, and water.*

TIP: *For a less fatty broth, refrigerate the soup overnight before adding the matzo balls. All the fat (called schmaltz) will rise and solidify on the surface, so you can easily scrape away and discard or save for other cooking uses—it's especially great for browning and flavoring vegetables or meats in place of oil or butter.*

KALE, SAUSAGE, AND WHITE BEAN SOUP

You want to be healthy, you say? Great, well, this soup is loaded with tons of kale (phytonutrients! fiber!) and beans (protein! more fiber! sexy . . .). But you also want it to be indulgent? Okay! Let's start with sausage. Let it crisp up and render out some of its delicious fat, redolent with fennel, chile flakes, and oregano, and let's use that fat to cook everything else, flavoring the whole pot.

To me, healthy eating should never be about deprivation. It should be about figuring out the smartest way to squeeze maximum pleasure out of a few choice indulgences so that healthy dishes are also happy ones.

MAKES 6 SERVINGS

- 3 tablespoons extra-virgin olive oil, plus extra for serving
- 2 mild or spicy Italian sausages
- 1 medium yellow onion, finely chopped
- 2 teaspoons kosher salt
- 5 garlic cloves, minced
- 1 tablespoon finely chopped fresh thyme leaves
- 2½ teaspoons sweet paprika
- Freshly cracked black pepper
- 6 cups chicken broth or vegetable broth (made from Vegetable Broth Concentrate, page 69)
- One 15-ounce can cannellini beans, drained and rinsed
- 1 bunch of Tuscan (lacinato) kale, washed, dried, ribs removed, and leaves roughly chopped (about 8 cups)
- 1 tablespoon finely chopped fresh parsley leaves
- ¼ cup finely grated Parmigiano-Reggiano cheese

In a large soup pot, heat 2 tablespoons of the oil over medium-high heat. Squeeze the sausage out of the casing and fry it, stirring often to crumble, until cooked through, 6 to 8 minutes. Use a slotted spoon to transfer the sausage to a plate and set aside, leaving the sausage renderings in the pan.

Reduce the heat to medium and add the remaining 1 tablespoon olive oil, the onion, and 1 teaspoon of the salt. Cook until the onion starts to caramelize and soften, stirring often to scrape up any browned bits from the bottom of the pan, about 5 minutes. Stir in the garlic, thyme, paprika, and pepper to taste. Cook until the garlic is fragrant, about 1 minute.

Add the broth and beans, increase the heat to high, and bring the soup to a strong simmer. Reduce the heat to medium-low and cook, stirring occasionally, for 20 minutes. Return the sausage to the pot along with the kale and remaining 1 teaspoon salt and cook until the kale is tender, about 10 minutes more. Taste and add more salt and pepper as needed.

Serve the soup with a drizzle of olive oil, and sprinkled with the parsley and Parmigiano.

TIP: *Bring any leftover soup to a boil, take it off the heat, and add enough shards of day-old country-style bread to absorb the broth. Pack it into a baking dish, drizzle with olive oil, and sprinkle with lots of Parmigiano-Reggiano. Bake in a 350°F oven to crisp the top layer and serve sprinkled with fresh torn basil for a classic Tuscan dish of* ribollita.

LAZY LENTIL PORRIDGE WITH CHILE-CUMIN DRIZZLE

I call this Lazy Lentil Porridge because it's what I make when I don't feel like having to think about what's for lunch. My daughter is guaranteed to eat it up (I leave the spicy drizzle off hers) and my husband and I love it, too. It's loaded with sweet carrots and onion; the cauliflower I sneak in there breaks down almost entirely but leaves a few nice bits of texture throughout, and the yellow lentils gently soften to become an ultracreamy but dairy-free base. It gets even better with time, so don't be afraid to make extra.

MAKES 4 SERVINGS

CHILE-CUMIN DRIZZLE

2 tablespoons ghee or butter

1 teaspoon cumin seeds

1 teaspoon crushed chile flakes

1 shallot, minced

1/2 teaspoon kosher salt

PORRIDGE

1 tablespoon extra-virgin olive oil

1 medium sweet onion, minced

1/2 teaspoon kosher salt

1 garlic clove, minced

1 teaspoon dried oregano

1/2 teaspoon ground cumin

1/4 teaspoon ground coriander

1 bay leaf

2 large carrots, peeled and finely chopped

Florets from 1/2 head of cauliflower, finely chopped

1 cup red or yellow lentils, rinsed

2 1/2 cups vegetable broth (made from Vegetable Broth Concentrate, page 69), store-bought low-sodium vegetable or chicken broth, or water

Freshly cracked black pepper

2 scallions, white and light-green parts only, finely chopped (optional)

To make the chile-cumin drizzle, in a small skillet, melt the ghee over medium heat. Add the cumin and chile flakes and fry the spices, stirring often, until the cumin is fragrant and toasted, about 1 minute. Add the shallot and salt and cook, stirring often, until it is softened and caramelizing, about 5 minutes. Remove from the heat and set aside to steep.

To make the porridge, in a medium pot, heat the olive oil over medium heat. Add the onion and salt and cook, stirring often, until the onion softens, 2 to 3 minutes. Add the garlic and cook, stirring often, until it is fragrant, about 30 seconds, then stir in the oregano, cumin, coriander, bay leaf, carrots, and cauliflower. Let cook, stirring, for 3 minutes, then add the lentils and toast for 1 minute, stirring.

Increase the heat to high, add the broth, and bring to a boil. Reduce the heat to low, cover, and cook, stirring occasionally, until the lentils are tender and have absorbed most of the liquid, 25 to 30 minutes. The porridge should be wet but thick, like Indian dal. Taste and add more salt and broth or water if needed. Add a few cracks of black pepper and stir to combine.

Ladle the porridge into a bowl and drizzle with the chile-cumin ghee. If desired, garnish with the scallions.

DERBY

POZOLE VERDE

I first had a version of this soup on a family outing to New Mexico when I was about twelve years old. We were taking a road trip *(road trip!)* around the Four Corners states, and it was on this same vacation that my parents decided to pick up an inebriated *(drunk!)* hitchhiker *(stranger!)* and pack him into the back of the car with all their children. Luckily, we survived, and he turned out to be perfectly sweet if a little lost. But the experience certainly stayed with me. . . .

We stopped at every rodeo, saw pueblo towns built right into the sides of mountains, and ate all the Tex-Mex we could find. My first taste of this soup was one of the memories that stuck. I'd never had so many flavors in one slurp of broth before—rich chicken broth at the base; tangy acid from the tomatillos and lime; onion, garlic, and jalapeño singing throughout, and a touch of sweetness at the back that always showed up just in time. The hominy totally blew my mind—it's such a strange, soft, "corn-y" thing to bite into, but it perfectly balances the brightness of the surrounding broth. It became the special soup I would search for every time we ate out, until I finally decided a few years ago to try my hand at re-creating the perfect one I'd had all those years ago in New Mexico.

MAKES 6 SERVINGS

- 5 medium tomatillos, husked, rinsed, and halved
- 1 small sweet yellow onion, halved (one half chopped, for serving)
- 1 jalapeño pepper, roughly chopped (seeded for less heat)
- 2 tablespoons pure maple syrup
- 2 medium garlic cloves, peeled
- 1 teaspoon ground cumin
- 1 teaspoon dried oregano
- 1/2 bunch of fresh flat-leaf parsley, roughly chopped (about 1 cup), plus extra for serving
- 4 cups (1 quart) hot chicken stock
- 4 bone-in, skin-on chicken thighs
- 2 teaspoons kosher salt
- 2 tablespoons extra-virgin olive oil
- Two 15-ounce cans hominy, rinsed and drained
- Grated zest from 1/2 orange plus 1/4 cup orange juice
- Freshly cracked black pepper
- Thinly sliced radishes for serving
- Diced avocado for serving
- Whole-milk yogurt or sour cream for serving
- 2 limes, cut into wedges, for serving

In a blender, combine the tomatillos, the whole onion half, the jalapeño, maple syrup, garlic, cumin, oregano, and parsley. Add 1 cup of the hot chicken stock and blend until completely smooth.

Season both sides of the chicken generously with the salt. Heat a large, heavy-bottomed pot over medium-high heat for 2 minutes. Add the olive oil, let it shimmer, and add the chicken thighs, skin-side down. Reduce the heat to medium and cook on both sides until browned and the chicken is cooked through, 15 to 20 minutes total. Transfer the chicken to a large plate.

Pour the tomatillo mixture into the pot and stir, scraping up any browned bits. Reduce the heat to medium-low and simmer until the sauce is reduced by half, 8 to 10 minutes.

Add the remaining 3 cups chicken stock and the hominy to the pot, then stir in the orange zest and juice. Bring to a boil, then reduce the heat to medium-low and simmer until the hominy is warmed through, about 10 minutes. Taste and adjust the seasoning with more salt and black pepper if needed.

While the pozole simmers, remove and discard the chicken skin from the thighs and pull the meat off the bone. Use your fingers or two forks to shred it, then divide it among serving bowls.

To serve, ladle some soup over the chicken and finish with chopped onion, radish, avocado, parsley, and a dollop of yogurt or sour cream. Serve with a lime wedge and the spiced chips from the carnitas, on page 245, or your favorite tortilla chip!

TIP: *If you can't find tomatillos, use green tomatoes (not quite the same, but close enough). If you can't find green tomatoes, use red ones! This soup is much less about the color or the specific ingredient than about finding that perfect balance of tart acidity and rich chicken broth.*

VEGGIE CHILI 'N' BEER

You may have had some pretty tasty chilies before. But I bet few have promised stick-to-your-ribs satisfaction *and* a totally vegetarian ingredients list. And still fewer will have made sure the whole blend comes together in a supreme broth of chipotle, tomato, and—you guessed it—beer! The frat boy's drink of choice adds tons of malty richness, so you will never miss the ingredients I've taken out to help keep this chili both light and filling.

The best part is, all you have to do is throw a bunch of ingredients into a pot and let it simmer away on the stove until you're ready to eat. The longer the flavors have to meld together, the better, but 30 minutes on the stove is all you need if you're in a time crunch.

MAKES 8 SERVINGS

- 2 tablespoons olive oil
- 1 large yellow onion, finely chopped
- 4 garlic cloves, smashed
- 1/4 cup tomato paste
- 2 medium zucchini or yellow squash, ends trimmed, diced
- One 16-ounce can chopped or diced roasted tomatoes (with juices) or 2 cups homemade Oven-Dried Tomatoes (page 162), chopped
- 2 bay leaves
- 1/2 tablespoon ground cumin
- 1 1/2 tablespoons dried oregano
- 1/2 tablespoon chipotle chile powder
- 1 tablespoon kosher salt
- Freshly cracked black pepper
- 1 chipotle pepper in adobo sauce, finely chopped, plus 1 to 2 tablespoons adobo sauce (depending on how smoky and spicy you like it)
- Two 15-ounce cans kidney beans, drained and rinsed
- One 15-ounce can black beans, drained and rinsed
- One 12-ounce bottle beer (I like a mellow beer, such as Corona, but most pale, mild lagers will work; a stout like Guinness would take over the flavor profile)
- 2 cups vegetable broth (or 4 teaspoons Vegetable Broth Concentrate, page 69, dissolved in 2 cups boiling water)
- Grated cheddar cheese for serving
- Sour cream for serving
- Diced avocado for serving
- 2 limes, cut into wedges, for serving

In a large heavy-bottomed pot, heat the oil over medium-high heat until it shimmers, about 2 minutes. Add the onion and garlic and cook, stirring often, until they are translucent, 2 to 3 minutes. Stir in the tomato paste and cook, stirring, until the color has deepened, 2 to 3 minutes. Stir in the zucchini and cook, stirring occasionally, until the zucchini starts to soften, about 5 minutes.

Stir in the tomatoes (with their juices), bay leaves, cumin, oregano, chipotle powder, salt, black pepper to taste, chipotle chile and adobo sauce, and beans. Pour in the beer and broth. The liquid should cover everything in the pot—if it doesn't, add water or more broth to cover.

Bring the chili to a boil, reduce the heat to medium-low, and simmer gently, stirring occasionally, for at least 30 minutes. Remove from the heat and taste; adjust the salt and pepper as needed.

Serve with some grated cheddar and a dollop of sour cream, then top with avocado and a squeeze of lime.

ROASTED TOMATO SOUP WITH GIANT CHEESY HERB CROUTONS

I'm the girl who drinks whole mugs of my grandfather's Staten Island Special spaghetti sauce (check out my book *Relish* for the recipe!), so suffice it to say I really like tomato soup. The natural sugars in tomatoes become much more present with a little oven time, and I love to balance that sweetness with these incredible giant cheesy herb croutons that also make for great party crackers if you're having guests over.

MAKES 6 SERVINGS

GIANT CHEESY HERB CROUTONS

1/2 cup grated Gruyère, cheddar, or Parmigiano-Reggiano cheese

Leaves from a few sprigs fresh oregano or thyme

1/2 teaspoon crushed chile flakes

1/2 teaspoon kosher salt

Freshly cracked black pepper

8 slices (1/2 inch thick) whole wheat sourdough, peasant loaf, or baguette

2 tablespoons extra-virgin olive oil

ROASTED TOMATO SOUP

3 1/4 pounds (about 5 large) beefsteak tomatoes, cored, halved, and sliced into wedges

1 medium yellow onion, peeled, halved, and quartered

3 garlic cloves, unpeeled

1 tablespoon finely chopped fresh thyme leaves

2 teaspoons kosher salt

Freshly cracked black pepper

3 tablespoons extra-virgin olive oil, plus more for drizzling

2 cups vegetable broth, homemade (using Vegetable Broth Concentrate, page 69) or store-bought, or water in a pinch (plus more if you want a thinner soup)

1/4 cup roughly chopped fresh basil leaves for serving

Adjust the oven racks so that the oven will fit both a large roasting pan (or 9 x 13-inch baking dish) and a rimmed baking sheet. Preheat the oven to 400°F.

To make the croutons, line a rimmed baking sheet with parchment paper. In a small bowl, combine the cheese, oregano, chile flakes, salt, and pepper to taste. Rub this mixture between your fingers to distribute the flavors and incorporate. Arrange the bread slices on the baking sheet and sprinkle with the herbed cheese. Drizzle the slices with the olive oil. Toast until the cheese is melted and golden brown, 10 to 12 minutes. Set aside.

At the same time, to make the soup, place the tomatoes, onion, garlic, thyme, salt, and pepper in a large roasting pan or a 9 x 13-inch baking dish. Drizzle with the olive oil and use your hands to toss to combine. Roast the vegetables until the tomatoes are very soft and juicy, about 30 minutes.

Let the tomatoes and onion cool slightly. Peel the garlic cloves. Transfer to a blender and puree until smooth (be sure to include any pan juices). Pour into a medium saucepan with the broth.

Taste and adjust the seasoning, and add more broth or water if you want a thinner soup. Serve warm, garnished with a crouton, a drizzle of olive oil, and a rain of fresh basil.

WARM SPRING PEA SOUP

This fresh pea soup has nothing to do with the traditional, thick pea and bacon version you may have tried. That one plays its part well on cold fall and winter days. But *this* pea soup celebrates the glory of sweet, delicate, fresh spring and summer peas. The broth in this all-veggie delight is lush with fresh pea puree and little rivulets of olive oil that dance over leeks, carrot coins, and bok choy. It's a winner if you're trying to have a lighter day that's full of flavor.

MAKES 4 SERVINGS

2 small heads baby bok choy

6 cups vegetable broth, homemade (using Vegetable Broth Concentrate, page 69) or store-bought

2 leeks, dark-green tops discarded, cleaned (see How to Clean Leeks, page 69); white and pale-green parts very thinly sliced

3 carrots, peeled and thinly sliced into coins

3 cups fresh or frozen peas

1/2 cup fresh mint leaves

1 teaspoon kosher salt, plus extra for serving

Extra-virgin olive oil for serving

Separate the bok choy ribs from the leaves. Slice the ribs on the bias into 1/4-inch-wide pieces; leave the bok choy leaves whole.

Bring the broth to a gentle simmer over medium-high heat and add the sliced leeks and carrot coins. Simmer until the vegetables are tender, about 10 minutes, then add the bok choy rib pieces and cook 1 minute longer. Use a slotted spoon to transfer all the leeks, carrots, and bok choy to a medium bowl. Add 2 cups of the peas, the mint, and salt to the broth and cook until the peas are just tender, 1 to 2 minutes.

Remove from the heat, set aside to cool slightly, then blend the soup with an immersion blender (or, working in batches, puree it in a stand blender). Take care when blending hot soup! Best to hold the lid on with a kitchen towel or potholder.

Return the soup to medium heat and bring to a simmer, then remove from the heat and add the remaining 1 cup peas and the bok choy leaves to heat through. Divide the leeks, carrots, and bok choy ribs among 4 bowls. Top with the soup. Serve drizzled with a little olive oil and a pinch of salt.

salads

Forget the rabbit food salads you may have suffered through with their sad blends of wilted leaves and spartan portions. The salads in this chapter are a celebration of vibrant vegetables and fruits, and some don't have any lettuce at all. There are roasted salads like the Plums with Tahini Dressing, and raw ones like the Brussels Sprout Salad with Pecorino and Capers. There are cool ones—like my grandmother's famous White Bean Salad with Celery—and warm ones, like the delectable Lentil-Citrus Salad. There are simple, flavorful dressings that will have you ditching your bottled standbys while tempting you back for seconds.

I am convinced that the reason French women don't get fat is because their health food tastes like the intoxicatingly delicious Carrot Salad with Parsley and Golden Raisins. I am also convinced that one of my all-time favorite meals is the Thai Niçoise Salad with spicy peanut-lime dressing. Surprise yourself—you're about to go salad wild.

KALE AND PLUM SALAD WITH MISO VINAIGRETTE

Kale chips, kale smoothies, kale candy . . . Kale is here to stay, and though we may be going a little overboard trying to find new and interesting ways to eat it, the traditional salad is still my favorite. Raw kale has the most vital nutrition, and since you're probably eating the stuff because you care about your body, allow me to introduce you to a way of eating it that takes good care of your taste buds, too.

If you've had raw kale and hated it, it probably just wasn't massaged. Yes, you read that right. Kale is an extremely sturdy (read: full of fiber) green that needs to be broken down a little bit before it will properly absorb delicious dressings and be easier to chew. The massage technique is really easy: Tear the kale into small pieces, getting rid of the sturdy ribs. Drizzle with a little olive oil and salt, then use your fingertips to pinch and press the leaves until they turn an even deeper green and begin to soften. Ahh, much better. Uptight kale is the worst. Massaged kale is going to be your jam.

MAKES 4 SERVINGS

1/4 small Vidalia onion, thinly sliced

2 tablespoons white wine vinegar

1 1/2 bunches (about 10 leaves) Tuscan (lacinato) kale, washed and dried, ribs removed and leaves torn into bite-size pieces (about 5 1/2 cups)

1/2 teaspoon kosher salt

Freshly cracked black pepper

2 teaspoons extra-virgin olive oil

1 tablespoon white miso

1 teaspoon sugar

1/4 cup grapeseed oil

2 plums, halved, pitted, and thinly sliced

In a food processor, combine the onion and vinegar and set aside for 5 minutes. This will gently pickle the onion so the flavor will be a bit more mild than straight up raw.

Place the kale in a large bowl, sprinkle with the salt and pepper to taste, and drizzle with the olive oil. Use your hands to massage the kale until the leaves soften, 2 to 3 minutes.

Add the miso and sugar to the food processor and pulse 2 to 3 times to combine, then turn the processor on and slowly drizzle in the grapeseed oil until the dressing is creamy. Drizzle the dressing over the kale and toss to combine. Garnish with the plums, then serve.

TIP: *If plums aren't in season, segmented citrus works well. Check out Segmenting Citrus on page 27.*

TIP: *Massaged kale yields a lovely, softened green that's much better able to drink up a tasty dressing than big pieces of raw kale. However, if you're looking for a crunchier salad and are handy with a knife, giving the kale more surface area without actually breaking it down will ensure you get a salad that holds on to its dressing and its crunch. The trick is to remove the sturdy ribs, and when you have 3 or 4 leaves, lay the largest one on the bottom and pile the others on top, then roll them up tight like a cigar. Now, slice across the "cigar" to form very thin ribbons of kale.*

SPINACH SALAD WITH CRISPY CHICKPEAS AND APPLES

I warn you now, make only as many of these as you're comfortable eating, because they'll *all* be gone. I'm about to introduce you to the addictive snack that is crispy, roasted (kind of fried) chickpeas. Take that mighty, protein-packed staple of salad bars everywhere, toss it with some chile powder and a tiny hit of sugar, and roast it to a glowing, crisp little nub that crunches delicately in your mouth and makes this spinach salad, flecked with crunchy-sweet apples and tangy vinaigrette, feel deliciously sinful and healthy all at once. Perfect.

MAKES 4 SERVINGS

One 15.5-ounce can chickpeas, drained, rinsed, and dried on a kitchen towel

5 tablespoons extra-virgin olive oil

1 teaspoon chipotle chile powder

1/2 teaspoon smoked paprika

1 1/2 teaspoons sugar

1 teaspoon kosher salt

Freshly cracked black pepper

3 tablespoons apple cider vinegar

1 small shallot, minced

1 teaspoon grainy mustard

1 red or green apple, peeled, cored, and diced (about the same size as the chickpeas)

4 cups baby spinach, washed and dried

1/4 cup chopped walnuts, toasted (see Toasting Nuts, page 14)

Preheat the oven to 400°F.

In a medium bowl, toss together the chickpeas, 2 tablespoons of the olive oil, the chipotle powder, smoked paprika, 1 teaspoon of the sugar, 1/2 teaspoon of the salt, and pepper to taste. Transfer the chickpeas to a rimmed baking sheet and toast in the oven, shaking the pan occasionally, until they are crisp and golden brown, 25 to 30 minutes. Transfer the chickpeas to a large plate to cool.

In a large bowl, whisk together the vinegar, shallot, mustard, and remaining 1/2 teaspoon each sugar and salt, then slowly drizzle in the remaining 3 tablespoons oil. Add the apple and spinach and toss to combine. Sprinkle the chickpeas and walnuts over the top and serve.

WHITE BEAN SALAD WITH CELERY

This is one of my grandmother's signature dishes (Hi, Grandmommy!). She took her whole family—all six children and Italian New Yorker husband—vegetarian in the seventies (some later rebelled), and she's been a longtime advocate for plant-based eating, even before veganism became the new black. In this salad, she has a generous hand with the vinegar and adds just enough oil to hold it all in line. Sweet onion, celery, and fresh herbs keep the salad light, fresh, and crisp, while the beans themselves are creamy and tender.

We love this at picnics—it keeps really well in the heat since there's no dairy in the dressing—and cold out of the fridge for late-night snacks. It's even better the day after it's made, as the beans soak up the dressing and tenderize even more.

MAKES 6 TO 8 SERVINGS

Two 15.5-ounce cans cannellini beans, drained and rinsed

4 celery stalks, thinly sliced into half-moons

1/2 small sweet onion, minced

2 tablespoons red wine vinegar

1 1/2 teaspoons Dijon mustard

1 small garlic clove, grated on a Microplane-style rasp

1 teaspoon kosher salt

Freshly cracked black pepper

1/4 cup extra-virgin olive oil

1/4 cup fresh parsley and/or basil leaves, roughly chopped

In a large bowl, combine the beans, celery, and onion.

In a small bowl, whisk together the vinegar, mustard, garlic, salt, and pepper to taste. While whisking, slowly drizzle in the olive oil, whisking until the vinaigrette is creamy and emulsified.

Pour the dressing over the beans and toss to combine. Sprinkle with the herbs and serve.

SHAVED BRUSSELS SPROUT SALAD WITH PECORINO AND CAPERS

There's a restaurant in New York City called Barbuto where the chef, Jonathan Waxman, has perfected (among many menu items) a version of this dish. Sadly for me, it's only available seasonally, and I live too far away to stop in for one nightly, or I would. So, I did what all resourceful gluttons do and tried to figure out how to make this beloved salad at home, where I could eat it to my heart's content. My version adds some capers for a little bite, and I love the extra salty creaminess of pecorino (sheep's milk) cheese, but you could totally use Parmigiano-Reggiano. Other than that, this is as close as I could come, and it makes me very happy.

By the way, slicing all these Brussels sprouts thin by hand is a form of hazing in some kitchens, but extremely necessary and worth the effort. To make it easier, invest in a slicer attachment for your food processer, or very carefully experiment with your mandoline.

MAKES 4 TO 6 SERVINGS

- 1 pound Brussels sprouts, stems trimmed and tough outer leaves removed
- 2/3 cup finely grated Pecorino Romano cheese, plus extra for serving
- 1/4 cup fresh lemon juice (1 to 2 lemons)
- 1/4 cup roughly chopped capers
- 1/2 teaspoon kosher salt
- Freshly cracked black pepper
- 1/2 cup extra-virgin olive oil
- 1 tablespoon finely chopped mint leaves (see The Best Way to Chop Fresh Herbs)

Using the slicing attachment of a food processor or a chef's knife, thinly shred the Brussels sprouts. Place them in a large bowl and toss with the cheese, lemon juice, capers, salt, pepper to taste, and the olive oil. Taste and add more salt if needed. For a crisp salad, serve immediately, sprinkled with more cheese and the mint. If the salad sits a bit, it will be wilted, but still delicious.

THE BEST WAY TO CHOP FRESH HERBS

The less you chop and crush your herbs on a cutting board, the less flavor you leave behind on that surface. Ideally, you want to make only one or two passes with your knife through fresh herbs. To make thin ribbons of fresh mint or basil leaves with minimal cuts, choose the largest leaves in the bunch, stack them, roll them tightly like a cigar, and thinly slice them crosswise to create thin and tender ribbons called chiffonade.

ROASTED PLUMS WITH TAHINI DRESSING

This recipe was actually concocted on the spot by Frances Boswell, food whisperer extraordinaire and the delicate hands that made every recipe in this book look so lush and photo-ready. We had extra plums left over from the kale salad, so she threw them on a baking sheet in the oven and forgot about them . . . until the wafting smell of roasting fruit caught all of our attention. The savory quality of the herbed sweet-sour plums, plus this incredibly creamy tahini and lemon dressing, is unthinkably tasty. Plus, it's a great way to use up fruit that is just about to turn.

MAKES 4 SERVINGS

- **2 pounds plums, halved and pitted**
- **2 tablespoons extra-virgin olive oil**
- **1 teaspoon kosher salt**
- **Freshly cracked black pepper**
- **1 tablespoon fresh thyme and/or oregano leaves, stripped from about 4 sprigs**
- **Tahini Dressing (recipe follows)**
- **Flaky sea salt for garnish**

Preheat the oven to 400°F. Line a baking sheet with parchment paper.

Arrange the fruit, cut side up, on the prepared baking sheet. Drizzle with the olive oil and season well with the salt and pepper to taste. Sprinkle the fruit with all but a pinch of the fresh herbs.

Place the baking sheet in the oven and immediately reduce the heat to 250°F. Roast until the fruit is very soft and juicy and starting to caramelize, about 2 hours. (Alternatively, turn off the oven after 1 hour and leave the fruit in the oven overnight. This will produce a more leathery result. Either way is good!)

Layer a plate with the roasted fruit, then drizzle with the tahini dressing. Sprinkle with the reserved fresh thyme or oregano and a pinch of flaky sea salt.

TAHINI DRESSING

MAKES ALMOST 2 CUPS

- **Juice of 2 lemons (about 6 tablespoons)**
- **1 cup raw tahini (sesame paste)**
- **1/2 teaspoon kosher salt**
- **1 ice cube**

In a medium bowl, combine 3 tablespoons of the lemon juice, the tahini, 3/4 cup water, salt, and the ice cube. Whisk vigorously until the mixture comes together. It should lighten in color and thicken enough that it holds an edge when the whisk is dragged through it.

Remove the ice cube if any remains unmelted and adjust the seasoning, adding more lemon juice and salt until the sauce is addictive—you will know. Scrape the sauce into a shallow serving dish and hide it from the eaters in your house until ready to serve.

WATERMELON-GOAT CHEESE SALAD

This is probably the easiest recipe in the book, and perhaps the one I crave most often. It's traditional in Turkey to have an afternoon snack of screamingly cold, fresh cut watermelon (So sweet! So juicy! So perfectly refreshing on a hot day!) accompanied by triangles of salty feta cheese. Watermelon can have such a range of flavors, from the outer rim that tastes faintly of cucumber to the luscious middle where all the sugar concentrates. The creaminess of the goat cheese (I find it sticks a little better to the melon than feta), the delicate kiss of good-quality olive oil, flakes of sea salt that glorify the sweetness, and a few cracks of black pepper make this my ultimate summer bite.

MAKES 4 SERVINGS

1/2 medium watermelon, sliced or cubed (about 4 cups), chilled

1/2 cup crumbled goat cheese

1/4 cup extra-virgin olive oil

Flaky sea salt

Freshly cracked black pepper

Arrange the watermelon on a platter and sprinkle the goat cheese over the top. Drizzle with the olive oil and season with a few pinches of salt and pepper to taste. Serve immediately.

SNOW PEA SLAW

This slaw is extra bright and crisp, loaded with snow peas—or sugar snap peas in summer—apple, thinly sliced cabbage, and a handful of chopped roasted, salted peanuts on top for good measure and a little fatty friend for your mouth. All you need for dressing is some olive oil and fresh lime juice and you have yourself a gloriously easy side that pairs perfectly with the easy crab cakes on page 208, or any sweet, delicate fish—even chicken!

MAKES 6 SERVINGS

- **1/2 pound snow peas, thinly sliced on the bias**
- **1 cup thinly sliced green or red cabbage**
- **1 small apple, halved, cored, and cut into thin matchsticks (I like Honeycrisp, but Granny Smith is nice and tart)**
- **2 scallions, finely chopped**
- **2 tablespoons fresh lime juice**
- **1 tablespoon extra-virgin olive oil**
- **1/2 teaspoon kosher salt**
- **1/2 teaspoon sugar**
- **1/2 cup salted roasted peanuts, chopped (or see Toasting Nuts, page 14, to roast raw peanuts)**

In a large bowl, combine the snow peas, cabbage, apple, scallions, lime juice, olive oil, salt, and sugar and toss to combine. Divide the salad among plates and serve sprinkled with the peanuts.

TIP: *This is an incredibly kid-friendly raw slaw. It's a little bit sweet from the apple with the familiar crunch of peanuts. If your family has to avoid peanuts, try salted roasted sunflower or pumpkin seeds (pepitas) instead!*

WARM LENTIL-CITRUS SALAD

I am a really, really big fan of lentils. They are incredibly filling (loaded with tons of fiber and protein) and absorb the flavor of whatever you serve them with—meaning they're even better as leftovers! They retain a beautiful al dente texture if you don't overcook them, giving you plenty of chew. I love to make a giant batch of this salad on Sundays and save some to throw over mixed greens with a sprinkle of goat cheese and extra dressing for easy lunches throughout the week.

MAKES 6 SERVINGS

- 1 cup dried green lentils (such as Le Puy)
- 1/2 yellow onion (slice it through the equator rather than through the root)
- 6 whole cloves
- 1 bay leaf
- 1 orange, segmented (see Segmenting Citrus, page 27), juice reserved
- 2 grapefruits, segmented (see Segmenting Citrus, page 27), juice reserved
- 1 small shallot, finely chopped
- 2 tablespoons red wine vinegar
- 1 teaspoon honey
- 1 teaspoon Dijon mustard
- 6 tablespoons extra-virgin olive oil
- 1 teaspoon kosher salt
- Freshly cracked black pepper
- 1 cup fresh flat-leaf parsley, roughly torn or chopped and stems minced

In a medium saucepan, combine the lentils and 4 cups water. Stud the onion half with the cloves and add it to the pot. Add the bay leaf and bring the lentils to a boil over high heat. Reduce the heat to medium-low and gently simmer until the lentils are tender, 25 to 30 minutes. Drain the lentils (discard the onion and bay leaf) and transfer the lentils to a large bowl.

In a medium bowl, whisk together the orange juice, grapefruit juice, shallot, vinegar, honey, mustard, olive oil, salt, and pepper to taste. Pour the vinaigrette over the warm lentils and toss to combine. Add the parsley, toss to combine, taste, and season with more salt and pepper if needed. Serve garnished with the orange and grapefruit segments. This salad is of course delicious cold, too—and even better the next day. Just wait to add the citrus until you are ready to eat to keep them bright and fresh.

ALL ABOUT LENTILS

Lentils are an incredibly versatile little legume. Typically, they fall into three categories: green (firmest texture after cooking, great for salads), brown (medium-firm texture, a little quicker cooking and slightly muddier, earthy flavor; these are the lentils you'll typically find in lentil soup), and red (soft and mushy when cooked with the sweetest natural flavor, making them ideal for creamy soups and dals). I prefer green lentils for this salad, like Le Puy (French green lentils).

BURST GRAPE AND RADICCHIO SALAD

Why cook grapes? Because, like roasted tomatoes, cooked grapes first caramelize their sugars in juicy little bombs, then burst and concentrate all their flavor into dainty morsels. The escaped juices become an intense infusion for this recipe's port vinaigrette, greeting the bitter crunch of endive, radicchio, and peppery arugula with a sweet little kiss. Because this salad is so unusual and has such vibrant flavor of its own, I love to pair it with naturally sweet meats cooked simply, such as a roasted chicken or grilled pork chop.

MAKES 4 SERVINGS

- 5 tablespoons extra-virgin olive oil
- 4 fresh thyme sprigs
- 1/2 teaspoon dried oregano
- 2 cups halved red grapes
- 1 teaspoon kosher salt
- 1/4 cup tawny port wine
- 3 tablespoons sherry vinegar
- Freshly cracked black pepper
- 2 heads of Belgian endive, ends trimmed, halved lengthwise, and thinly sliced crosswise
- 2 cups baby arugula
- 1 head of radicchio, cored, halved, and thinly sliced
- Small wedge of Parmigiano-Reggiano cheese
- Lemon wedges for serving

In a medium skillet, heat 2 tablespoons of the olive oil over medium-high heat. Add the thyme sprigs and oregano and cook until they start to sizzle, 30 seconds to 1 minute. Add the grapes and salt and toss to combine. Turn the heat to medium-low and cook, stirring often, until the grapes soften, about 10 minutes.

Pour in the port, bring to a simmer for 2 minutes or until reduced by half, then remove from the heat and let sit 5 minutes more. Transfer to a medium bowl and whisk in the sherry vinegar and remaining 3 tablespoons olive oil. Taste and season with salt and pepper as needed.

In a large bowl, combine the endive, arugula, and radicchio. Drizzle half of the vinaigrette over the greens and toss to combine. Add more dressing if desired. Transfer to a large platter and spoon the remaining vinaigrette (including the grapes; discard the thyme sprigs) over the top.

Use a vegetable peeler to shave thin ribbons of Parmigiano over the salad. Serve with lemon wedges.

SAINT'S SALAD WITH GINGER-MAPLE VINAIGRETTE

This is one of *many* "garbage" salads I make toward the end of the week when I have a few bunches of kale I bought on Monday still waiting to be eaten, maybe some leftover rice or quinoa, and a few apples at the ready. The magic is in the ginger-maple vinaigrette. It is downright transformative. Seriously, this salad has converted so many former kale haters it deserves sainthood—hence, Saint's Salad.

Get chopping and prepare to enjoy the salad that eats like a meal, though it works very nicely as a hearty side to roasted chicken (oh, or the baby back ribs on page 248 if you want to embrace your inner Saint and Sinner, too).

MAKES 4 SERVINGS

SALAD

- 1/4 cup pine nuts, hazelnuts, or walnuts
- 1 bunch Tuscan (lacinato) kale, washed, dried, and ribs removed
- 1 1/4 cups cooked wild rice or long-grain brown rice
- 1 apple, peeled, cored, and finely diced
- 1/2 cup pomegranate seeds (optional)

DRESSING

- 1 inch fresh ginger
- 1 small garlic clove
- 2 tablespoons white wine vinegar
- 1 1/2 teaspoons maple syrup
- 1 teaspoon kosher salt
- Freshly cracked black pepper
- 1/4 cup extra-virgin olive oil or grapeseed oil

To make the salad, toast the pine nuts in a medium skillet over medium heat until they are golden brown, shaking the pan often, 2 to 3 minutes. (If using hazelnuts or walnuts, see Toasting Nuts on page 14 for how to toast.) Set the nuts aside to cool on a plate.

Stack a few kale leaves and roll them like a cigar, then thinly slice them crosswise into ribbons. Add the kale, rice, and apple to a large bowl.

To make the dressing, peel the ginger and grate it on a Microplane-style rasp into a medium bowl. Gather the grated ginger in your fingers and squeeze to release the ginger juice, then discard the pulp. Grate the garlic into the bowl with the ginger juice. Whisk in the vinegar, maple syrup, salt, and pepper to taste. Slowly whisk in the olive oil to emulsify.

Pour the dressing over the salad and toss to combine. Let the salad sit for 10 minutes, then sprinkle with the nuts and pomegranate seeds (if using) and serve.

VARIATION: *This salad is a perfect Thanksgiving side dish with dried cherries and toasted pecans used in place of the pomegranate seeds and pine nuts.*

CUCUMBER, PEACH, AND FETA SALAD

I started making this salad as a riff on the traditional Greek shepherd salad of tomatoes, cucumbers, onions, and feta. I swapped in peaches for tomatoes (you could totally do both, especially at the height of summer when you need to be seizing every opportunity to enjoy their brief moment of perfectly ripe juiciness). Instead of onion, I love the slightly sweeter and muted taste of chives. And that little bit of grainy mustard in the dressing is a welcome surprise.

MAKES 4 SERVINGS

- 1 English (seedless) cucumber or 4 Persian (mini) cucumbers, sliced into thin rounds
- 2 peaches, peeled, halved, pitted, and thinly sliced
- 1/4 cup crumbled feta cheese (preferably Belgian or French)
- 2 tablespoons balsamic vinegar
- 1 small garlic clove, grated on a Microplane-style rasp
- 1 teaspoon grainy mustard
- 1 teaspoon honey
- 3/4 teaspoon kosher salt
- Freshly cracked black pepper
- 3 tablespoons extra-virgin olive oil
- 1/4 cup chopped fresh chives

On a platter, alternate slices of cucumber and peaches. Crumble the feta over the top.

In a small bowl, whisk together the vinegar, garlic, mustard, honey, salt, and pepper to taste. While whisking, slowly drizzle in the olive oil until the dressing is creamy and emulsified.

Drizzle the dressing over the salad and serve sprinkled with the chives.

VARIATION: *In the winter I like to make this salad with grapes instead of peaches.*

VARIATION: *Feta cheese can have a very assertive, salty flavor. To make the salad mellower, substitute ricotta salata or goat cheese.*

THAI NIÇOISE SALAD

I know I wrote this book, and I should love all my recipes equally, but this is my salad queen. Overflowing with a variety of colorful veggies—crisp romaine lettuce, crunchy bean sprouts and cabbage, juicy cucumbers and tomatoes, creamy fingerling potatoes, peppery paper-thin radishes—all doused in a vibrant, gently spicy peanut-lime dressing with a shower of fresh herbs, it just feels like total abundance and pure opulence. How many salads can you say that about? Long live the queen.

MAKES 4 SERVINGS

PEANUT-LIME DRESSING

- 1/3 cup extra-virgin olive oil
- 1/4 cup fresh lime juice (3 to 4 limes)
- 2 tablespoons reduced-sodium soy sauce
- 1 1/2 teaspoons toasted sesame oil
- 2 teaspoons sugar
- 1 teaspoon kosher salt
- Freshly cracked black pepper
- 1 small shallot, roughly chopped
- 1 inch fresh ginger, peeled and roughly chopped
- 1 garlic clove, roughly chopped
- 1/2 Fresno chile (red jalapeño; optional), roughly chopped
- 1/2 cup roasted peanuts (if salted, reduce the amount of salt in the dressing)

SALAD

- 2 large eggs
- 1/2 cup fingerling potatoes, halved, or 1 medium red potato, cut into bite-size pieces
- 1 teaspoon kosher salt
- 2 cups shredded romaine lettuce
- 2 medium carrots, grated (about 1 cup)
- 1 English (seedless) cucumber, peeled (optional) and finely chopped
- 1 cup bean sprouts
- 1 cup shredded red cabbage
- 1/2 cup halved cherry tomatoes
- 1/2 cup thinly sliced radishes
- 1/2 cup roughly chopped or hand-torn fresh mint or cilantro leaves, plus extra for serving

To make the dressing, in a food processor, combine everything but the peanuts and blend until combined. Add the peanuts and pulse until they are roughly chopped.

To make the salad, place the eggs in a medium saucepan and fill with water to cover. Bring the water to a boil, cover, remove from the heat, and set aside for 9 minutes. Scoop the eggs out of the saucepan and transfer to a bowl of ice water.

Return the pan of water to a boil and add the potatoes and salt. Boil the potatoes until they're tender, about 10 minutes, then add them to the ice water. Drain, peel the eggs, and cut them into quarters. Set the eggs and potatoes aside.

Arrange the lettuce on a platter and scatter the carrots, cucumber, bean sprouts, cabbage, tomatoes, radishes, and herbs over the top. Add the potatoes and the egg. Drizzle with the peanut-lime dressing.

ZUCCHINI RIBBONS WITH MINT AND POMEGRANATE

If you can use a vegetable peeler, you can make this very fancy looking but extremely simple salad. Ribbon after ribbon of delicate zucchini is scattered with ruby red pomegranate seeds, fresh mint, and pistachios. None of the flavors competes with or overwhelms the others, but every mouthful contains little bursts, a gentle crunch, and a lingeringly refreshing velvet bite.

MAKES 4 SERVINGS

1/3 cup pistachios

3 medium zucchini

1 1/2 tablespoons extra-virgin olive oil

Juice of 1 lime

1 teaspoon kosher salt

2 tablespoons finely chopped fresh mint

1/3 cup pomegranate seeds

Preheat the oven to 350°F. Spread the pistachios on a rimmed baking sheet and toast 5 to 6 minutes, until golden. Transfer them to a plate to cool.

Place the zucchini on a cutting board and slice off the ends. Use a vegetable peeler to shave the zucchini into ribbons, then transfer them to a medium bowl.

In a small bowl, whisk together the olive oil, lime juice, and salt. Drizzle it over the zucchini and toss to combine. Add the mint and toss to combine. Transfer to a serving bowl and use your fingers to fluff the ribbons. Sprinkle with the pistachios and pomegranate seeds and serve.

CARROT SALAD WITH PARSLEY AND GOLDEN RAISINS

I first had a salad like this at lunch when I was working a banking job in London and had escaped for the weekend to visit college friends in Paris. We sat at a little café people-watching and catching up, tearing at a perfect crusty-chewy baguette that we slathered with butter and salt, and balancing our carb fest with this light and refreshing but gratifyingly crunchy salad. On days when I'm in need of a quick mental vacation, I whip this up—it's so simple, I bet you'll have it memorized the first time you make it.

MAKES 4 SERVINGS

- **2 cups matchstick-cut carrots (see Tip)**
- **2 tablespoons golden raisins**
- **1/3 cup roughly chopped fresh flat-leaf parsley, plus extra for garnish**
- **1/4 cup extra-virgin olive oil**
- **Juice of 1 lemon**
- **1/2 teaspoon kosher salt**
- **2 tablespoons slivered almonds**

In a large bowl, combine the carrots, raisins, parsley, oil, lemon juice, and salt. Toss to mix and let sit 5 minutes, so the carrots and raisins can absorb the dressing. Serve sprinkled with more parsley and the almonds.

TIP: *You can buy bagged matchstick carrots at most grocery stores, often near where they have broccoli slaw in bags. Or you can practice your knife skills and cut planks and then strips of carrot. Or you can grate them on a box grater, though the salad won't have quite the same texture.*

VARIATION: *You can fry the almonds in a bit of butter or olive oil to add a little indulgent flare to this dish. Just add 2 teaspoons fat to a skillet over medium heat and fry the nuts until golden brown. Pour any remaining fat over the carrots along with the nuts when dressing.*

BOMB BROCCOLI SALAD

Raise your hand if you just can't get enough raw broccoli. No takers? Yeah, me neither—until I came up with this crazy salad. *It's so good!*

Some people have extra beer or mayo in their fridge. Our family has extra broccoli. Like, four heads too many. This salad came out of one such dire occasion when we had way too much and it needed to be used ASAP. I decided to make a dressing out of the motley crew of assorted condiments I had in my fridge, and it ended up sort of Asian and entirely delicious. Bonus: Raw things come together in minutes, so hurry up and make this and send me a picture! Can't wait for you to start your own broccoli revolution.

MAKES 4 SERVINGS

2 tablespoons almond butter, at room temperature

1 inch fresh ginger, peeled and grated

1½ tablespoons honey or 2 teaspoons sugar

1 tablespoon diced hot cherry peppers

Juice of 2 limes (about 3 tablespoons)

6 tablespoons extra-virgin olive oil

1 shallot, minced

Kosher salt and freshly cracked black pepper

1 large head of broccoli

¼ cup salted roasted peanuts, finely chopped

In a large bowl, whisk together the almond butter, ginger, honey, peppers, and lime juice. While continuing to whisk, drizzle in the olive oil to emulsify, then stir in the shallot. Add salt and pepper to taste. This dressing can be made a day in advance and refrigerated—the longer it sits, the more flavorful it will be, as the shallot has time to infuse it.

To prepare the broccoli, remove the stems from the florets. Use a paring knife to slice off the fibrous outer layer on the stems, then finely chop the tender stalk. Finely chop the florets. The more finely chopped, the better, for more surface area to soak up the dressing!

When ready to serve, add the broccoli to the dressing and toss with the peanuts for added crunch. Serve immediately or let sit 20 minutes to marinate. Devour.

sandwiches

2013
LES
DOMANIERS
THE SOURCE
THE MAKER
ESTD 1882
Maldon
SEA SALT
FLAKES
Ball
MEDITERRANEAN
GOURMET
MOROCCAN HARISSA
100% Natural

and snacks
Nutrition Facts
HOT
SPREAD
Nutrition Facts

Standard sandwiches may tend to feel a little "weekday" when what you're craving is lunchtime opulence worthy of the weekend. Fortunately, that's all about to change. The variety of options you can house between two slices of bread (or a lettuce wrap) is endless, and the sandwiches and snacks in this chapter are comforting, portable, cultural chameleons. Herein, you'll find everything from the far-flung Seared Garlic-Lime Shrimp Banh Mi and Herby Falafel to my familiar-with-a-twist Philly Cheesesteak Quesadillas or Balsamic Onion and Pear Grilled Cheese. I dare you to keep reading and find out which sandwich prompted me to describe it as "a unicorn of lacey, fried perfection." I promise it's not a ham and cheese.

SEARED GARLIC-LIME SHRIMP BANH MI

I love any pickled veggie, and sandwiches loaded up with pickles are a personal must because they add incredible crunch and a juicy tanginess to every bite. Tons of fresh herbs pretty much anywhere and definitely on sandwiches also make me very, very happy. Best of all, both of these boosters give you tons of flavor with virtually no calories.

The shrimp in this recipe cook in minutes, which is why I end up choosing them for this sandwich more often than not, but you could absolutely sub in chicken breast or a mild white fish like mahi mahi or catfish. This is one of our favorites to make, wrap tightly in foil, and take with us for picnics in the park on beautiful spring weekends.

MAKES 4 SANDWICHES

PICKLED VEGETABLES

- 2 tablespoons rice vinegar
- 1 tablespoon Worcestershire sauce
- 1/8 teaspoon sugar
- 1/2 teaspoon kosher salt
- 1/4 small red onion, thinly sliced
- 2 medium carrots, peeled and grated
- 1 medium daikon, peeled and grated
- 1 red bell pepper, thinly sliced
- 1 medium jalapeño, thinly sliced on the bias

SEARED SHRIMP

- Zest of 1 lime
- Juice of 1/2 lime
- 2 garlic cloves, minced
- 1/2 teaspoon kosher salt
- Freshly cracked black pepper
- 1 pound medium shrimp, peeled and deveined
- 2 teaspoons canola oil

BANH MI

- 1/4 cup mayonnaise
- 2 tablespoons Sriracha sauce (optional)
- 1 large baguette, halved horizontally
- 1 avocado, pitted, peeled, and thinly sliced
- 12 fresh basil leaves, torn or roughly chopped
- 12 fresh mint leaves, torn or roughly chopped

To make the pickled vegetables, in a medium bowl, whisk together the vinegar, Worcestershire sauce, sugar, and salt until the sugar and salt are dissolved. Add the onion, carrots, daikon, red pepper, and jalapeño and set aside for at least 30 minutes (the pickles can be refrigerated in an airtight container for up to 3 days; they will get softer and spicier as they sit).

To make the shrimp, in a medium bowl, whisk together the lime zest, lime juice, garlic, salt, and pepper to taste. Add the shrimp and toss to combine.

In a large nonstick skillet, heat the oil over medium-high heat. Lift the shrimp out of the bowl and place them on a paper towel for just a second to absorb any moisture, then add them to the skillet. Cook the shrimp until they start to curl and are golden brown, 1 1/2 to 2 minutes. Turn and cook on the other side until the shrimp are just cooked through, about 1 minute—to borrow from Clinton Kelly, they should make a "C" shape, not an "O" shape. Transfer to a plate.

Preheat the broiler to high.

For the banh mi, in a small bowl, combine the mayonnaise and Sriracha (if using). Open the baguette wide so the cut sides face up and arrange on a baking sheet. Spread the mayonnaise mixture on the cut sides of the baguette. Broil for 2 to 3 minutes, until warmed through, taking care that it doesn't burn.

Layer the shrimp on the bottom half of the baguette and top with some of the pickled vegetables. Place the avocado slices, basil, and mint on top. Use a serrated knife to cut the baguette crosswise into 4 sandwiches and serve.

TIP: *Serve the shrimp and pickled vegetables with a drizzle of Sriracha mayo over rice, with noodles, or in lettuce wraps if you want a less traditional take on the banh mi.*

CURRIED EGG SALAD SANDWICH WITH DRESSED GREENS

Our family doesn't eat a lot of tuna (tasty, but high in mercury = not good), so egg salad is our easy lunch staple. It's filling and packed with protein, and it travels nicely, too.

This version takes the classic components of deviled eggs—Dijon mustard, mayo, and a dash of paprika—and adds some exotic flair with curry powder, along with the crunch of fresh celery and red onion. I love it topped with dressed watercress if you can find it—the peppery bite is unbeatable—but arugula works perfectly, too.

MAKES 4 TO 6 SERVINGS

8 large eggs

1/3 cup mayonnaise

2 teaspoons whole-grain or Dijon mustard

2 teaspoons apple cider vinegar

1 teaspoon Madras curry powder

1/2 teaspoon smoked paprika

1 teaspoon kosher salt

Freshly cracked black pepper

2 large celery stalks, minced

1/2 small red onion, minced

1 tablespoon finely chopped fresh thyme and/or mint leaves

Juice of 1/2 lemon

1 tablespoon extra-virgin olive oil

1 1/2 cups watercress or arugula

8 to 12 slices whole-grain bread, toasted

In a saucepan large enough to hold the eggs without crowding, cover the eggs with room temperature water. Set the pan over high heat and bring to a boil. Remove from the heat, cover, and let the eggs sit for 9 minutes. Transfer them to a bowl of ice water to cool. Peel the cooled eggs. The yolks should be bright yellow, with just the faintest bit of wetness toward the center—this will make your dressing extra creamy.

Finely chop the eggs and place half of them in a medium bowl. Use a fork to mash them until smooth.

Add the mayonnaise, mustard, vinegar, curry powder, paprika, 3/4 teaspoon of the salt, and pepper to taste and stir to combine. Stir in the celery, onion, and herbs. Fold in the remaining eggs.

In a medium bowl, whisk together the lemon juice, olive oil, and remaining 1/4 teaspoon salt. Add the watercress and toss to coat the leaves with the dressing.

Divide the egg salad among 4 to 6 pieces of toast. Top each with some of the dressed watercress and serve open-faced (or add a slice of toast on top to make a full sandwich).

TIP: *I like to toast a slice of bread and then, while it's still hot, use a serrated knife to slice it in half horizontally to make two really thin slices of bread from one for a sandwich top and bottom that ends up being the perfect ratio of bread to filling! Alternatively, you can serve the egg salad in large frilly Bibb lettuce leaves or stuffed into an avocado half.*

SUPER BOWL SUB

Two Super Bowls ago, John and I found ourselves housesitting with my little brother, Oliver, on Super Bowl Sunday. We hadn't made any plans for festivities, and about an hour before kickoff, we all realized we were so *hungry*! We raced to the supermarket, grabbed a bunch of stuff off the shelves, and flew home so the boys wouldn't miss a minute of the game. Of course, I was much more interested in creating a spectacular sandwich.

This came together with literally no planning, and the result was preposterously delicious, so we've kept making it. We also discovered that weekend that leftovers make for an excellent late-night snack if you find yourself rooting around the fridge at midnight.

MAKES 4 SERVINGS

6 tablespoons mayonnaise

6 tablespoons ketchup

2 tablespoons whole-grain mustard

3 tablespoons chopped bread-and-butter pickles

1/2 teaspoon kosher salt

Freshly cracked black pepper

1 ciabatta loaf, halved horizontally

8 slices pepperoni

8 slices smoked or roasted deli turkey

1/4 red onion, thinly sliced

1 Fresno chile or pickled jalapeño, thinly sliced

4 slices Monterey Jack or pepper Jack cheese

1 cup thinly sliced radicchio (from 1 medium head)

2 tablespoons extra-virgin olive oil

1 1/2 teaspoons red wine vinegar

1/2 teaspoon dried oregano

Preheat the broiler to high.

In a small bowl, stir together the mayonnaise, ketchup, mustard, pickles, 1/4 teaspoon of the salt, and pepper to taste. Arrange the ciabatta cut sides up on a rimmed baking sheet and spread with the mayo mixture.

Place the pepperoni in an even layer over the bottom half of the ciabatta. Follow with the turkey, onion slices, chile, and cheese. Broil for 3 minutes, or until the cheese melts.

Meanwhile, in a medium bowl, toss the radicchio with the olive oil, vinegar, oregano, the remaining 1/4 teaspoon salt, and pepper to taste.

Arrange the radicchio on top of the cheese, pouring any remaining oil-vinegar dressing over the top half of the sandwich. Set the top half of the sandwich on the bottom half and press down to compress. Slice crosswise into 4 equal pieces and serve.

FETA AND DILL SIGARA BOREKS

One of my all-time favorite eating experiences has to be Turkish breakfast at my grandparents' home when I visit them in Istanbul every summer. The morning meal is an onslaught of mini-plates, piled with ripe tomatoes, crisp cucumbers, a variety of fresh fruits (Cherries! Watermelon! Peaches!) and salty cheeses, local honey and olive oil, baked eggs, a Turkish version of bagels (called *simit*), and best of all, a mountain of golden brown, fresh-out-of-the-oil, crispy *sigara borek*.

There really is no wrong time of day to indulge in delicately fried phyllo dough, surrounding mashed feta cheese, fresh dill, and parsley. You will just as likely find these being served as a lunch side or dinner appetizer. I add shredded carrots and phyllo scraps to my version to keep the stuffing light and just a touch sweet.

MAKES 20 PASTRIES

- **2 medium carrots, peeled and grated (about 1 cup)**
- **1 cup crumbled feta cheese (4 ounces)**
- **1/4 cup finely chopped fresh dill**
- **1/4 cup finely chopped fresh parsley leaves**
- **2 large eggs, separated**
- **1/2 teaspoon kosher salt**
- **6 (9 x 14-inch) sheets phyllo dough, thawed if frozen**
- **Extra-virgin olive oil**

In a medium bowl, combine the carrots, feta, dill, parsley, egg yolks, and salt.

In a small bowl, whisk the egg whites until frothy and set aside.

Unwrap 3 sheets of the phyllo dough and stack them so one is placed nicely on top of the next. Use a chef's knife to cut the dough into about 10 triangles (either right triangles or isosceles) no wider than 4 to 5 inches at the base. The smaller the *sigara borek*, the better—the filling will cook evenly and quickly. The rolled "cigars" should be roughly the size of your ring finger. Finely chop any scraps or torn pieces of phyllo and add them to the filling for extra crunch.

Place a tablespoon of the dill-feta mixture in the center of the base of each triangle (take care not to overstuff the cigar, otherwise the filling will come out when you fry it; you're using about half the filling on these 10 triangles), then gather the base of the dough and roll it over the filling. Tuck the edges in as you roll to trap the filling (as you would a burrito) and continue rolling until you have just 1 inch of dough left at the top. Repeat with the remaining triangles. Lightly dip or brush the remaining 1-inch tip of each cigar with the egg white wash and press it gently on the cigar to seal. Place the cigars on a lightly oiled plate. Repeat with the remaining sheets of phyllo and remaining filling. Cover the cigars with a slightly damp kitchen towel while you heat the oil to prevent the phyllo dough from drying out.

Pour 1 inch of oil into a straight-sided, heavy-bottomed skillet and heat over medium-high heat until an instant-read thermometer reaches 325°F (any hotter and the phyllo will brown too quickly, before the inside is cooked). The oil will shimmer, and will spit if you splash a little water in the pan.

Add 4 to 5 cigars to the hot oil and fry on all sides until golden brown, 3 to 4 minutes, using a fork to turn the cigars often so they brown evenly and don't stick to the bottom of the pan. Use a slotted spoon or frying spider to transfer the *boreks* to a paper-towel-lined plate to cool while you fry the rest.

Eat warm or at room temperature (they're crispiest within a few hours of frying).

KOREAN FRIED CHICKEN SANDWICH WITH SPICY HONEY AND MISO AÏOLI

All over New York, Korean fried chicken chains have been cropping up. And the addictive spicy-sweet glaze and TV-commercial-ready crunch typically found on their wings makes the only question: *Why did it take so long?*

John and I don't get to go out to eat as often as we used to with little munchkins running around, so I've spent a lot of time trying to re-create dishes we love in our home kitchen. The thing that took me the longest was figuring out how to get the tender but extra-crispy coating that Korean chicken achieves. It's not flaky, packed with shards of seasoned flour and buttermilk like Southern fried chicken. And it's not a thick, breadcrumb coating, either. It is a unicorn of lacey, fried perfection.

My goal was to figure out the easiest method, using the most common ingredients, to make the best at-home version of this dish. I tested a bunch of techniques—tenderizing the chicken in buttermilk overnight; dunking it into a variety of possible flours; adding alcohol (beer and vodka) to a wet batter, per a tip from Michael Symon. All versions of this chicken were delicious . . . but I discovered the most minimal process actually yielded my favorite results. All you need for supercrispy fried chicken is a coating of cornstarch and baking powder, seasoned with salt, pepper, and a little smoked paprika.

The miso aïoli and spicy honey glaze are my favorite backup dancers for the star act, chicken. Sometimes I'll skip the buns entirely and just use a crisp lettuce shell—the better to taste it all, my dear!

MAKES 4 SERVINGS

FRIED CHICKEN THIGHS

- 1 cup cornstarch (cake flour or Wondra flour also work great to provide a thin, crunchy, even coating, but cornstarch is the crunchiest)
- 1 teaspoon baking powder
- 1/2 teaspoon smoked paprika
- 1 teaspoon kosher salt
- Freshly cracked black pepper
- 4 boneless, skinless chicken thighs, cut crosswise into 3 strips
- Peanut oil, for frying
- 4 potato buns
- 8 iceberg lettuce leaves

(Ingredients continue on the next page.)

To make the chicken, in a medium bowl, whisk together the cornstarch, baking powder, smoked paprika, salt, and pepper to taste. Add the chicken pieces and turn to coat them in the cornstarch mixture.

Pour 1 1/2 inches of oil into a heavy-bottomed, straight-sided skillet and heat the oil until an instant-read thermometer reaches 375°F. Set a wire rack over a paper bag or paper towels (to absorb the oil) and have at the ready.

While the oil heats, make the spicy honey glaze. In a large bowl (big enough to hold the chicken), whisk together the honey, Sriracha, rice vinegar, soy sauce, chives, cayenne, and salt. Set the glaze aside.

To make the miso aïoli, in a small bowl, whisk together the mayonnaise, miso, garlic, and salt. Cover the bowl with plastic wrap and refrigerate.

SPICY HONEY GLAZE

3 tablespoons honey

1½ tablespoons Sriracha sauce

1 tablespoon rice vinegar or lemon juice

1 tablespoon low-sodium soy sauce

2 tablespoons finely chopped chives

⅛ teaspoon cayenne pepper

¼ teaspoon kosher salt

MISO AÏOLI

¼ cup mayonnaise

1 tablespoon white or yellow miso

1 garlic clove, grated on a Microplane-style rasp

¼ teaspoon kosher salt

Add a few pieces of chicken to the oil, dropping it in away from you, so the oil doesn't splatter toward you. (Don't overcrowd the skillet or the temperature of the oil will drop and the chicken will be greasy.) Fry the chicken, turning the pieces midway through cooking, until they are browned and crisp on both sides, about 6 minutes total. Use a slotted spoon or frying spider to transfer the chicken to the wire rack. Repeat with the rest of the chicken.

While the chicken is hot, add it to the bowl with the glaze and toss to coat.

Divide the aïoli among the 4 buns and add 1 lettuce leaf to each bottom bun half. Top with a few pieces of fried chicken and a second lettuce leaf, then the top bun half, and serve. Any leftover chicken is great chopped up over a salad the next day, though I've never had this happen.

BREADING BREAKDOWN

Whenever you're "breading" something, the traditional rule of thumb is that you want to follow the three steps of FEB: Flour. Eggs. Breadcrumbs. In this case, we are taking it down to just one step for a light and supercrispy coating of just seasoned cornstarch and baking powder. If you want a thicker, more traditional fried chicken, you can dip the cornstarch-coated chicken into whisked eggs, and then into a third bath of breadcrumbs (panko works great) or more of the cornstarch mixture.

AVOCADO TOAST WITH LEMON-CHILE OIL

Gone are the humble days of simple mashed avocado on toast. We've reached the age of avocado toast enlightenment—and with good reason. (A) It's delicious. (B) It's so easy. And (C) it's healthy. The good fats in avocado, while calorie-dense, are absolutely critical to helping your body function at its best (your brain especially). They may also help you get the best hair, skin, and nails of your life.

This recipe takes me on a trip to Italy . . . Sicily, to be precise. Each piece is anointed with Lemon-Chile Oil, a pantry "superbooster" I keep on hand to brighten up a variety of dishes. A shower of fresh basil keeps us feeling bright and fancy. Because sure, avocado toast is healthy, but that's not really why we eat it.

MAKES 4 SERVINGS

- 4 slices (1/2 inch thick) country-style bread, toasted
- 2 garlic cloves, peeled and halved lengthwise
- 1 avocado, halved and pitted
- Flaky sea salt and freshly cracked black pepper
- Lemon-Chile Oil (recipe follows)
- 1/2 lemon (optional)
- 1/2 tablespoon thinly sliced fresh basil

Rub each piece of toast with half a garlic clove, then discard the garlic.

Smash one-fourth of the avocado on each toast. Season with salt and pepper to taste, then drizzle with the lemon-chile oil. Squeeze juice from the lemon (if using) over all toasts. Let a little basil rain onto each piece.

LEMON-CHILE OIL

This oil makes a fantastic finishing drizzle for fish, chicken, vegetables, or even soup or pasta. For more sensitive palates, reduce the chile flakes to just a pinch. To store, remove the zest and refrigerate the oil in a glass container for up to 1 month, or keep on the counter for up to 1 week away from heat and direct sunlight.

MAKES ABOUT 1/4 CUP

- 2 lemons
- 1/4 cup extra-virgin olive oil
- 1/2 teaspoon crushed chile flakes

Using a vegetable peeler, remove the zest from the lemons in strips, being careful not to grab too much of the bitter, white pith under the yellow skin. Transfer to a medium saucepan. (Reserve the lemons for another use.)

To the saucepan with the lemon zest, add the oil and chile flakes. Stir to combine and submerge the lemon zest, then warm the oil over medium heat. When the oil is fragrant and just starts to bubble, remove from the heat and set aside to cool at least 10 minutes.

PHILLY CHEESESTEAK QUESADILLAS

This recipe is a nod to my Philly roots (Born and raised! For my first six months, anyway. . . . Go, Eagles!), and the technique works great for reimagining any leftover meat you might have around your house—rotisserie chicken, steak, pulled pork, tempeh (hehe), you name it!

MAKES 4 QUESADILLAS

2 tablespoons unsalted butter

2 fresh oregano sprigs

1 teaspoon kosher salt

1 cup thinly sliced leftover steak (or chicken or pork)

2 tablespoons extra-virgin olive oil

1 medium onion, halved and thinly sliced

1 teaspoon dried oregano

1/2 teaspoon sugar

1 red bell pepper, cored, seeded, and thinly sliced

5 cremini (baby bella) mushrooms, stemmed, caps thinly sliced

Four 8-inch flour tortillas

1 cup (4 ounces) shredded Monterey Jack cheese or low-moisture mozzarella

Melt the butter in a medium skillet over medium heat with the oregano sprigs and 1/2 teaspoon of the salt. Swirl, then add the steak. Baste the meat with the butter and cook until it's warmed through, then transfer it to a plate. Discard the oregano. To cook fresh steak, let it come to room temperature before adding it to the pan with the butter and oregano, then sear it to your desired doneness. Let rest 10 minutes, then slice into strips.

Wipe out the skillet and return it to medium-low heat, add 1 tablespoon of the olive oil, the onion, dried oregano, sugar, and the remaining 1/2 teaspoon salt and cook, stirring often, until the onion is deeply golden brown and caramelized, 20 to 30 minutes. (If you're in a rush, increase the heat to medium, sweat the onions for 5 minutes and move along.) Stir the bell pepper into the skillet and cook until the peppers are soft, about 5 minutes. Transfer this mixture to a medium bowl.

Add the remaining tablespoon of the oil and the mushrooms to the pan and cook for 2 minutes without moving the mushrooms. Stir the mushrooms and cook until they start to shrink and their liquid begins to evaporate, about 2 minutes more. Return the onions and peppers to the skillet, toss to warm through, then transfer the mixture back to the bowl and wipe out the pan using tongs and a wet paper towel.

Set the skillet back over medium heat. Place 1 tortilla in the skillet and sprinkle half evenly with 2 tablespoons of the cheese. Top the cheese with one quarter of the vegetables and meat, then another 2 tablespoons of cheese. Gently fold the tortilla in half and press it down with a spatula or heavy plate. When the bottom of the tortilla is golden brown, about 3 minutes, use a spatula to carefully flip it over and continue cooking until the other side is browned, 2 to 3 minutes more. Repeat with the remaining 3 tortillas.

Transfer the quesadillas to a cutting board and let sit 2 minutes, then use a pizza cutter to slice them into wedges. Serve hot.

HARISSA AND MINT CHICKEN SAMOSAS

The angel on your shoulder tells you to go for the ground chicken, but the devil on your shoulder reminds you that taste is king—what do you do? Make these chicken samosas. They stay light but flavorful with a blend of breast and thigh meat (your butcher can freshly grind the combination for you), and extra juicy with plenty of smoky-spicy harissa, sweet-sour apricots, and fresh herbs. Wrap it all up in buttered phyllo dough and you have a present for your mouth. If you don't feel like fighting with papery thin sheets of phyllo, a simple puff pastry or empanada dough will work great to form delightful chicken dumplings that you can bake or fry.

MAKES 12 SAMOSAS

SAMOSAS

- 1 tablespoon extra-virgin olive oil
- 1 teaspoon brown mustard seeds
- 1 large red onion, finely chopped
- 1 teaspoon kosher salt
- 8 dried apricots, finely chopped
- 1 teaspoon ground cumin (preferably from toasted whole seeds; see Tip)
- 1 teaspoon ground turmeric
- 1/2 teaspoon ground coriander
- 3/4 pound ground chicken, made from skinless thighs and breasts (ask your butcher to grind it fresh for you—don't be shy!)
- 1 tablespoon apricot jam (optional)
- Heaping 2 tablespoons harissa paste
- 1/4 cup finely chopped fresh mint or cilantro stems (save the leaves for the dipping sauce)
- 1 stick (4 ounces) unsalted butter, melted

(Ingredients continue on the next page.)

To make the samosas, in a large skillet, heat the oil over medium heat. Add the mustard seeds and when they begin to sizzle, stir in the onion and 1/2 teaspoon of the salt. Cook, stirring often, until the onion softens and browns around the edges, 5 to 6 minutes. Continuing to stir, add the apricots and cook another 2 minutes. Stir in the cumin, turmeric, and coriander and cook, stirring often, until fragrant, about 30 seconds.

Crumble the chicken into the pan and add the remaining 1/2 teaspoon salt. Cook, using a wooden spoon to stir and break up the chicken, until the chicken is cooked through, 5 to 6 minutes. Remove from the heat and transfer the chicken mixture to a medium bowl. Stir in the apricot jam (if using) and harissa and set aside to cool slightly, then refrigerate until completely chilled. You can speed this process along if you spread the mixture out into a thin layer on a baking sheet before refrigerating.

Preheat the oven to 350°F.

Stir the mint or cilantro stems into the chicken mixture. Turn the chicken mixture onto a cutting board and finely chop it into small bits (or pulse it in a food processor).

Set the melted butter next to a work surface. Line a rimmed baking sheet with parchment paper. Place 3 sheets of phyllo dough on the work surface, one on top of the other. Brush some of the melted butter on the top sheet—just enough to thinly coat the phyllo. With the long side nearest to you, slice the phyllo into 4 equal strips (3 to 4 inches wide). Place about 2 tablespoons of filling at the lower end of a strip and fold the bottom up over the filling as though you are

9 (9 x 14-inch) sheets phyllo dough, thawed if frozen

DIPPING SAUCE

1/2 cup yogurt

1/4 cup finely chopped fresh cilantro or mint leaves (or a combination of the two)

1 tablespoon fresh lime juice

1/2 teaspoon honey (optional)

1/2 teaspoon ground cumin (preferably from toasted whole seeds; see Tip)

1/2 teaspoon kosher salt

folding a flag. For the next fold, angle the left corner up toward the right side to make a triangle, then turn the triangle up to the left. Continue to fold until the samosa is completely wrapped in a triangle shape. Repeat with the remaining 3 strips, then brush each samosa all over with more melted butter, using the butter to "glue" any rough edges or corners together. Place the samosas on the baking sheet. Repeat with the remaining sheets of phyllo and remaining filling.

Bake the samosas for about 25 minutes, or until they are golden brown, turning the baking sheet midway through cooking. Set them aside to cool.

To make the dipping sauce, in a medium bowl, stir together the yogurt, herbs, lime juice, honey (if using), cumin, and salt. Serve with the samosas.

FRESHLY GROUND SPICES

Ground cumin works fine in this recipe, but if you want to grind some fresh, it's pretty easy and adds a bright flavor that sometimes gets lost in packaged spices. Heat a medium skillet over medium heat. Add the cumin seeds and toast, shaking the pan often, until they smell fragrant, 2 to 3 minutes. Transfer to a medium plate to cool, then pulverize in a spice grinder. Toasted cumin can be stored in an airtight container in a cool, dark, and draft-free spot for up to 3 months.

ZUCCHINI AND DELICATA SQUASH PANINI WITH MUHAMMARA

The combination of savory squash and nutty, slightly sweet *muhammara* (a fruity walnut-bell pepper spread) pairs perfectly in this sandwich, though you could just as easily skip the bread and eat them on their own as a side, or over mixed greens in a salad, or over brown rice for a hearty meal. Psssst . . . this recipe is also secretly vegan. That's my favorite part about good, healthy cooking—when no one even notices it's happening, because the food doesn't feel as if it's "missing" anything. It's just delicious.

MAKES 2 PANINI

1/2 small kabocha squash, scrubbed, halved, and seeded

1/4 teaspoon garlic powder

1/2 teaspoon kosher salt

1/4 teaspoon ground cumin

1 small zucchini, ends trimmed, sliced on a slight bias into 1/4-inch-thick planks

3 tablespoons extra-virgin olive oil

4 slices whole wheat bread

Muhammara (recipe follows)

12 large basil leaves, roughly chopped

Preheat the oven to 350°F.

Cut the squash in half again, then carefully slice each half into 1/4-inch-thick slices.

In a small bowl, mix together the garlic powder, salt, and cumin. Drizzle the zucchini and squash slices with some of the olive oil and season with the spice blend. Roast the squash and zucchini in a single layer on a baking sheet. The squash will need about 40 minutes, flipping halfway through. The zucchini can go in for the last 10 to 15 minutes (flip them after 7 or 8 minutes). Remove when all the veggies are golden brown, with a few crisp bits.

Lightly drizzle one side of each of the bread slices with the remaining olive oil. Turn the bread oiled side down and spread each slice with a heaping tablespoon of *muhammara*. Add the kabocha squash and zucchini to half of the bread and layer the basil on top. Sandwich with the remaining slices of bread, oiled side up.

Place the sandwiches in a skillet over medium heat and press down with a heavy plate or pan. After 2 minutes, flip and replace the plate or pan (careful! It's hot). Grill the sandwiches until toasted and golden, 1 to 2 minutes more. Halve and serve. (P.S. This recipe also works great with a panini press or on the grill if you have one.)

MUHAMMARA

Traditionally served as part of a Middle Eastern mezze course, this slightly piquant and sweet roasted red pepper, walnut, and molasses spread takes sandwiches to a whole new level.

MAKES ABOUT 1¼ CUPS

- 1 slice whole wheat bread, roughly torn
- ½ cup walnut pieces, toasted (see Toasting Nuts, page 14)
- 3 large garlic cloves, roughly chopped
- 1 cup jarred roasted red peppers, drained and blotted dry
- 1 tablespoon fresh lime juice or lemon juice
- 1 tablespoon pomegranate molasses (or ½ tablespoon regular molasses and ½ tablespoon raspberry jelly)
- 1 teaspoon kosher salt
- ¼ teaspoon crushed chile flakes

In a food processor, pulse the bread until it looks like medium breadcrumbs. Add the toasted walnuts and garlic and pulse until finely ground. Add the roasted peppers, lime juice, pomegranate molasses, salt, and chile flakes and process until the mixture is creamy, 10 to 15 seconds. Transfer the mixture to a medium bowl and set aside.

ROASTING PEPPERS

You can quickly make your own charred bell peppers to replace the jarred roasted red peppers by carefully using tongs to rotate a red bell pepper over the open flame of your stove, allowing the fire to burn and char the pepper skin on all sides. Alternatively, place an oven rack in the upper third of your oven, throw a couple of peppers on an aluminum-foil-lined baking sheet, and roast them under the broiler, 6 to 8 minutes, using tongs to rotate them every so often to get all sides blackened. Watch carefully so they don't go up in smoke! Place the hot peppers in a bowl and cover with plastic wrap to steam. When cool enough to handle, use your fingers to peel away the charred skin and pull out the stem and seeds. You can store these in olive oil up to 1 week in the refrigerator.

BUTTERNUT SQUASH AND RICOTTA TOAST

There's a restaurant here in New York City called ABC Kitchen where there's always a wait, morning, noon, and night, in a city with tens of thousands of restaurants to choose from, because the food is just that good. When you eventually sit down, you must immediately order one of their seasonal toasts. My all-time favorite is the squash toast they serve in fall: lovingly whipped Kabocha squash and caramelized onions with the faint tang of a well-timed splash of vinegar, piled high on a thick piece of sourdough bread and garnished with a dazzling array of pepitas, scallions, chiles, and other little bits and bobs that I am always too greedy to take notice of as I relish bite after bite. I always wish I'd ordered two.

This recipe is my home-kitchen ode to ABC's perfection.

MAKES 8 SERVINGS

1 lime

1/4 cup extra-virgin olive oil, plus extra for serving

1/4 cup pumpkin seeds (pepitas)

1 1/4 teaspoons kosher salt, plus a few pinches for the toast

1 yellow onion, minced

1 1/4 pounds butternut squash, peeled, seeded, and cut into 1/2-inch chunks (about 4 cups)

Freshly cracked black pepper

1 tablespoon apple cider vinegar

1 tablespoon pure maple syrup

8 slices (1/2 inch thick) country-style bread

1 cup ricotta cheese or goat cheese

Flaky sea salt

1 tablespoon finely chopped chives or scallions

1 Fresno or jalapeño pepper, thinly sliced (optional)

Grate the zest of the lime, then cut the lime into wedges.

In a medium nonstick skillet, heat 1 tablespoon of the olive oil over medium heat. Add the pumpkin seeds and cook, tossing often, until they brown, 2 to 3 minutes. Stir in the lime zest and 1/4 teaspoon of the kosher salt, cook for 15 seconds, and transfer to a plate.

Add 2 tablespoons of the oil to the skillet and increase the heat to medium-high. Add the onion and 1/2 teaspoon of the kosher salt and cook, stirring often, until the onion begins to soften and brown, 3 to 4 minutes. Add the squash, the remaining 1/2 teaspoon kosher salt, and black pepper to taste. Reduce the heat to medium-low, cover, and cook, stirring often, until the squash is tender, about 20 minutes. Uncover, increase the heat to medium-high, and sauté until the mixture starts to sizzle, 1 to 2 minutes.

Add the vinegar and maple syrup, bring to a simmer, and stir to glaze the squash and onions. Remove from the heat and use a fork or potato masher to smash the mixture until it is semismooth.

Adjust an oven rack so it is 3 to 4 inches from the heat source and preheat the broiler to high. Place the bread on a rimmed baking sheet and drizzle with the remaining tablespoon olive oil and season with a few pinches of kosher salt. Broil 2 to 3 minutes, until browned, then turn the bread over and broil the other side 1 to 2 minutes, until browned (watch the bread closely as broiler intensities vary).

Divide the smashed squash mixture among the toasts and squeeze a lime wedge over the squash. Dollop 2 tablespoons ricotta on top of each slice, then season with flaky sea salt and a drizzle of olive oil. Serve sprinkled with the chives, Fresno pepper (if using), and toasted pepitas.

VARIATION: *If you feel like it, skip the olive oil drizzle in favor of the Lemon-Chile Oil on page 127.*

BALSAMIC ONION AND PEAR GRILLED CHEESE

I will never tire of the endless array of delicious grilled cheeses out there in the world. I've sampled my fair share, and though the classic American on white does not disappoint when you want a throwback—the *second* the cheese cools, it totally seizes up and becomes more closely related to Silly Putty than anything worth eating. Don't waste your time on an average indulgence. Let's go big and make it count.

This recipe doesn't have a lot in the way of healthy selling points, so I'll jump to the maddeningly delicious part that includes balsamic caramelized onion, Gouda cheese, and the totally unexpected, sweet and creamy pear. Every health nut needs a weakness, and mine will have to be this sandwich for now . . . and maybe cookie dough later.

MAKES 2 SERVINGS

4 tablespoons (1/2 stick) unsalted butter

1 sweet yellow onion, sliced into 1/4-inch-thick rounds

1/2 teaspoon kosher salt

2 tablespoons balsamic vinegar

1/2 teaspoon sugar

4 slices whole-grain sandwich bread

1 tablespoon mayonnaise, at room temperature

1 cup grated Gouda cheese (Cheddar, Havarti, Gruyère, or Taleggio all work)

1 semiripe pear, peeled, halved, cored, and thinly sliced

Freshly cracked black pepper

In a medium nonstick or stainless skillet, melt 2 tablespoons of the butter over medium heat. Add the onion and salt and cook, stirring often, until the onion begins to soften and caramelize but retains some texture, 8 to 10 minutes. Add the vinegar and sugar and let the liquid reduce and coat the onion, about 2 minutes.

Spread one side of each bread slice thinly with mayonnaise (it gives an insanely crunchy, golden brown crust to the bread, with the faintest hint of sweetness). Turn 2 slices of bread mayo side down and sprinkle with half of the cheese. Add a few pear slices and cracks of pepper, top each with one-fourth of the onion, and sprinkle with the remaining cheese. Set the 2 other bread slices on top of the cheese, mayo side up. The remaining onion can be stored in a sealed container in the fridge for up to 3 days, or in the freezer for up to 2 months.

Wipe out the skillet and melt the remaining 2 tablespoons butter over medium heat. Place the sandwiches in the skillet and reduce the heat to medium-low. Set a large, heavy plate or pan on top of the sandwiches to press them down. Cook the sandwiches until one side is golden brown, 2 to 3 minutes.

Carefully remove the plate (it might be hot!) and use a spatula to flip the sandwiches over. Replace the plate and toast the second side until golden brown, another 2 to 3 minutes. Transfer each sandwich to a plate, slice, and serve.

HERBY FALAFEL

I fancy myself something of a falafel connoisseur. Ever since I was a kid, I've loved the way the crunchy outer shell cracks open to reveal (in good cases!) a vibrant green interior, fragrant with fresh herbs and crumbling, tender chickpeas. I never get sick of eating them, because every recipe is unique. Each cook and food truck patron has his or her perfect ratio of herb to spice to legume. Some are dense and heavy, some are light and airy; some have tons of herbs, some just a few flecks; some add tons of flour or eggs to bind, others are all but falling apart.

This is my favorite recipe, tested and tweaked over the years to use exactly the (admittedly, heavy-handed) amount of fresh herbs I love, plenty of crumbly chickpeas, and just a touch of baking powder to keep the whole thing light and crisp. The true test: Philomena eats these things by the handful, and so does everyone else who can reach the plate.

MAKES ABOUT 22 FALAFEL BALLS (SERVES 4)

1½ cups dried chickpeas (canned will leave your falafel mix too wet to handle)

4 large garlic cloves, roughly chopped

½ sweet yellow onion, roughly chopped

1 cup roughly chopped fresh parsley leaves and stems (more or less one big bunch of parsley, all but the last inch! Stems contain tons of flavor.)

½ cup roughly chopped fresh mint and/or cilantro leaves

1½ teaspoons ground coriander

1¼ teaspoons ground cumin

1 tablespoon kosher salt

2¼ teaspoons baking powder

2½ tablespoons all-purpose flour

Grapeseed or vegetable oil, for frying (in a pinch, a combo of butter and oil works, too)

Tahini Dressing (page 97), for serving

In a pot, combine the chickpeas with water to cover by 2 inches. Bring the water to a boil over high heat, simmer the chickpeas for 1 minute, cover the pot, remove from the heat, and let the chickpeas sit in the hot water for 1 hour. Measure out ¼ cup of the chickpea liquid and set aside. Drain off the rest, then rinse the chickpeas under cold water. Turn them out onto a rimmed baking sheet lined with paper towels to drain.

In a food processor, combine the garlic, onion, parsley, mint, ground coriander, cumin, and salt and pulse 15 to 20 times, until the mixture is well combined and almost a paste. Add all but ½ cup of the chickpeas and pulse until the blend forms a crumbly looking mixture, scraping the bowl if needed.

In a small bowl, mix together the baking powder and 2 tablespoons of the reserved chickpea cooking liquid. Add it to the chickpea mixture and pulse 3 times, then sprinkle the flour over the top and pulse 3 more times. (If preparing this mixture more than 1 hour ahead, do not add the baking powder blend and flour until 1 hour before cooking.) Add the reserved ½ cup whole chickpeas and pulse 5 times. They will be roughly chopped but incorporated, and will give the falafels nice texture throughout. Scrape the mixture into a bowl, cover with plastic wrap, and refrigerate for 1 hour.

Pour 2 inches of oil into a heavy-bottomed pot and heat until an instant-read thermometer reaches 350°F. You can also test the oil by dropping a small amount of falafel mix in to see if it sizzles. Line a plate with paper towels and set it near the stovetop.

Remove the falafel mixture from the refrigerator and roll it into balls about the size of a golf ball. Don't pack the balls too tightly; just enough so that they hold together. Working in small batches, fry the falafel for 3 to 4 minutes, turning often until they are golden brown on all sides, crisp on the outside, and cooked through the middle (you may *have* to bite into one to test, oh shucks!). Take care not to overfill the pan or you will drop the cooking oil temperature. Use a frying spider or slotted spoon to transfer the falafel to the paper-towel-lined plate to drain.

Serve hot with the tahini dressing on the side.

TIP: *For a full-on falafel experience, load up a whole wheat pita with a slather of the Tahini Dressing on page 97, some shredded cabbage and chopped tomatoes, your favorite pickles, a few fresh falafel balls, and—for a hit of spice—a drizzle of harissa paste. Or serve these on toothpicks for a great party bite! Think of them wherever you might use a meatball.*

VARIATION: *Add a chopped jalapeño or other green chile in with the herbs if you want it spicy! You can also add 1 whisked egg to the mix to help it bind together more, but I prefer a bit of a crumbly texture, and I think the balls stay lighter and fresher without it. If yours are too wet or falling apart, you can add a sprinkle more flour to the chickpea mix.*

vegetables

U.S. POSTAGE
Skirt Steak
Chx Wing
~~Chx Tender~~
Beef Skewer Satay
Meatballs

As new trends in food go, one of the most exciting for me has been the current celebration of vegetables as the main event. It used to be that restaurants would practically pay you to take a side of flavorless sautéed spinach with an overpriced steak the size of your head. Now, there are whole culinary empires devoted to meals made up almost entirely of bountiful, beautiful vegetables.

Having a small portion of high-quality meat as an accoutrement to a wealth and variety of fresh vegetables—rather than the other way around—is a win for palates and pants buttons alike (and increasingly, it seems that a plant-based diet is the key to a quality long life, so here's to that!). The trick is to create veggie dishes that are so abundant and flavorful that nothing seems to be missing. To feast on Harissa-Roasted Carrots with Crispy Caper Gremolata, Raw Beet Carpaccio, Sugar-and-Thyme-Basted Onions, and Spaghetti Squash Cacio e Pepe is to dine like a king and still be able to slip into the queen's slinky gown.

SWEET POTATOES WITH FRESH CHERRIES AND PECANS

I go insane for this delectable combo of sweet potato and pecans made bright with fresh cherries, crisp crumbled cauliflower, parsley, and lime. This is my kind of rich, abundant healthy eating: a glorious pile of colors and flavors that leaves my body full and fueled and my mouth extremely happy.

MAKES 4 SERVINGS

- **1/3 cup pecan pieces, roughly chopped**
- **2 sweet potatoes, quartered lengthwise, or 1 1/4 pounds winter squash, sliced into 1/2-inch-thick pieces (kabocha, delicata, and pumpkin work well)**
- **3 tablespoons extra-virgin olive oil**
- **1 1/2 teaspoons kosher salt**
- **1/4 teaspoon crushed chile flakes**
- **1 cup finely chopped cauliflower florets**
- **1/4 cup finely chopped fresh flat-leaf parsley (leaves and stems)**
- **1/2 small shallot, minced**
- **Zest and juice of 1/2 lime**
- **1/2 cup fresh Bing cherries (though Rainier are gorgeous when they're in season!), halved and pitted, or 1/4 cup dried cherries**
- **1/2 cup crumbled goat cheese (optional)**
- **Flaky sea salt**

Preheat the oven to 375°F.

Place the pecans on a rimmed baking sheet and toast until fragrant and golden brown, 7 to 8 minutes. Transfer to a plate and set aside.

Place the sweet potatoes or squash on the baking sheet and drizzle with 1 tablespoon of the oil. Sprinkle with 1 teaspoon of the kosher salt and the chile flakes and roast for 30 to 35 minutes, until browned and tender, turning the potatoes or squash midway through cooking. Transfer them to a platter.

Place the pecans in a medium bowl. Stir in the cauliflower, parsley, shallot, lime zest, lime juice, and the remaining 2 tablespoons oil and 1/2 teaspoon kosher salt.

Serve the pecan mix over the sweet potatoes and sprinkle with the cherries, goat cheese (if using), and flaky sea salt.

RHUBARB BARS
PAT 3/4 OF DRY
SAUCE, SPREAD EVENLY.
SPRINKLE REMAINING
SPRINKLE WITH 3/4 - 1
BAKE AT 350°F FOR 30
WHEN SLIGHTLY COOL, CUT IN
YUM!

SPICED BUTTERNUT SQUASH WITH MINT YOGURT

Heyo. Me again, with another veggie dish that I actually crave. This time, it's sweet butternut squash, roasted to perfection with a crazy concoction of spices I came up with playing in my mom's spice cabinet. She is *obsessed* with these little black seeds called nigella, which have an amazingly rich onion flavor (you can order them online as nigella seeds, *kalonji*, or black onion seeds, or find them in a Middle Eastern specialty store). I'm officially on the bandwagon. In fact, I call for them in my Everything-Bagel Biscuits (page 49), too, and if you end up getting them for this recipe, I guarantee you will find loads of delicious uses for them. I just got up and made myself a cracker spread with labneh (Greek yogurt would work), sliced cucumbers, nigella seeds, flaky salt, and a drizzle of olive oil. How's that for (self-)implanted cravings?

Back to squash. If you're a fan of candied yams, go for the little bit of brown sugar I call for in the spice blend to help caramelize the tops of the squash in the oven. It really plays magically with the tart-creamy yogurt I like to drizzle on top. But if you want to leave it off, no harm done.

The truffle salt suggestion is me being naughty because I love truffles and truffle salt is the closest I'm going to get to eating them regularly. Please, make lots extra of this squash, because it's a dream to eat cold or hot, and you'll want more tomorrow if you finish it all tonight.

MAKES 4 TO 6 SERVINGS

- **1 large (about 4 pounds) butternut squash, peeled**
- **1/4 cup extra-virgin olive oil**
- **1 tablespoon dark or light brown sugar (optional)**
- **1 teaspoon nigella seeds (optional)**
- **1 teaspoon dried oregano**
- **1 teaspoon garlic powder**
- **1/2 teaspoon ground cumin**
- **1 1/2 teaspoons kosher salt (or sub 1 teaspoon with 1/2 teaspoon truffle salt—say whaaaaaat?)**
- **1/4 teaspoon crushed chile flakes**
- **1 cup Greek yogurt (or labneh, if you have it)**
- **2 tablespoons finely chopped fresh mint leaves**
- **Zest of 1 lemon**

Preheat the oven to 350°F.

Separate the neck of the squash from the round bottom. Halve the bottom and scoop out the seeds. Slice each half into 2 or 3 wedges. Halve the neck lengthwise, then slice it crosswise into 1/2-inch-thick half-moons. You want all the pieces to be roughly the same thickness so they roast evenly.

In a large bowl, toss the squash with the olive oil and turn it out onto a rimmed baking sheet. In a small bowl, combine the brown sugar and nigella (if using), the oregano, garlic powder, cumin, 1 teaspoon of the kosher salt (or 1/2 teaspoon truffle salt), and the chile flakes. Sprinkle the mixture over the squash. Roast for about 40 minutes, until the squash is browned and a fork easily slips into the center. For extra dark and crisp edges, let it go 1 minute under the broiler at the very end.

Meanwhile, in a small bowl, combine the yogurt, mint, lemon zest, and remaining 1/2 teaspoon salt. If you want dollops, leave as is. If you prefer more of a drizzly texture, loosen the mixture with a tablespoon or two of water. Serve the squash anointed with mint yogurt.

SUNCHOKES WITH ROASTED GARLIC AÏOLI

I like to think of these as the healthy veggie equivalent of steak fries. Sunchokes (also called Jerusalem artichokes), if you haven't had one before, land somewhere between an artichoke and a potato in texture and flavor, and the mushrooms roast up and become extra tender and crisp around the edges. And there aren't many things in life that wouldn't be better with a side of roasted garlic aïoli. You can also make the aïoli with Vegenaise if you want to keep this dish totally vegan.

These go play in the oven and leave me plenty of time to take care of other business, so I love making a big plate for dinner parties—whether it's just me and the family or a whole host of hungry people.

MAKES 4 SERVINGS

3/4 pound sunchokes, cut crosswise into 1/2-inch pieces

8 garlic cloves, unpeeled

2 tablespoons extra-virgin olive oil

2 1/2 teaspoons kosher salt

Freshly cracked black pepper

8 ounces mixed mushrooms (such as oyster mushrooms and shiitakes), ends trimmed, mushrooms halved or quartered if large

1/4 cup mayonnaise (or Vegenaise if you want to make this dish vegan)

2 tablespoons fresh lemon juice

1 tablespoon finely chopped fresh parsley leaves

Set a rimmed baking sheet in the oven and preheat the oven to 425°F.

In a large bowl, toss together the sunchokes, garlic, 1 tablespoon of the olive oil, 1 teaspoon of the salt, and a few cracks of black pepper. Remove the baking sheet from the oven, turn the mixture out onto it and shake it to spread evenly. Roast for 15 minutes.

Meanwhile, in the same bowl, toss the mushrooms with 1 teaspoon of the salt and the remaining 1 tablespoon oil.

Add the mushrooms to the baking sheet with the sunchokes. Roast for 10 minutes, stir, then roast about 10 minutes longer, or until the sunchokes are golden and a fork pierces the center of one. Remove from the oven and transfer the garlic cloves to a cutting board to cool.

When the garlic is cool enough to handle, squeeze it out of the skins and into a small bowl. Use a fork to mash them, then stir in the mayonnaise, lemon juice, and remaining 1/2 teaspoon salt.

Sprinkle the sunchokes and mushrooms with parsley and serve them with the aïoli for dipping.

BROCCOLI AND CAULIFLOWER "GRATIN"

This is a perfect side dish or veggie main if your family does Meatless Mondays—which I hope you do! Hunks of roasted cauliflower and broccoli bathed in an herbed garlic oil, topped with melting cheese and a sprinkle of toasty breadcrumbs—ooh, come to mama. While many people throw the broccoli stems away, they're great peeled and thinly sliced into a salad (sort of like a radish), and they're excellent roasted in this preparation because they retain so much texture. If you want to try a variation, slabs of butternut squash also are quite delicious with this technique. And if you don't feel like cutting veggie steaks, simple florets of broccoli and cauliflower work just as well.

MAKES 4 SERVINGS

1 tablespoon unsalted butter

1/4 cup whole wheat panko breadcrumbs

1 1/2 teaspoons kosher salt

3 tablespoons extra-virgin olive oil

4 medium garlic cloves, minced or pressed

1/4 teaspoon crushed chile flakes (optional)

2 1/2 pounds cauliflower (1 medium head), cut crosswise into 1- to 1 1/4-inch-thick slabs

1 1/4 pounds broccoli (2 or 3 stalks), stems peeled and broccoli halved lengthwise

1 cup grated sharp cheddar cheese or Gruyère

1 cup grated Gouda cheese

Freshly cracked black pepper

Preheat the oven to 425°F. Set a rimmed baking sheet on the middle rack while the oven preheats.

In a medium skillet, melt the butter over medium-high heat. Add the panko and toast, stirring often, until fragrant and deeply golden brown, 2 to 3 minutes. Transfer to a bowl, sprinkle with 1/2 teaspoon of the salt, and stir to combine.

In a large bowl, whisk together the olive oil, garlic, the remaining salt, and the chile flakes (if using). Add the cauliflower and broccoli and toss to combine, making sure the garlic oil gets into all the crevices of the vegetables.

Pull the baking sheet out of the oven and pour the veggie mixture out onto it. Roast for 15 to 20 minutes, until the veggies start to brown but aren't totally tender, turning them over midway through cooking so both sides brown evenly. Remove the pan from the oven, sprinkle the veggies with the cheeses, and roast for 5 minutes, or until the cheese is nicely melted.

Transfer to a platter and serve sprinkled with the toasted breadcrumbs and additional salt and pepper to taste.

VARIATION: *If you want to gussy this dish up for a dinner party, boost the breadcrumbs with some tasty additions. In a small bowl, use your fingers to blend together 1/2 cup finely chopped parsley stems and leaves, 1 tablespoon finely chopped fresh mint, and 2 tablespoons golden raisins. Add to the breadcrumbs and toss to combine. Rain this mix all over the top of a pile of the broccoli and cauliflower hot out of the oven.*

RAW BEET CARPACCIO

This recipe barely needs writing down. I like beets any which way, but I'm especially partial to skipping a long roasting or boiling process in favor of a shaved raw plate. The more often you can eat fruits and veggies raw, the more they'll be able to do for you because all their integral enzymes, vitamins, and nutrients remain intact.

I love the particular crunch of thinly sliced beets, sweet but just a touch earthy. You can use this mix on top of another salad, thrown over yogurt or grains, or just on their own. A few dollops of warmed goat cheese (check out the Variation below) are also quite nice with the coolness of the beets.

MAKES 4 SERVINGS

- **1/4 cup extra-virgin olive oil**
- **2 tablespoons red wine vinegar**
- **1 teaspoon honey**
- **2 teaspoons chopped fresh tarragon**
- **1/2 teaspoon kosher salt**
- **Freshly cracked black pepper**
- **8 small to medium red or golden beets, scrubbed and rinsed**
- **Flaky sea salt**

In a small bowl, whisk together the olive oil, vinegar, honey, tarragon, salt, and pepper to taste.

Peel the beets or, if they're organic, scrub extra well and leave the skin on. Slice them extra thin with a mandoline—please be *very* careful!

Arrange the beets on a plate and spoon the vinaigrette over the top—the beets will drink it up! Finish with a pinch of flaky sea salt.

VARIATION: *For extra decadence, roll little patties of goat cheese in flour, then in a whisked egg, and then coat with crushed nuts (pecans, almonds, or hazelnuts work great) or panko breadcrumbs. Pan-fry them in a little olive oil or butter until golden brown and lay them on top of the beets.*

EGGPLANT CAPONATA

It seems as if every Italian family must have its own version of caponata. They'll almost always include eggplant, tomatoes, onions, and pine nuts, plus something briny, such as capers or olives, and something sweet, such as currants or raisins. The medley of these flavors never ceases to excite me: There's so much for the mouth to play with.

The thing that makes each version unique is the ratio of each item to the others. I like to go a little heavier on the olives, capers, and currants, because I think these bright pops of flavor, plus the daintiest pour of balsamic vinegar right at the end, really set caponata apart from eggplant in tomato sauce. But I give you leave to tweak the ratios to your liking! There's no wrong way to eat this classic Italian staple.

P.S. For a novel spin on eggs, try frying one up and serving over leftover caponata. . . . Oooh, so good for breakfast, lunch, or dinner!

MAKES 4 SERVINGS

1/4 cup pine nuts

2 tablespoons extra-virgin olive oil

1 pound Italian eggplants (about 2), cut into 1/2-inch dice

1 teaspoon kosher salt

Freshly cracked black pepper

1 medium red onion, finely chopped

2 tablespoons tomato paste

3 medium garlic cloves, minced

1/3 cup dried currants

1/3 cup pitted oil-cured olives, roughly chopped to about the same size as the currants and capers

2 tablespoons capers

1/2 cup canned crushed tomatoes (or buy canned whole peeled tomatoes and crush them with your hands)

Set a large nonstick skillet over medium-low heat and add the pine nuts. Cook, shaking the pan often, until the nuts are golden brown, 2 to 3 minutes. Watch them closely! The difference between toasty and charred is literally all of 20 seconds. Transfer to a plate.

Add 1 tablespoon of the oil to the pan and heat over medium-high heat. Add the eggplant and cook, stirring occasionally, until it is browned on all sides and starting to soften, about 8 minutes (if the eggplant browns too quickly, turn the heat to medium-low). Stir in 1/2 teaspoon of the salt and pepper to taste and cook for 30 seconds, then transfer the eggplant to a medium bowl and cover the bowl with plastic wrap (this will help steam the eggplant to finish the cooking).

Add the remaining 1 tablespoon of oil to the skillet along with the onion and remaining 1/2 teaspoon salt and cook until the onion starts to soften, 2 to 3 minutes. Add the tomato paste and stir it around the pan to begin to caramelize and coat the onion. Reduce the heat to medium-low and cook the onion and tomato paste until the paste is a deep, rusty red and the onion is completely soft, 4 to 6 minutes. Stir in the garlic and cook until it is fragrant, about 1 minute.

1½ tablespoons balsamic vinegar

12 fresh basil leaves, roughly torn

Add the currants, olives, and capers and toss to warm them through, about 1 minute, then add the crushed tomatoes. Return the eggplant to the pan and stir everything together. Cover and cook 15 to 20 minutes over low heat (I like my eggplant really well done and soaked through with the sauce, though some cooks will take it off the heat after just a few minutes here). Stir in the vinegar. Remove from the heat and adjust the seasoning with additional salt and pepper, if needed. Stir in the pine nuts and top with the basil when ready to serve.

TIP: *I don't salt the eggplant here, which others often do to remove some of the bitterness. I find that salting makes the eggplant texture more leathery and I like soft, creamy bites in this dish.*

TIP: *Kids love the sweet-salty flavor of caponata. They might not be up for eating it straight on toast, but try tossing it with pasta and adding lots of grated Parmigiano-Reggiano cheese. I find adults like this version quite a lot, too.*

PICKLED KIRBYS

I've mentioned my love of pickles before. They're my go-to snack, either on their own for something light and crisp, or sliced thin and used to top a "sandwich" of chips and cheese when I'm hovering around the kitchen island, catching up with friends over a pantry-raid spread. I love the bite of the vinegar and the way the smell makes your mouth water before you've even tasted one. These Kirby coins are extra crisp, but the technique is perfect for almost any combination of veggies you might desire to soak in a bath of vinegar, sugar, and herbs. I've included a few of my favorite pickle combos in the sidebar on the next page, if you're looking for inspiration.

MAKES 1 QUART

1 pound Kirby cucumbers (4 to 6, depending on size), sliced into 1/4-inch coins

3 large fresh dill sprigs

1/2 cup sugar

3 garlic cloves, peeled

2 tablespoons kosher salt

2 teaspoons coriander seeds

1 teaspoon yellow mustard seeds

1 1/2 cups distilled white vinegar

Add one-third of the cucumber slices and 1 dill sprig to a quart-size mason jar. Layer in more cucumber slices, another dill sprig, the rest of the cucumber slices, and the final dill sprig.

In a medium saucepan, combine 1/2 cup water with the sugar, garlic, salt, coriander, and mustard seeds and bring to a boil over high heat. Add the vinegar, reduce the heat to medium-low, and simmer for 2 minutes. Remove from the heat and pour the hot brine and all the additions over the cucumbers (the brine should completely submerge the cucumber slices—if it doesn't, add more vinegar to cover). Set the mixture aside to cool for 20 minutes.

Screw the lid onto the jar and refrigerate for at least 1 day before using the cucumbers. The pickles will keep for up to 3 weeks in the refrigerator.

TIP: *You can pickle green beans, beets, carrots, red bell peppers, or even a mix of vegetables. Start with a whole bunch of vegetables on the counter and let your kids create their own custom pickle jars!*

TIP: *Kirby cucumbers usually have fewer (and smaller) seeds than traditional cucumbers. English (seedless) cucumbers and Persian (mini) cucumbers also work well for pickles.*

SOME OTHER PRETTY PICKLES

PICKLED VIDALIAS

Substitute 2 large Vidalia onions for the cucumbers. Halve the onions and thinly slice. Add 1 teaspoon whole black peppercorns to the spice mix in the brine and replace 1/2 cup of the white vinegar with balsamic vinegar. To make the onions a little spicy, add 2 dried red chiles to the brine. (Red or white onions also work here.)

TACO PICKLES

Substitute 4 medium carrots, peeled and thinly sliced crosswise and on the bias, for the cucumbers. Add 2 jalapeños, thinly sliced crosswise and on the bias. Substitute 6 cilantro sprigs for the dill sprigs. Swap cumin seeds for the mustard seeds.

PICKLED GOLDEN BEETS

Peel and halve 3 medium golden beets, then cut them into 1/2-inch-thick slices to use in place of the cucumbers. Replace 1 cup of the white vinegar with apple cider vinegar. Instead of dill, use fresh thyme sprigs.

CHILI-GLAZED GREEN BEANS

Whenever I order Chinese food delivery, I find myself filled with MSG and regrets. It might just be the delivery places around me here in New York City—or what I'm ordering, or the gusto with which I devour it—but it's the truth. Still, every now and then, I'm hit with an irresistible desire for the wok-seared, sweet and spicy Chinese-style green beans. In an effort to spare myself tomorrow's sodium-swollen puffy face, I make this version at home instead. They're great on their own or under seared shrimp, chicken, or beef.

MAKES 4 SERVINGS

- **1 tablespoon sambal oelek (an Asian chili sauce), Sriracha sauce, or diced hot cherry peppers plus a little of their vinegar**
- **2 tablespoons low-sodium soy sauce**
- **1 tablespoon honey**
- **1 tablespoon grated fresh ginger**
- **1 large garlic clove, finely chopped**
- **1 tablespoon plus 1/2 teaspoon kosher salt**
- **1 pound green beans, ends trimmed, halved on the bias**
- **1 tablespoon grapeseed oil**
- **1/2 cup salted roasted peanuts (or see Toasting Nuts, page 14, to roast raw peanuts), roughly chopped**

In a small bowl, combine the sambal oelek, soy sauce, honey, ginger, and garlic.

Bring a medium saucepan of water to a boil with 1 tablespoon of the salt. Add the beans and blanch until al dente, 6 to 8 minutes. Drain in a colander and place under running cold water to stop the cooking process (or transfer the beans to an ice water bath).

Heat a large skillet over high heat for 2 minutes. Add the oil and when it shimmers, add the beans. Season with the remaining 1/2 teaspoon salt and cook, shaking the pan often, until the beans get some color and blister in places, 3 to 4 minutes.

Add the sambal mixture to the skillet and toss the beans to coat. Cook for 1 minute, then transfer the beans immediately to a serving dish. Top with the peanuts and serve hot.

OVEN-DRIED TOMATOES

I confess that I don't (currently) can or preserve many things besides pickles, but I make an effort for roasted tomatoes. Weirdly, I don't love the taste of store-bought sun-dried tomatoes—they're always a little too acidic and leathery for me—but when you roast tomatoes slowly with a little olive oil, garlic, and fresh herbs, something miraculous happens. They become tender, sweet, and concentrated with rich, tomato flavor without any of the bite some raw tomatoes can have.

These roasted tomatoes are amazing piled high on a piece of toast for a simple bruschetta. I wouldn't say no to a little fresh mozzarella or burrata underneath, either. I love to pack them in oil with the roasted garlic from the pan—the resulting tomato oil is great for vinaigrettes or garnishing soups, pastas, and pizzas.

MAKES 2 CUPS

8 medium tomatoes, cored and quartered

1 teaspoon dried oregano

Leaves from 8 fresh thyme sprigs

1 teaspoon sugar

1 teaspoon kosher salt

Freshly cracked black pepper

1/4 cup extra-virgin olive oil, plus extra for storage if needed

2 garlic cloves, unpeeled

Preheat the oven to 350°F.

Place the tomatoes in a baking dish or pan large enough so that they can all sit in a single layer.

In a small bowl, mix together the oregano, thyme, sugar, salt, and pepper to taste. Sprinkle the herb mixture over the tomatoes, then drizzle generously with the olive oil. Toss the garlic cloves into the pan.

Roast until the tomatoes are dark red, very tender, and start to brown on the bottom, checking after 40 minutes, and allowing them to cook a little longer as needed. Set them aside to cool in the dish.

Use right away, or pack the tomatoes and any juices into a pint-size airtight container for storage. Squeeze the roasted garlic into the jar with the tomatoes, then cover with olive oil to preserve them. Refrigerate for up to 1 week, or freeze for up to 3 months.

TIP: *For an amazing tomato addition to sandwiches and quiche—anywhere you want that great tomato flavor but not necessarily all the wetness, slice the tomatoes into 1/4-inch rounds as pictured to the right and drizzle with olive oil and sprinkle with fresh thyme, salt, and pepper. You can then roast them low and slow at 250°F for about 3 hours (this will give you the most natural sweetness); or speed things along at 400°F for about 30 minutes or until they are dried but still tender.*

SHREDDED ROOT VEGETABLE PANCAKES

Fried potato in all its forms is endlessly comforting. French fries, obviously delicious. Potato chips, my guiltiest of pleasures (but I actually feel very little guilt because I enjoy them so much). Combine potatoes with some shredded onion, a few seasonings, and some binders, and you have delicious potato pancakes. The only problem is that potatoes, though a vegetable, aren't that good for you. Especially when fried. They're pretty high on the glycemic index, meaning they create a sugar spike (and resulting crash) in your body, much the same way other white foods do (white rice, white bread, white sugar, etc.).

In the hope of having my (pan)cake and eating it too, I've subbed in some veggies with less of that sugar hit—rutabagas and parsnips—that offer a similar texture and slightly lighter flavor. These root vegetable pancakes are a gift to eggs everywhere for brunch, served under a little crème fraîche and smoked salmon for a party app, or simply paired with sour cream and applesauce for an ideal sweet-savory combo anytime.

MAKES 8 PANCAKES (4 SERVINGS)

2 cups of shredded rutabaga, parsnips, or sweet potato (from about 2 medium vegetables), shredded on the medium holes of a box grater

1 medium yellow onion, grated on the medium holes of a box grater

3 large egg whites, beaten

1/4 cup all-purpose flour, plus more if needed so mixture just holds together

1 teaspoon kosher salt

Freshly cracked black pepper

1/2 cup coconut or grapeseed oil

Flaky sea salt

1/4 cup sour cream or crème fraîche

2 scallions, finely chopped

Place the grated root veggies and onion in a large kitchen towel and wring out any liquid, then add them to a medium bowl.

Stir in the egg whites. Stir in the flour, salt, and pepper to taste.

In a large skillet, heat 1/4 cup of the oil over medium-high heat. Use a scant 1/4 cup measure to scoop pancakes into the skillet, using the bottom of the measuring cup to spread the mixture into 1/2-inch-thick patties. Cook until the first side is deeply golden brown and crisp, 3 to 4 minutes, then turn the pancakes over and brown the other side, 3 to 4 minutes more. Transfer the pancakes to a wire rack to cool slightly. Work in batches so you don't overcrowd the pan, adding more oil to the pan as needed.

Serve the pancakes topped with a few pinches of flaky sea salt, a dollop of sour cream, and a sprinkle of scallions.

VARIATION: *If you want these guys a little spicy, mince 1/2 a jalapeño or Fresno chile and add it to the mixture before frying.*

SPAGHETTI SQUASH CACIO E PEPE

I made this on a whim one day when I had a spaghetti squash that had been sitting on my counter a little too long. I halved it, scooped out the seeds, drizzled it with a little olive oil and a sprinkle of garlic salt, and roasted it. I probably forgot about it in the oven, because I came back and it was dark, dark brown. But taking off the top layer, I found the inside was perfectly cooked. And the dark bits were actually kind of delicious themselves.

As I peeled and scraped out the fluffy spaghetti strands inside, it dawned on me that it might be just the vehicle for the Parmesan I had sitting in the fridge. A few minutes later, I was feasting on *cacio e pepe*-style roasted spaghetti squash. And because the flavors of *cacio e pepe* are so mild—really just cheese and pepper—I actually like it even better on the delicate squash than on traditional pasta, where it's so easy to lose the seasoning. I've dolled it up since that first fateful dish, opting for garlic cloves rather than garlic salt. But it is easy, filling, and deceptively indulgent either way.

MAKES 4 SERVINGS

- **1 medium spaghetti squash (about 2 3/4 pounds), halved lengthwise and seeded**
- **4 tablespoons extra-virgin olive oil**
- **1 teaspoon kosher salt**
- **2 garlic cloves**
- **1/2 cup grated Parmigiano-Reggiano cheese**
- **Freshly cracked black pepper**

Preheat the oven to 400°F.

Place both squash halves cut side up on a rimmed baking sheet, drizzle each half with 1 tablespoon of the olive oil, and season each with 1/2 teaspoon of the salt. Use a Microplane-style rasp to grate 1 garlic clove over each half, then rub it into the squash.

Roast the squash for 45 minutes to 1 hour, until a fork easily slips all the way through and the flesh fluffs into spaghetti-like strands.

Let the squash cool for 10 minutes, then shred it with a fork. Transfer the strands to a large bowl. Add the Parmigiano and remaining 2 tablespoons olive oil, then toss and season with additional salt and pepper to taste.

ASPARAGUS "FRITES"

I end up cooking asparagus like this a few times a week, because it goes so quickly and no one ever thinks he or she got enough. It's a ridiculously easy preparation to make when you feel like your weeknight dinner needs a vegetable.

I let the asparagus roast a little longer than most people would, but as they get that deep, dark golden brown color, they're also getting extra crispy. There's a part of me that feels as if I'm eating "healthier" French fries (hence the "frites") when I have them, which I'm totally okay with.

MAKES 6 SERVINGS

1 pound medium to medium-thick asparagus

3 tablespoons extra-virgin olive oil

1/2 teaspoon garlic powder

1 teaspoon kosher salt

Preheat the oven to 350°F.

Hold each asparagus spear at the middle and bend the spear near the woody end to snap it off—about an inch or so should snap off (discard the woody ends). Place the asparagus on a rimmed baking sheet.

In a small bowl, combine the oil, garlic powder, and salt. Drizzle the mixture over the asparagus and roll the spears in the mixture to evenly coat them.

Roast the spears for 20 to 25 minutes (depending on thickness), until the tips turn deeply golden brown and become crisp, shaking the baking sheet occasionally to distribute and roast all sides evenly.

Transfer to a platter and serve.

TIP: *You can use 1/2 teaspoon garlic salt in place of the garlic powder and kosher salt if you have it.*

SUGAR-AND-THYME-BASTED ONIONS

Roasting onions is as easy as cranking your oven to 400°F, throwing a few unpeeled on a baking sheet, and letting them go until the onions are all blistered skin on the outside that you peel away to reveal melting sweetness on the inside (about 1 hour, depending on your onions). Even this basic technique yields wonderful results, because slow-cooking onions brings all their natural sugars to the surface, so that, layer by layer, each has its own unique caramel flavor.

But this particular recipe is not your average roasted onion. Instead of simply roasting, we're going to baste the onions in a glorious sweet-savory combination of sugar, thyme, and rich broth. Imagine French onion soup made waistline friendly (though the gobs of stringy, melting cheese are certainly welcome in the original).

Served hot, these onions are a great addition to steak or grilled chicken. For a lovely starter, dip slices of baguette into the onion drippings at the base of the baking dish, then pull the onions apart and layer atop. Since these do take some time to cook, better to make a few all at once and then keep them in the fridge to use all week long to make even simple meals look—and taste—as if they took you hours.

MAKES 4 SERVINGS

4 medium yellow or red onions, peeled and halved crosswise

2 tablespoons extra-virgin olive oil

2 teaspoons kosher salt

3/4 cup vegetable broth (made from Vegetable Broth Concentrate, page 69) or chicken broth, plus more as needed

Leaves from 4 fresh thyme sprigs

4 large garlic cloves, roughly chopped

1 teaspoon sugar

2 bay leaves

1 tablespoon unsalted butter

Preheat the oven to 350°F.

Place the onions in a baking dish or casserole that will fit them all snugly (a 1 1/2-quart baking dish works well). Drizzle the onions with the oil and use your hands to evenly coat them, then season generously with the salt and arrange them in the dish cut side up.

In a small bowl, whisk together the broth, thyme, garlic, and sugar and pour the mixture over the onions. Add the bay leaves to the baking dish and cover with foil.

Roast the onions for 45 minutes to 1 hour, until they are very tender, removing the foil and using a spoon to baste them every 20 minutes or so (add 1/4 cup of broth or water to the baking dish if needed so the pan bottom isn't dry).

Remove the foil and place a pinch of butter on top of each onion, then return to the oven for another 10 minutes uncovered, until the tops are golden brown.

Let the onions cool for 10 minutes, then serve them with their sauce.

HARISSA-ROASTED CARROTS WITH CRISPY CAPER GREMOLATA

These roasted carrots get a little extra love from harissa paste, which makes them smoky and a little bit spicy, depending on the harissa you choose. And I love pairing them with a light and zingy gremolata that I boost with crispy capers. You could absolutely deep-fry rinsed and well-dried capers to get an even crunchier, crispier garnish, but I find roasting them on the baking sheet with the carrots gets a very similar result with less cleanup.

MAKES 4 SERVINGS

SPICED CARROTS

- 2 tablespoons extra-virgin olive oil
- 1½ tablespoons harissa paste (more or less, depending on how strong and spicy the harissa is; see Tip)
- 1 teaspoon kosher salt
- Freshly cracked black pepper
- 12 medium carrots, peeled, stems trimmed
- 2 teaspoons honey
- 2 tablespoons chopped toasted hazelnuts (see Toasting Nuts, page 14; optional)

CRISPY CAPER GREMOLATA

- 3 tablespoons capers, patted dry
- 1½ tablespoons extra-virgin olive oil
- ⅓ cup finely chopped fresh mint or parsley
- Zest and juice of ½ lemon
- Zest and juice of ½ orange
- 1 garlic clove, minced or grated
- ¾ teaspoon kosher salt
- Freshly cracked black pepper

Preheat the oven to 400°F. Use a little of the oil to lightly grease a rimmed baking sheet.

To make the spiced carrots, in a large bowl, whisk together the remaining oil, the harissa, salt, and pepper to taste. Add the carrots and toss to combine and coat. Spread them on the baking sheet. Scrape out any spice mixture that sticks to the bottom of the bowl and drizzle it over the carrots.

Roast the carrots for 20 minutes, then shake the pan to redistribute the carrots. Reduce the heat to 375°F and roast 20 to 25 minutes longer, until the carrots are browned and tender.

Meanwhile, 15 minutes before the carrots are done, start the gremolata. Toss the capers with ½ tablespoon of the olive oil and spread them in a single layer on one side of the carrot pan. Drizzle the carrots with the honey and return the pan to the oven.

While the carrots finish roasting, make the rest of the gremolata. In a small bowl, stir together the mint, lemon zest, lemon juice, orange zest, orange juice, garlic, salt, pepper to taste, and the remaining 1 tablespoon olive oil.

Serve the carrots on a platter sprinkled with the gremolata and topped with crisped capers and toasted hazelnuts (if using).

TIP: *If you can't find harissa, substitute a blend of ¾ teaspoon ground cumin, ½ teaspoon garlic powder, and a pinch of crushed chile flakes.*

pasta and grains

I'm part Italian, and pasta is practically a way of life for us. Especially growing up in a family where at least a few members were vegetarian at any given time, a variety of pasta and grain dishes were always in heavy rotation. After sampling hundreds—maybe thousands—of delectable preparations, I've concluded that there's no reason to waste a single calorie ever on pasta or grains that are anything less than carbtastically divine.

If you've been relying on boxed grain combinations or jarred sauces, this chapter is going to bring you into the light. With pasta or grain as the elegantly simple carrier for any combination of sauce and add-ons, it's time to say hello to some of the easiest homemade masterpieces out there. Whether it's learning to love your greens with a forkful of Rigatoni with Green Monster Pesto and Kale Chips; venturing vegan in a bowl of Cashew Soba Noodles with Fried Shallots; staying light with Quinoa Salad with Lemon, Herbs, and Feta; or going for gold with Sweet Corn Ravioli with Tarragon-Butter Broth, there's a little something for everyone.

And here's one little secret that is going to change your pasta game forever (it was the first thing Mario Batali ever taught me about Italian cooking, and you'll be amazed what a difference it makes): The pasta water is often the most neglected step of pasta cooking, and it is the key to a great finished dish.

So what makes great pasta water? The right amount of salt, which is roughly 2 teaspoons of kosher salt per quart (it sounds like a lot, but remember you're draining most of that water away—this is just so your pasta is well seasoned as it cooks). And how does great pasta water beget great pasta? Three simple steps: First, you salt it appropriately. Second, you never, ever, *ever* add oil to the pasta water. Giving your noodle this slippery slick of oil will mean it can't soak up all the delicious flavor of that sauce you labored over. Third, when you drain the pasta, it's a good idea to save a little pasta water (1/2 cup or so), because you always want to finish your pasta in the pan with the sauce, and adding a few splashes of pasta cooking water with all its leftover starch will help to thicken and bind the sauce right onto your noodle for the perfect result. And now that you're basically Italian too, let's eat! *Cin-cin!*

salt-n-pepa

You most likely have a big cylinder of Morton's table salt sitting in your spice cabinet that you use almost everywhere salt is required. If you are into "finishing salts," you may also own a box of Maldon Sea Salt Flakes. Two salts seems like plenty, so you may be wondering (a) why I call for kosher salt in many of my recipes, (b) what kosher salt is and whether it's worth buying, and (c) why can't you just use table salt instead? OK, here's the quick breakdown.

All these salts have basically the same chemical composition (NaCl, baby. Hey hey junior year chem!), with the addition of some minerals and/or anticaking agents in the case of table salt. Table salt is made up of extremely regular cubes of salt, meaning they fit quite nicely into measuring equipment. Kosher salt, on the other hand, is often flaked and irregular, meaning that tablespoon for tablespoon, you'll get about twice as much table salt as kosher salt into the same space (which means if you're going to sub table salt for kosher, you need to reduce the quantity by half for the same amount of saltiness).

The reason I like kosher salt—I use Diamond Crystal—is that it's a simple way to avoid oversalting because the flakes are easy to pick up between your fingers and use to evenly season your food. In soups or stews where the salt gets dissolved, this isn't as important, but for meats, salads, etc., where you want even salt distribution, kosher does the trick, whereas the fine grains of table salt make it a little bit harder to eyeball. Sea salt is its own ball game because it can come in all kinds of shapes and sizes, and comes with its own assortment of slight flavor variations based on the minerals in the water from which it was harvested. It can also be quite expensive, so if you're going to invest in it, reserve it for times when you want to add a bright burst of salinity or crunch to a meal right before serving—it's not worth using if it's going to get dissolved.

Keep in mind: You can always add more salt, but it's nearly impossible to get rid of too much salt in a finished dish (yes, throwing a peeled, raw potato in soup sometimes works to soak up some salt, or a little acid like vinegar or lemon juice to mute the taste, but the result is still not as good as the perfectly salted version). The amounts I've included in these recipes are my preference, but you should always taste the food and season the way you like before serving!

Speaking of which, salt is often paired with its bestie, pepper. As with all spices, freshly cracked is going to give you the most vibrant flavor, so ditch the bland, preground pepper languishing on your shelf and invest in a simple pepper mill. This way, you will always have pepper with the freshest, most peppery bite. Plus, you can customize to a fine grind for soups and sauces (this is also really easy to achieve by throwing whole peppercorns into a spice grinder), all the way on up to a coarse grind for steaks and heartier meals. If you don't have a pepper mill, a "pinch" of pepper is roughly 1/8 teaspoon and will generally do the trick, or you can just skip it entirely.

RIGATONI WITH GREEN MONSTER PESTO AND KALE CHIPS

I call pretty much anything I whir in the blender into a green sauce of some kind "green monster." I give Philo a green monster breakfast smoothie in the mornings, which is just banana, avocado, yogurt, a huge handful of frozen spinach, and water to blend. She loves it—and the name might have something to do with that. I also make a green monster dressing that's basically tons of fresh herbs, a little jalapeño, peanuts, olive oil, honey, and tons of lime juice that we eat with everything from crudités to samosas. So when I made up this extra-healthy, greens-packed pesto, it was only natural to call it green monster pesto.

This is one dish I can rely on to be ready in the time it takes to throw a bunch of stuff into a blender and boil water for pasta, especially if you skip the kale chips step (but don't, because they add a desirably crispy garnish to this dish, and are an excellent snack for the cook!). I tend to keep a bunch of sautéed greens on hand in the fridge to toss together with a healthy grain, a dollop of yogurt, and a drizzle of olive oil for fast lunches, and this blend often uses up any leftovers. The cooked garlic mutes the aggressive taste some raw garlic pestos can have, and the nuts, oil, and cheese blend to creamy perfection, enveloping the greens and making them delicious for palates of all ages. Green monster magic!

MAKES 4 SERVINGS

2 bunches Tuscan (lacinato) kale, washed, dried, and ribs removed

1/2 cup plus 3 tablespoons extra-virgin olive oil

Kosher salt

1 pound rigatoni

2 medium garlic cloves, sliced

1 cup fresh basil leaves

1/2 cup finely grated Pecorino-Romano cheese, plus extra for serving

Freshly cracked black pepper

1/2 cup walnuts or pine nuts

Adjust one oven rack to the upper-middle position and the other to the lower-middle position and preheat the oven to 350°F.

Roughly tear half of the kale into bite-size pieces and add them to a large bowl. Toss with 1 1/2 tablespoons of the olive oil and 1/2 teaspoon salt. On 2 baking sheets, arrange the pieces of kale in a single layer, with the leaves overlapping as little as possible, so they don't steam. Roast for 10 to 12 minutes, until the leaves are crisp, switching the pans from top to bottom and vice versa after 5 minutes and shaking the pans to loosen and redistribute the leaves. Set the kale aside to cool on the baking sheets.

Bring a large pot of salted water to a boil over high heat. Add the rigatoni and cook it 1 minute less than the package instructs. Reserving 1/2 cup of pasta water, drain the pasta.

Meanwhile, in a large skillet, heat 1½ tablespoons of the olive oil over medium heat. Add the remaining kale and sauté for 2 minutes. Add the garlic and toss to distribute. Cook until the garlic is fragrant and the greens are wilted, another 1 to 3 minutes. (This process works perfectly with spinach, chard, escarole, or any other green you'd like to use up.)

In a food processor, combine the basil, Romano, ½ teaspoon salt, and pepper to taste and process until well combined. Add the sautéed kale and the walnuts and pulse while drizzling in the remaining ½ cup olive oil until the texture is smooth. Add a spoon or two of pasta water to loosen the mixture if needed.

Toss the pasta with the kale pesto. Serve sprinkled with kale chips and more Romano.

WHEAT BERRIES WITH SWEET POTATO AND CHARRED CHILE VINAIGRETTE

Whether millet, barley, farro, quinoa (actually a seed), or a slew of others, grains are here to satisfy as a versatile (and supernutritious) canvas to use with any combination of veggies, dried fruits, proteins, and flavorful dressings you can imagine. And, if you're looking for an easy way to stretch your meals and make leftovers look endlessly appealing? Congratulations, you've found it.

This grain salad capitalizes on the incredibly nutty and chewy wheat berry. It's a particularly tasty combo with sweet potatoes and gently tart dried apricots. And you also get the heat of charred Fresno chiles, which are slightly less spicy than jalapeños—for the most part. Every once in a while, you end up with a hell-fire Fresno and it's all over, so better to taste a little bit before you add the whole thing to the dressing. You can also scrape out the seeds and ribs (white parts) for less heat.

MAKES 6 SERVINGS

1½ cups wheat berries
1½ teaspoons kosher salt
1 medium sweet potato, peeled and cut into ½-inch pieces
2 Fresno chiles (red jalapeños)
4 tablespoons extra-virgin olive oil
½ cup slivered or sliced almonds
½ teaspoon curry powder
2 tablespoons fresh lime juice
2 tablespoons finely chopped fresh chives
Freshly cracked black pepper
½ cup chopped dried apricots

In a large pot, combine the wheat berries with water to cover by 2 inches. Add 1 teaspoon salt and bring to a boil over high heat. Cook uncovered until the wheat berries are tender, about 1 hour. Drain and rinse under cold water to stop the cooking. (These can be made a day ahead and stored in the fridge if desired, but the salad is great warm if you make them fresh.)

Preheat the oven to 375°F.

Arrange the sweet potato pieces and whole chiles on a rimmed baking sheet and toss with 2 tablespoons of the olive oil and 1 teaspoon salt. Roast for 25 to 30 minutes, until the vegetables are browned and tender and the chiles are charred, stirring a few times throughout roasting. (If the chiles aren't charred enough, you can transfer the roasted vegetables to a bowl, then return the baking sheet with the chiles to the oven to broil until they're dark.) Transfer to a medium bowl and set aside. Leave the oven on.

In a bowl, combine the almonds and curry powder and toss to coat. Sprinkle the almonds on the baking sheet and toast them for 6 to 8 minutes, until golden brown. Toss once at the halfway point. Set the almonds aside on the baking sheet.

Finely chop the chiles (leave the charred skin on) and place them in a large bowl. Whisk in the lime juice, chives, ½ teaspoon salt, and pepper to taste, then drizzle in the remaining 2 tablespoons olive oil.

(For a smooth vinaigrette and to avoid chopping, you can puree all the dressing ingredients in a blender.)

Add the wheat berries and apricots and toss to combine, then fold in the sweet potato. Sprinkle the almonds on top and serve.

TIP: *If you buy organic sweet potatoes, there's no need to peel them. You can keep all the fiber and nutrition of the skin intact. Simply give them a good scrub with a vegetable brush (a new nail brush works great) and cut as usual.*

SWEET CORN RAVIOLI WITH TARRAGON-BUTTER BROTH

When I was a kid, my parents would load me and my three siblings into our gray Ford station wagon and trundle us all down to the Jersey shore on summer weekends to visit my grandparents. The torture of being in a cramped car for hours, singing along for the umpteenth time to the only CD we had with us, was quickly forgotten when we pulled up to a farm stand about twenty minutes from our destination to load up on the freshest green beans, juiciest peaches, and sweetest corn.

My dad is famous in our family for insisting that good corn on the cob spend less than 3 minutes in boiling water, and he would fight with my grandmother, who held firm that corn needs 30 minutes to sweeten and tenderize properly. The tender, barely cooked corn at the center of this ravioli, anointed with buttery corn-and-tarragon broth, is the best of both worlds.

MAKES 4 SERVINGS

2 large ears of corn, shucked

1/2 large sweet onion (such as a Vidalia or Maui), roughly chopped

1 bay leaf

1 Parmigiano-Reggiano rind (optional—a few chunks of Parmigiano-Reggiano cheese also work) plus 1/2 cup finely grated Parmigiano-Reggiano cheese

1/3 cup ricotta cheese

1 small scallion, white part only, minced

Kosher salt

8 sheets fresh pasta (sometimes sold as lasagna sheets)

Cornmeal for dusting

2 tablespoons cold unsalted butter, cut into small pieces

2 tablespoons minced fresh tarragon leaves

Freshly cracked black pepper

Slice the kernels from 1/2 ear of corn and place them in a medium bowl. Using the medium holes of a box grater, grate the rest of the corn off the cobs into the same bowl. Set this corn mash aside.

Add the corncobs to a large saucepan (halve them if they are too long) along with the onion, bay leaf, and Parmigiano rind (if using). Add 6 cups water and bring the mixture to a simmer over high heat. Reduce the heat to medium-low and gently simmer the corn broth for 20 minutes. Remove from the heat and set aside to steep and cool.

To the corn mash, add the grated Parmigiano, ricotta, scallion, and 1/2 teaspoon salt. Stir the filling to combine.

Place the pasta sheets on a clean work surface and cut each one into four even squares about 4 inches wide. Set half the squares aside, and spread the other half out on your workspace.

Spoon about 2 teaspoons of filling onto each square. Using your finger or a pastry brush, paint the edges of each square with cool water, then top it with one of the reserved pasta squares. Seal the edges with your fingers and press out any air around the filling. If you're OCD/fancy, trim the edges with a paring knife or pizza wheel.

Lightly dust a baking sheet with cornmeal and place the prepared ravioli on top; refrigerate until ready to boil.

Bring a large pot of salted water to a boil over high heat.

While the water comes to a boil, make the tarragon-butter broth. Strain the cooled corn broth through a fine-mesh sieve into a large

skillet (discard the cobs and solids). Bring the broth to a simmer over medium-high heat, add 1 teaspoon salt, reduce the heat to medium-low, and cook until the volume is reduced by one-fourth, about 5 minutes. Whisk in the cold butter, 1 piece at a time, until the sauce is slightly thickened. Whisk in the tarragon. Taste and season with more salt if needed and pepper to taste.

Add the ravioli to the gently boiling water and cook until they rise to the surface (the amount of time will depend on the thickness of the pasta, but generally it should take about 3 minutes). Test one to make sure the outer rim of the pasta is cooked and the filling is hot throughout. Use a slotted spoon to transfer the ravioli to four shallow bowls. Divide the broth over the top and serve.

CAULIFLOWER AND ZUCCHINI ORECCHIETTE

I'm a big fan of using vegetables or beans (cannellini or Great Northern work especially well) to bulk up pasta dishes. They add tons of flavor and texture, and they also let me use less pasta but still have the sensation of eating a big ol' bowl. In this case, cauliflower takes on all the same flavor as the pasta, so you barely notice when you're having bites that are mostly veggie. The zucchini gets a lovely char, especially if you leave it in the pan just a smidge too long and don't move it too much while it's in there; and it adds a ton of juiciness and flavor of its own. The rich, creamy dollops of ricotta melt delicately over the warm pasta, making the whole thing ultracreamy with very little actual cheese. And I love the splash of fresh mint right at the end.

MAKES 4 SERVINGS

Kosher salt

8 ounces orecchiette, or other shaped pasta such as farfalle or shells

3 tablespoons extra-virgin olive oil, plus extra for serving

1 small head of cauliflower, cored and divided into bite-size florets (about 3 cups)

1 medium zucchini, halved lengthwise and thinly sliced crosswise

4 garlic cloves, minced

1/2 teaspoon crushed chile flakes (optional)

2 tablespoons white wine (optional)

2 tablespoons unsalted butter

1/2 cup ricotta cheese

2 tablespoons finely chopped fresh mint

Bring a large pot of salted water to a boil over high heat. Add the pasta and cook it 1 minute less than the package instructs. Reserving 1/2 cup of the pasta water, drain the pasta.

In a large skillet, heat 2 tablespoons of the olive oil over medium-high heat. Add the cauliflower, season with 1 teaspoon salt, reduce the heat to medium, and cook, stirring often, until it loses its raw white color, 2 to 3 minutes.

Increase the heat to medium-high and drizzle in the remaining 1 tablespoon olive oil. Add the zucchini and cook until the vegetables start to brown, 3 to 4 minutes. Don't move them around too much; just toss them halfway through the cooking to get color on the other side. Season with another 1/2 teaspoon salt.

Reduce the heat to medium and stir in the garlic and chile flakes (if using). Cook until the garlic is fragrant, about 30 seconds. Add the wine (if using) or 2 tablespoons of the reserved pasta water and scrape up any browned bits in the bottom of the pan.

Add the pasta, butter, and 2 more tablespoons of the pasta water and cook, shaking the pan and stirring often, until the pasta is al dente and the butter is melted, about 1 minute.

Divide the pasta among bowls and top each with a few dollops of the ricotta. Serve sprinkled with the mint.

CASHEW SOBA NOODLES WITH FRIED SHALLOTS

This is the bowl of noodle heaven I reach for when I'm craving something decadent and creamy, but I'm pretending to be good—or maybe I'm pretending to be bad? Cashews, soy sauce, fresh lime juice, and toasted sesame oil flavor this luxurious vegan sauce. The cool, crisp cucumber and gentle scattering of fresh scallions balance out the richness all around, but a shower of fried shallots is what takes this dish to another level. Boom.

MAKES 4 SERVINGS

Kosher salt

6 ounces soba noodles

1 cup cashews, toasted and whole (see Toasting Nuts, page 14), plus 1/4 cup roughly chopped toasted cashews

3 medium shallots—1 roughly chopped and 2 thinly sliced crosswise into rings

6 tablespoons grapeseed oil

2 tablespoons soy sauce

1 tablespoon fresh lime juice

1 tablespoon toasted sesame oil

2 teaspoons sugar

1/8 teaspoon cayenne pepper

1 English (seedless) cucumber, chopped into bite-size cubes

4 scallions, thinly sliced

1 Fresno chile, thinly sliced (optional)

Bring a large pot of salted water to a boil. Add the noodles and cook according to the package instructions. Reserving 1/3 cup of the cooking water, drain the noodles and rinse them under cold water to stop the cooking.

In a food processor, process the 1 cup whole cashews into a butter—this will take 2 to 3 minutes, scraping down the sides and bottom of the bowl as necessary. Add the chopped shallot, 4 tablespoons of the grapeseed oil, the soy sauce, lime juice, sesame oil, sugar, 1/2 teaspoon salt, and the cayenne and process to combine. Add the reserved 1/3 cup pasta water and continue to process until the sauce is very creamy and smooth.

In a medium nonstick skillet, heat the remaining 2 tablespoons grapeseed oil over medium-high heat. Add the shallot rings and cook, stirring often, until they begin to brown around the edges, 3 to 4 minutes. Reduce the heat to medium and keep cooking, stirring often, until they are crisp and deeply caramelized, about 4 minutes longer. Add the chopped cashews and 1/2 teaspoon salt and continue to cook until the cashews are glossy, 1 to 2 minutes.

In a large bowl, combine the soba noodles and cashew butter sauce and toss to combine. Serve in bowls showered with the cucumber, scallions, and the fried shallot mixture. If you're feeling frisky, add the chile for a nice pop of heat!

VARIATION: *Cashews make for a very rich nut butter. You could use peanuts or almonds instead, or simplify the recipe by starting with 1 cup of high-quality store-bought cashew, almond, peanut, or sunflower butter.*

CRISPY BROWN RICE PILAF WITH MERGUEZ AND DATES

I'm a lifelong fan of the buttery rice pilafs that come along with so many Middle Eastern and Indian meats and fish dishes. The trick is to parboil the rice before finishing the cooking process in butter or oil so that each grain is surrounded in salty fat. Then it's up to the cook whether to add different dried fruits, nuts, spices, or citrus zest. All these textures and flavors work together to create the perfect accompaniment to the main meal—but why not put it all together in one epic explosion of rice, meat, and flavorings?

I use the devilish renderings of merguez sausage to bloom the rice and play off this spicy flavor by cooking dates (nature's candy) and slivered almonds in with the grain. The dates become softly sticky, while the nuts lose their crunch in favor of a tender bite. This is pure comfort food, but I used brown rice so we can enjoy it that much more. I get you.

MAKES 4 SERVINGS

1½ cups long-grain brown rice

3 teaspoons kosher salt

1 tablespoon extra-virgin olive oil

2 merguez sausages

1 medium red onion, finely chopped

1 tablespoon unsalted butter

2¼ cups chicken broth or water (or a combination)

½ cup chopped, pitted Medjool dates (about 8 dates)

½ cup slivered almonds

Bring a large pot of water to a boil over high heat. Add the rice and 2 teaspoons salt and cook, uncovered, until the rice is cooked on the outside but still quite raw on the inside, about 20 minutes. Drain in a sieve and rinse with cold water to stop the cooking. Turn the rice out onto a rimmed baking sheet lined with a clean kitchen towel.

In a large skillet, heat the oil over medium heat. Squeeze the sausage out of its casings (discard the casings) and cook until it is browned, stirring often to crumble, about 5 minutes. Use a slotted spoon to transfer the sausage to a large plate and set it aside (you'll use any fat that collects on the plate later).

Add the onion and ½ teaspoon salt to the pan and cook, stirring often, until the onion starts to brown around the edges, 4 to 5 minutes. Add the butter. When it melts, add the parboiled rice and stir to quickly coat. Let it warm for 1 minute, then add the broth and/or water, dates, almonds, and ½ teaspoon salt. Bring the liquid to a simmer, still over medium heat.

Use the end of a wooden spoon to poke about 6 holes through the rice. Reduce the heat to medium-low and cook, uncovered and without stirring, until the liquid level has reduced and doesn't rise above the rice, 8 to 10 minutes.

Cover the pan and reduce the heat to low. Cook until all the liquid is absorbed, 10 to 15 minutes more. Remove from the heat. Remove the lid, cover the pot with a piece of paper towel, then return the lid to hold it in place. Let the rice sit covered and steaming for 5 minutes.

Return the sausage and accumulated juices to the pilaf and fluff the rice with a fork, taking care to leave the crispy layer of rice at the bottom of the pan intact. Turn the rice out onto a platter. Use a spatula or wooden spoon to scrape up the crispy, browned bits at the bottom of the pan. Serve them on top of the rice.

TIP: *In this method, the rice is parboiled first, then gently sautéed before steaming. By not stirring or moving the bottom layer of rice, we're ensuring tender, individual grains (not gloopy lumps), and a crisp bottom layer of socarrat. And don't skip the final 5-minute steam off the heat—this is crucial for perfectly fluffed grains.*

QUINOA SALAD WITH LEMON, HERBS, AND FETA

The biggest mistake I see people make when they're trying to get more healthy grains into their meals without sacrificing flavor is that they forget a simple principle: Grains love to get dressed! They play very nicely with bold vinaigrettes and take on tons of delicious flavor the longer they sit.

The combination of lemon, herbs, and feta in this mix is classic. I love making a good-size portion of cooked quinoa (or millet or brown rice) at the start of the week that I'll then use as the base for easy grain salads like this one. They're perfect to take to work or on the road (or plane!) for a filling, simple meal that's equal parts healthy and delicious.

MAKES 4 SERVINGS

1/3 cup almonds, toasted (see Toasting Nuts on page 14), roughly chopped

1/2 cup quinoa

3 teaspoons kosher salt

1/2 cup fresh or thawed frozen peas, or chopped sugar snap peas, or shelled edamame

2 lemons

Two 15.5-ounce cans chickpeas, drained and rinsed

1/2 cup roughly chopped fresh mint leaves

1/2 cup roughly chopped fresh flat-leaf parsley

1/4 cup chopped fresh dill

3 tablespoons extra-virgin olive oil

Freshly cracked black pepper

1/2 cup crumbled feta cheese

Preheat the oven to 350°F.

Place the almonds on a rimmed baking sheet and toast until fragrant and golden brown, 7 to 9 minutes. Transfer to a plate and set aside to cool.

In a fine-mesh sieve, rinse the quinoa under running water until the water runs clear. In a small saucepan over medium-low heat, toast the quinoa, stirring constantly, until a faintly nutty aroma emerges. Add 1 cup water and 1 teaspoon salt and bring to a boil. Reduce the heat to low, cover, and simmer gently until the quinoa is tender and has absorbed all the water, about 15 minutes. Fluff the quinoa with two forks, place a sheet of paper towel over the pot, cover, and let steam off the heat for at least 5 minutes. The quinoa should be light and fluffy with no remaining wetness. Turn the quinoa out into a large bowl and set aside.

Rinse and fill the saucepan with water and 1 teaspoon salt. Bring it to a boil, add the fresh peas to cook until they are tender, bright green, and no longer starchy, about 2 minutes. Drain and dunk in a large bowl of cold water to stop the cooking.

Zest one of the lemons into the bowl of quinoa. Add the chickpeas, peas, mint, parsley, and dill.

Squeeze the juice of both lemons into the bowl, then add the olive oil, 1 teaspoon salt, and pepper to taste, and toss to combine. Taste and add more salt or pepper if needed. Crumble the almonds and feta on top just before serving.

CAULIFLOWER ALFREDO MAC 'N' CHEESE

This is my spin on the comfort food classic. I use cauliflower puree to bulk up the cheesy béchamel sauce of traditional mac 'n' cheese. With the addition of creamy ricotta and the salty umami bomb of Parmigiano-Reggiano (and a little butter), you'll never notice anything missing—or anything added.

I also like to go for a pasta made with an alternative flour, since the sauce is the main show here and provides a great opportunity to expose picky taste buds to more nutritious noodles. Artichoke flour pasta is my favorite, since it doesn't get overly sticky like rice flour versions and it has better texture than whole wheat varieties. Quinoa pasta options are also good. Whatever your pasta choice, it's mac 'n' cheese you can feel *veggie* good about (oh, I'm hilarious).

MAKES 4 SERVINGS

1 medium head of cauliflower, cut into bite-size florets and stem pieces (about 4 cups)

1 cup whole milk

Kosher salt and freshly cracked black pepper

2 tablespoons unsalted butter

8 ounces elbow macaroni

3 tablespoons extra-virgin olive oil

2 large shallots, minced

1/2 cup vegetable broth (optional), made with Vegetable Broth Concentrate (page 69)

1/2 cup ricotta cheese

3/4 cup finely grated Parmigiano-Reggiano cheese

1/4 teaspoon freshly grated nutmeg

1/2 cup whole wheat panko breadcrumbs

1/4 cup finely chopped fresh flat-leaf parsley

1/2 teaspoon dried basil

In a medium saucepan, combine the cauliflower, milk, 1 teaspoon salt, and pepper to taste. Bring the milk to a simmer over medium heat, reduce the heat to medium-low, partially cover, and gently cook, stirring occasionally, until the cauliflower is tender, 10 to 12 minutes.

Carefully transfer the cauliflower and milk to a blender (working in batches if needed—it will be very hot and you don't want to overfill the blender). Add the butter and pulse a few times to release the steam, then puree until smooth.

Bring a large pot of salted water to a boil. Add the macaroni and cook it 3 minutes less than the package instructs. Reserving 1/2 cup of cooking water, drain the pasta.

While the pasta cooks, in a large, deep skillet, heat 1 tablespoon of the olive oil over medium heat. Add the shallots and 1/2 teaspoon salt and cook, stirring often, until the shallots are tender, 2 to 3 minutes. Add the cauliflower puree and the veggie broth. Stir to combine.

Stir the ricotta, 1/2 cup of the Parmigiano, and the nutmeg into the sauce, then add the macaroni and stir to combine. If the pasta seems dry, add some of the pasta water or more vegetable broth.

Preheat the broiler. Then, in a small bowl, mix together the panko, parsley, basil, 1/4 teaspoon salt, and the remaining 1/4 cup Parmigiano and 2 tablespoons olive oil. Rub between your fingers to combine.

Pour the pasta mixture into a greased 9 x 13-inch baking dish. Sprinkle the seasoned panko over the top and broil just 1 or 2 minutes, until the topping is a deep golden brown.

VARIATION: *You can add pureed sweet potato or squash to the cauliflower blend for a slightly sweeter combo. Just add a little extra pasta water or veggie or chicken broth to loosen the mix if it seems too thick.*

MILLET "BURRITO BOWL"

When I was pregnant with my son, John Jr., all I wanted in life was Mexican food. *Every. Single. Day.* It may be true what they say about boy-driven cravings—it's all about the frat food.

This was a dish I came up with to satisfy some of those cravings in a mindful way, rather than constantly caving to my ultimate weakness: chips and salsa (which I would happily have eaten for breakfast, lunch, and dinner). The millet is hearty and filling, and the beans provide a good amount of protein and fiber, which helped keep me full . . . especially useful because I always seemed to be hungry. I love to throw the peppery arugula and radishes in this mix because they lighten it up a bit and give good crunch. The dressing is bright and tangy, with lots of lime and toasted cumin. If you go for the extras, a ladle of salsa and little dollop of sour cream at the end makes it all very messy, but very, very delicious. (If you're pregnant or nursing, be sure to use a pasteurized variety when you choose your cheese!)

MAKES 8 SERVINGS

Kosher salt

1½ cups millet

4 tablespoons extra-virgin olive oil

2 teaspoons whole cumin seeds

¼ cup fresh lime juice (3 to 4 limes), plus 1 lime cut into wedges for serving

¾ teaspoon ground coriander

Freshly cracked black pepper

One 15-ounce can pinto or black beans, drained and rinsed

4 radishes, halved and thinly sliced

4 scallions, finely chopped

4 cups baby arugula or torn arugula

¾ cup crumbled Cotija, feta, or goat cheese

¼ cup roasted and salted pumpkin seeds (pepitas)

Salsa and sour cream for serving (optional)

Bring a large pot of salted water to a boil over high heat. Add the millet and cook until the millet is tender, about 20 minutes. Drain and rinse under cool water, shaking out as much water as possible. Transfer the millet to a large bowl and toss with 1 tablespoon of the olive oil.

Add the cumin seeds to a small skillet set over medium heat. Toast until it smells fragrant, about 2 minutes. Transfer to a spice grinder or mortar and pestle to gently crush, or tip out onto a cutting board and use a heavy-bottomed pot to do the same.

In a small bowl, combine the cumin, lime juice, coriander, 1 teaspoon salt, and pepper to taste. Whisk in the remaining 3 tablespoons olive oil.

Add the pinto beans, radishes, scallions, and arugula to the bowl with the millet. Drizzle in the dressing and toss with a fork to combine. Sprinkle with the cheese and pumpkin seeds and serve with a lime wedge, plus salsa and sour cream on the side, if desired.

TIP: *Add even more protein by stirring in shredded cooked chicken or salmon, or a dose of healthy fat with chopped avocado.*

SPICY SHRIMP PASTA WITH FAT BOY BREADCRUMBS

This shrimp pasta goes down *almost* too easily. Peeled shrimp cook extremely quickly, which is convenient if you're ready to eat now and still haven't figured out what to make. The rest of the sauce is chunky, rustic tomato, garlic, onion, and fresh basil—an amazing basic sauce with or without the shrimp if you want to dip your toe into homemade heaven. Sometimes it's the simplest preparations that are the most satisfying.

Mario Batali introduced me to the idea of breadcrumbs on pasta. At first I thought he was crazy. But, as with so many Mario-related things, his crazy turned out to be genius. I've included my version of his famous Fat Boy breadcrumbs—pebble-size pieces of golden brown crispness that add tons of texture you never knew your pasta was missing.

MAKES 4 SERVINGS

3/4 pound medium shrimp, peeled and deveined

Kosher salt

2 slices (1/4 to 1/2 inch thick) Italian country-style bread, cut into 1/2-inch cubes

4 tablespoons extra-virgin olive oil

1 pound spaghettini

5 garlic cloves, finely minced

3/4 teaspoon crushed chile flakes

1/2 teaspoon dried oregano

1/2 sweet onion, minced

1/4 cup white wine or chicken broth

1 pint cherry tomatoes, halved

1/2 cup chiffonade-cut basil leaves

Thirty minutes before you are ready to cook, place the shrimp in a bowl and season with 1/2 teaspoon salt. Set aside on the counter to come to room temperature.

Preheat the oven to 300°F.

Spread the bread cubes on a rimmed baking sheet and toast for 10 minutes, or until golden brown, shaking the pan intermittently to redistribute. Use a heavy-bottomed pan to crush them into crumbly pieces.

Transfer the breadcrumbs to a large skillet, drizzle them with 1 tablespoon of the olive oil and 1/2 teaspoon salt, and toss to combine. Heat the skillet over medium heat and toast the breadcrumbs until golden brown and crisp, shaking the pan often, about 6 minutes. Turn the breadcrumbs out onto a large plate.

Bring a large pot of salted water to a boil. Add the spaghettini and cook it 1 minute less than the package instructs. Reserving 1/2 cup of the pasta water, drain the pasta.

In a large skillet, combine 2 tablespoons of the oil, the garlic, chile flakes, and oregano. Cook over medium heat until the garlic is fragrant, about 1 minute, taking care not to let it sit still and burn. Add the shrimp and cook until they start to turn bright pink, shaking the pan often, 1 to 2 minutes. Transfer the shrimp to a large plate (it's okay if they're not cooked all the way through—they will finish cooking with the pasta; you just want a good sear on both sides. Don't place them in a bowl or they could steam and overcook).

Increase the heat to medium-high and add the remaining 1 tablespoon oil, the onion, and 1/2 teaspoon salt. Cook until translucent, 2 to 3 minutes. Add the wine to deglaze the pan, using a wooden spoon to loosen any browned bits that are sticking to the bottom.

When the wine is reduced by half, about 2 minutes, add the tomatoes. When the tomatoes start to burst, about 5 minutes, reduce the heat to medium and return the shrimp to the pan to finish cooking, about 1 minute longer.

Remove the pan from the heat and add the pasta and a few tablespoons of pasta water to emulsify and thicken the sauce. Shake the pasta in the pan, stirring constantly with a wooden spoon, until the sauce is velvety and the pasta is al dente, 1 minute more. Add the basil and toss to combine.

Divide among bowls and serve topped with the breadcrumbs.

THAI VEGETABLE CURRY WITH COCONUT RICE

Don't be scared! I know this recipe calls for a few (ahem, a lot) more ingredients than most in this book, but the result—especially if you don't live near a good Thai restaurant—is well worth the effort. And most of the skill is just in procuring all the ingredients—the actual cooking is very hands-off as you let the broth gurgle and simmer its way to an edible Thai escape.

Thai curries are much less about the spice associated with Indian curries, and more about the incredible blending of rich, creamy coconut milk with fresh, light, aromatic herbs such as lemongrass, mint, ginger, Thai basil, garlic, and chiles . . . and, often, a pinch of something sweet, such as palm or date sugar (I've also tried condensed milk to great delight). You can buy curry paste in the ethnic foods aisle of most grocery stores—or order online—and it's a great addition, because it will bring in the marinating flavors of Thai chiles, spices, and Kaffir lime leaves that can sometimes be hard to find.

Though I love to get sticky rice when I go out to eat this sort of food, I've found it basically impossible to make when I'm cooking at home, so I turn to this easy coconut brown rice alternative. Regular brown rice works absolutely fine, too—and is probably the better choice if you're looking for a lighter meal. But if you're throwing a party, make the coconut rice. . . .

MAKES 4 SERVINGS

COCONUT RICE

1 cup long-grain brown rice (such as jasmine)

1 cup light coconut milk

1/2 teaspoon kosher salt

Optional additions: a split vanilla bean, a strip or two of citrus zest, a few cardamom pods

VEGETABLE CURRY

2 tablespoons grapeseed or olive oil

1 medium red onion, cut into 1-inch pieces

2 lemongrass stalks, tougher outer layer removed, tender inner reed minced

2 tablespoons finely chopped peeled fresh ginger

3 garlic cloves, minced

(Ingredients continue on the next page.)

To make the coconut rice, preheat the oven to 350°F.

Place the rice in a fine-mesh sieve set over a large bowl and cover with cold water. Swish the rice around until the water becomes cloudy, then lift the sieve out of the bowl and discard the water. Repeat 2 or 3 times, until the water doesn't become cloudy when the rice is swished.

Transfer the rice to a 1 1/2- to 2-quart baking dish. Pour the coconut milk, 1 cup water, and the salt over the rice and stir to distribute. Include the optional additions now, if desired. Give the rice a stir, then cover with foil and bake for 50 minutes, or until all the liquid is absorbed. Remove the foil and discard, then use a fork to fluff the rice. Cover with a kitchen towel and let sit at least 5 minutes to finish steaming. (Leave the oven on for the peanuts and coconut; see step 6.)

To make the curry, heat the oil in a large pot over medium-high heat. Add the onion and cook, stirring often, until it softens, about 3 minutes. Stir in the lemongrass, ginger, and garlic and cook, stirring often, until it is fragrant, 1 to 2 minutes. Stir in the curry paste and toast with the aromatics, 1 to 2 minutes.

2 tablespoons store-bought red (or green) Thai curry paste

2 cups quartered cremini (baby bella) mushrooms

2 cups bite-size broccoli florets

2 cups shredded napa cabbage or red cabbage

Kosher salt

1 cup vegetable broth, homemade (from Vegetable Broth Concentrate, page 69) or store-bought, or water

1/2 cup light coconut milk

1/2 tablespoon sugar (optional)

Freshly cracked black pepper

1 cup sugar snap peas or snow peas, thinly sliced

GARNISHES (ALL OPTIONAL, ALL DELICIOUS)

1/4 cup roasted peanuts

3 tablespoons unsweetened dried coconut

Kosher salt

1 cup fresh Thai basil leaves

1/4 cup fresh mint leaves

1 jalapeño, thinly sliced

1 lime, cut into wedges

1/2 pound bean sprouts

Stir in the mushrooms, broccoli, cabbage, and 1 teaspoon salt and cook, stirring often, until the mushrooms release their liquid, 5 to 6 minutes. Stir in the broth or water, coconut milk, and sugar (if using). Bring the liquid to a simmer and cook until the broccoli is tender, 6 to 8 minutes. Remove from the heat, add salt and pepper to taste, stir in the snap peas, and cover.

Meanwhile, if you're going for the garnishes, arrange the peanuts and coconut on a rimmed baking sheet and toast in the oven for 4 minutes, or until the peanuts are shiny and the coconut is golden brown, shaking the pan to redistribute the mixture once or twice. Remove from oven and sprinkle with 1/4 teaspoon salt—yes, the coconut too!

Keep the rice and curry separate until you are ready to eat. I like to serve this dish family style: Ladle the curry into one bowl and the rice into another. Place these on the table, along with a platter of Thai basil, mint leaves, thinly sliced jalapeño, and lime wedges. Let people make their own bowls, topped with a mound of raw bean sprouts and a sprinkle of the peanuts and toasted coconut blend for a lovely crunch.

TIP: *A rice cooker is one gadget I think everyone should have in her home. It will save you so much time and countless batches of soggy or accidentally burned rice. If you have one, skip the rice baking in the oven and just throw the rice, coconut milk, water, salt, and flavorings into your rice cooker! Don't skip the rinsing or steaming steps, though.*

VARIATION: *Swap in any kind of vegetables you like. Kale and Swiss chard work beautifully instead of cabbage; instead of mushrooms try eggplant; instead of broccoli use cauliflower. This curry is a great use for any odds and ends in the fridge.*

seafood

There are two things that make seafood wonderful in my mind: First, though seafood is generally light, it's also supremely and uniquely flavorful, meaning you really don't have to do much to it. And second, for the most part, the less you cook it, the better it tastes, meaning your meal is on the plate fast.

Fresh seafood should taste like the sea. If you associate it with the stuff your cat eats, you've likely been cooking it too long—it may seem counterintuitive, but the longer you cook fish, the fishier it tastes—or buying old product.

When it comes to picking fresh fish, rely on your nose: There should not be any strong, fishy smell. If you can see eyes, they should be clear, not milky. On crustaceans, you want shiny, hard shells that are intact, not chipped or cracked. And whenever possible, buying them live will ensure you the best, freshest flavor!

Once you have your hands on the quality stuff, I can't wait for you to try the Smoky Salmon and Avocado Wedge Salad (think healthy BLT) and the Mussels Provençal with Toasts. And if you're looking for a gateway seafood recipe, my Crab Cakes with Snow Pea Slaw (try adding a poached egg on top of the crab cakes for a killer brunch!) and Pan-Fried Calamari with Charred Jalapeño Chimichurri are easy eating.

CRAB CAKES WITH SNOW PEA SLAW

The perfect crab cake should barely hold together because it's almost entirely made of crab, with just the tiniest bit of creamy mayonnaise and a small handful of breadcrumbs to bind it and add a layer of flavor and texture that doesn't fight the crustacean. I love it served with a crispy snow pea and apple slaw and a rémoulade filled with fresh herbs and a pop of mustard.

MAKES 4 SERVINGS

RÉMOULADE

1/2 cup mayonnaise

1 small garlic clove, finely grated

1 1/2 tablespoons capers, roughly chopped

1 1/2 tablespoons whole-grain mustard

1 tablespoon ketchup

1 tablespoon finely chopped fresh chives

1 tablespoon finely chopped fresh flat-leaf parsley

1 1/2 teaspoons hot sauce (I love Frank's RedHot or Cholula)

1 1/2 teaspoons fresh lime juice

1/2 teaspoon kosher salt

Freshly cracked black pepper

CRAB CAKES

1/4 cup mayonnaise

1 large egg

1 tablespoon fresh lime juice

1 teaspoon Old Bay seasoning

1/2 teaspoon kosher salt

1/2 cup panko breadcrumbs

8 ounces jumbo lump crabmeat

1 tablespoon extra-virgin olive oil

Snow Pea Slaw (page 99)

To make the rémoulade, in a medium bowl, whisk together the mayonnaise, garlic, capers, mustard, ketchup, chives, parsley, hot sauce, lime juice, salt, and pepper to taste. Cover with plastic wrap and refrigerate until serving.

To make the crab cakes, in a medium bowl, whisk together the mayonnaise, egg, lime juice, Old Bay, and salt. Add the panko and crabmeat and toss with a fork to combine. Shape the mixture into 4 patties.

In a large nonstick skillet, heat the oil over medium heat. Fry the crab cakes on both sides until golden brown, 3 to 4 minutes on each side. Transfer each to a plate. Serve with snow pea slaw and rémoulade.

SEA BASS ROASTED OVER CITRUS

This is such a gorgeous and simple fish preparation, perfect for entertaining or treating yourself to a party of one. The citrus perfumes the fish from above and below, tenderizing and flavoring all the while. Pulling it out of the oven is a treat for the eyes as well as the mouth, with wheels of glowing orange, pink, and yellow surrounding the succulent white fish and garnished with a few sprigs of fresh herbs. These days, with less time to hover around a stove, I'm an especially big fan of fancy-looking dishes that are made entirely in the oven. With minimal preparation, this dish goes in easy and 20 minutes later comes out ready to present to the hungry horde . . . so you can do whatever domestic goddesses choose to with all that extra free time.

MAKES 4 SERVINGS

4 tablespoons plus 2 teaspoons extra-virgin olive oil

2 fresh oregano sprigs

3 garlic cloves—1 smashed and 2 thinly sliced

1 ruby red grapefruit, sliced into thin rounds

2 oranges, 1 halved and 1 sliced into thin rounds

2 limes—1 sliced into thin rounds, 1 zested and juiced

10 fresh thyme sprigs

1⅓ pounds sea bass fillet (wild striped bass is also great)

1½ teaspoons kosher salt

Freshly cracked black pepper (optional)

Flaky sea salt to garnish (optional)

Preheat the oven to 475°F.

In a small bowl, combine 2 tablespoons of the olive oil, the oregano, and smashed garlic and set aside to steep.

Grease a 9 x 13-inch baking dish with 2 teaspoons of the oil. Shingle the grapefruit, orange, and lime slices on the dish bottom. Scatter half the thyme sprigs over the fruit.

Set the fish fillet skin side down in the baking dish, squeeze both orange halves on top to release the juice, then drizzle the fish and citrus with the remaining 2 tablespoons oil. Rub generously with the sliced garlic (leave it on the fish to cook), and sprinkle everything with the salt and, if desired, pepper to taste. Scatter the remaining thyme sprigs over top.

Roast for 18 to 20 minutes, until the fish is firm around the edges, the sides of the fish are opaque, and the thickest part of the fish gives slightly when pressed.

Serve straight from the baking dish or transfer to a platter. Finish with the lime juice and zest, flaky sea salt if you have it, and spoon some of the oregano-scented oil on top.

OVEN

MUSSELS PROVENÇAL WITH TOASTS

Each summer my family loves to visit a restaurant up in Maine called Street & Co., where they serve the most insane mussels—sweet, tender, saline—bathed in a rich broth of butter and white wine and an impossible amount of minced garlic. The mussels steam and drink up the essence of this bath, flavoring every plump morsel. After you devour the mound of mussels, hunks of fresh sourdough bread are on standby to sop up any remaining broth. Are you drooling yet? You should be.

This is the version I make at home when Maine is out of reach. I've added a ton of fresh herbs to my broth, which allows me to cut down on the butter just a smidge without skimping on flavor. The trick to great mussels is to cook them quickly, and to pour plenty of tasty wine into the steam bath for them to drink up—remember, you want them to steam, not boil, so make sure there's enough liquid to coat the bottom of the pan, but none of the mussels should be entirely submerged. A wide, heavy-bottomed pan works best, ideally with a lid, though covering with foil and a baking sheet will work.

The other trick (and this is more of a personal preference thing) is to channel your inner mermaid when you eat them: Use the empty shell of one mussel like pincers to pluck each tender mussel from its own shell and pop it into your mouth. Or you can take all the mussels out of their shells and toss them in the broth to be eaten with a spoon or scooped up with bread for an equally delicious enterprise. A splash of cream into the broth at this point has also been known to happen, but leave out the lemons if you go this route.

MAKES 4 SERVINGS

4 pounds mussels

6 tablespoons (3/4 stick) unsalted butter

3 shallots, minced

1/2 teaspoon kosher salt

8 garlic cloves, minced, plus 1 whole clove for rubbing the toasts

2 teaspoons finely chopped fresh thyme leaves or flat-leaf parsley

1 bay leaf

1 cup dry white wine

1/2 to 1 cup low-sodium chicken, fish/shrimp, or vegetable broth

(Ingredients continue on the next page.)

Discard any mussels that have severely cracked or crushed shells. Give any that are slightly open a few taps on the countertop—if they close on their own, it means they're still healthy, alive, and good to eat! If they stay open, toss them.

Place the mussels in a colander and set it under cold running water to rinse them clean. Pull out any hairy beards (these will make your broth grainy and cloudy) and scrub the shells with a sponge or clean nail brush to loosen any grit, then rinse again. Place mussels in a large bowl of clean water and set aside.

In a large Dutch oven, melt 4 tablespoons of the butter over medium heat. Add the shallots and the kosher salt and sauté until softened, about 4 minutes. Add the minced garlic, thyme, and bay leaf and cook, stirring often, until the garlic is fragrant, 1 to 2 minutes. Add the wine, increase the heat to medium-high, and simmer until the liquid is reduced by half, about 2 minutes. Add the broth and bring to a simmer. You want the mussels to steam, not boil, so if the liquid

- 1 baguette, halved horizontally and quartered crosswise
- 2 tablespoons extra-virgin olive oil
- Flaky sea salt
- 2 lemons, halved
- 12 fresh basil leaves, roughly torn
- 2 teaspoons finely chopped fresh chives
- 2 tablespoons finely chopped fresh flat-leaf parsley

comes up more than 1 inch in the pan, just use a little less broth. The wine is what's most important for a good steam.

Just before you drop the mussels in to steam, toast the bread: Preheat the broiler to high. Place the baguette pieces on a rimmed baking sheet. Drizzle with the olive oil and sprinkle with flaky salt. Set the lemons cut side up on the pan with the baguettes. Broil the bread and lemons until they are both browned, 2 to 3 minutes for the bread; the lemons might take a minute or two longer (watch the bread and lemons closely, as broiler intensities vary). Set the bread and lemons aside. Rub the bread with the remaining garlic clove.

Add the mussels to the pot, cover, and let them steam until just open, 3 minutes or so. As soon as they open, take them off the heat or they will overcook and get rubbery. Use a slotted spoon to transfer the mussels to a large bowl. Swirl the remaining 2 tablespoons butter into the broth; taste and add kosher salt if needed. Discard the bay leaf and return the mussels to the pot.

Serve family style, or divide the mussels among four bowls. Sprinkle the basil, chives, and parsley into the broth, swirl, and ladle over the mussels. Serve immediately with a pile of baguette toasts and a charred lemon half for each person to squeeze over the mussels before eating.

TIP: *This preparation works great with clams, too!*

POACHED SALMON WITH DILL TZATZIKI

Every home cook should know how to poach salmon. I love it for an easy lunch or dinner, or beautifully presented for brunch. It's a very basic technique that yields perfectly seasoned and cooked salmon (or chicken) every single time. What you choose to top it with can vary widely—from punchy rémoulade to elegantly simple crème fraîche. I like mine with tangy-tart yogurt mixed with a generous handful of fresh dill, cucumber, and garlic for an easy, filling lunch or light dinner.

MAKES 4 SERVINGS

SALMON

- 1 tablespoon coriander seeds
- 1 teaspoon black peppercorns
- 1 bay leaf
- 1 lemon, lime, or orange, thinly sliced
- Four 6- to 8-ounce center-cut salmon fillets, pin bones removed (see Tip)
- 2 teaspoons kosher salt
- Freshly cracked black pepper

TZATZIKI

- 1 small cucumber
- 1 medium garlic clove
- 1/2 cup Greek yogurt
- 2 tablespoons finely chopped fresh dill
- 1 tablespoon fresh lemon or lime juice
- 1/2 teaspoon kosher salt

To make the salmon, in a large, deep skillet, toast the coriander seeds and peppercorns over medium heat, shaking the pan often, until the coriander is fragrant, 1 to 2 minutes. Add enough water to fill the pan to 3 inches and add the bay leaf and citrus slices. Bring the liquid to a boil over medium-high heat, reduce the heat to medium, and simmer 10 minutes.

Season the salmon with the salt and pepper to taste and set it in the simmering water. Reduce the heat to medium-low and very gently simmer the salmon until the edges are firm, 5 to 6 minutes for a 1 1/4-inch-thick fillet (thinner or thicker fillets will need about 1 minute less or 1 minute more time to cook through). Remove from the heat and let the salmon sit in the poaching broth for 5 minutes.

To make the tzatziki, grate the cucumber on the medium holes of a box grater. Place it in a colander or fine-mesh sieve and press out as much liquid as possible, then transfer it to a medium bowl. Use a Microplane-style rasp or garlic press to add the garlic to the cucumber. Add the yogurt, dill, lemon juice, and salt and stir to combine.

Set the salmon on a paper towel to absorb the extra moisture, then place each fillet on a plate. Serve with a dollop of tzatziki.

TIP: *To remove pin bones, run your hand over the salmon to feel for little spiny bumps. Use tweezers to remove the bones.*

TIP: *To cook salmon evenly, you need a piece of fish that's evenly thick across. An easy way to achieve this is to ask your fishmonger for center-cut fillets.*

SMOKY SALMON AND AVOCADO WEDGE SALAD

There are few things that handle hunger or cure a hangover quite like a BLT sandwich with avocado. I didn't grow up eating a ton of meat, so my exposure to this gem of a sandwich happened in college (I know, pity me). Of course, I made up for lost time.

I started making this salad as a way to get a similar (but let's be real, it's salmon—not bacon) fix in a healthier way. The salmon gets coated with smoked paprika and plenty of salt, then drizzled with maple syrup to create a delicious smoky-sweet crust. I pair it with the traditional BLT components plus avocado and my homemade herbed buttermilk dressing to create salad magic.

MAKES 4 SERVINGS

DRESSING

1/2 cup buttermilk

3 tablespoons crème fraîche or Greek yogurt

1 tablespoon distilled white vinegar or fresh lime or lemon juice

2 tablespoons finely chopped fresh tarragon

1 tablespoon finely chopped fresh chives

1 tablespoon finely chopped fresh parsley

1/2 teaspoon kosher salt

Freshly cracked black pepper

SALAD

1 teaspoon extra-virgin olive oil

2 teaspoons smoked paprika

1/2 teaspoon kosher salt

Two 6- to 8-ounce skin-on salmon fillets (preferably center cut), pin bones removed (see Tip, page 215)

1 tablespoon maple syrup

1 small head of iceberg lettuce, cored and quartered

1 avocado, pitted, peeled, and sliced

12 cherry tomatoes, halved

1 lime, cut into wedges for serving

To make the dressing, in a small bowl, whisk together the buttermilk, crème fraîche, white vinegar, tarragon, chives, parsley, salt, and pepper to taste. Cover with plastic wrap and refrigerate until serving.

To make the salad, adjust the oven rack to the upper-middle position and preheat the broiler to high. Line a rimmed baking sheet with foil.

In a small bowl, mix together the olive oil, paprika, and salt. Coat the top and sides of the salmon with the paprika mixture and set the salmon fillets on the baking sheet.

Broil the salmon for 5 to 6 minutes, until the center is firm when pressed lightly. Brush or drizzle the maple syrup over each fillet and broil for 3 to 4 minutes longer, until the salmon flakes easily and is just turning opaque in the center.

Transfer the salmon to a plate to cool, then use a fork to pull the salmon into large flaky shards.

Set an iceberg wedge on each plate. Add a few avocado slices and tomatoes, then a mound of the flaked salmon. Spoon the dressing over the top and serve with a lime wedge.

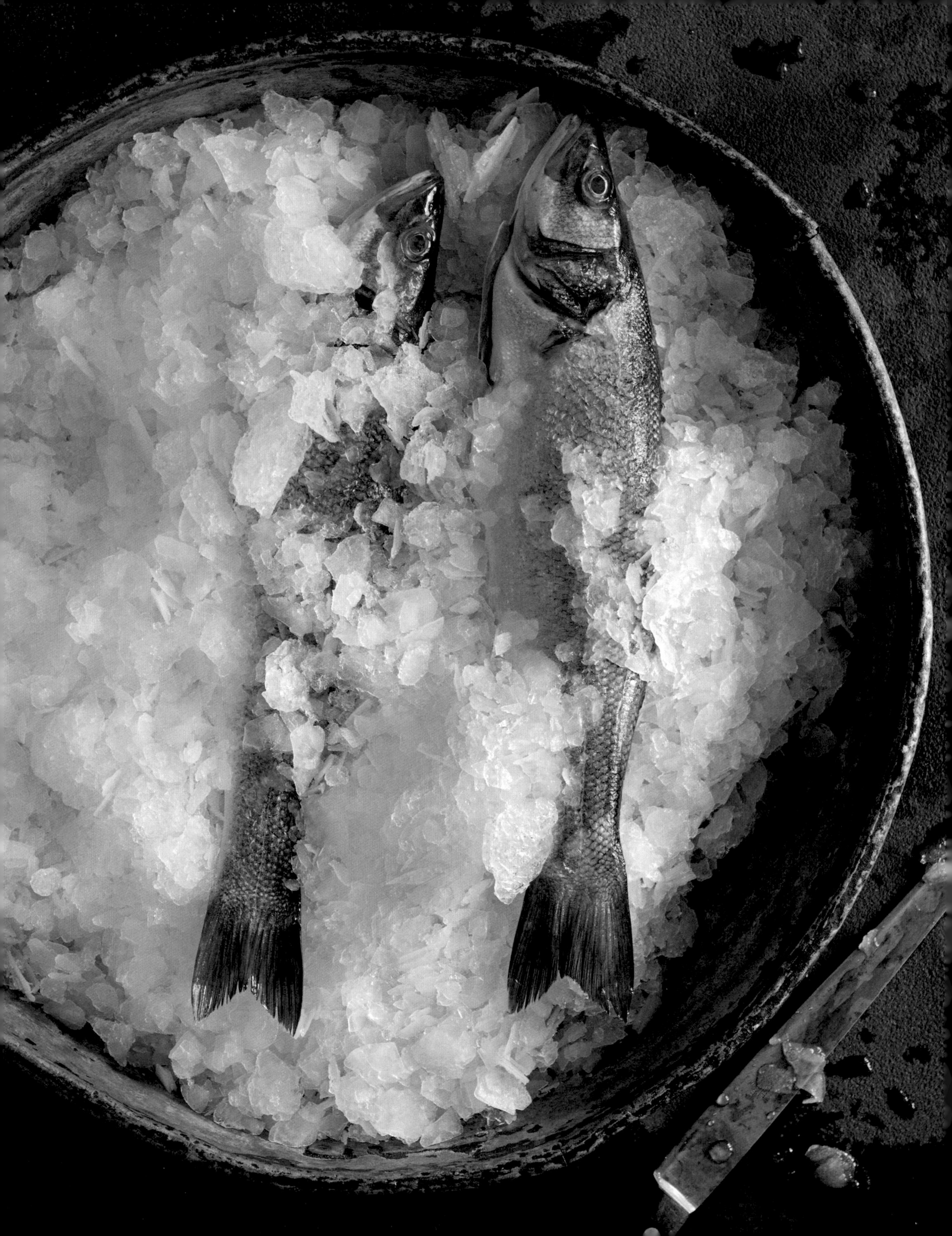

WHOLE ROASTED BRANZINO

This is one of those rare recipes that you'll know by heart the first time you make it. Even better, it's finished in 20 minutes and is always a hit at our family table. The only hard part is getting good-quality fish—it's a good bet that line-caught will be the most flavorful if you can find it. The rest is just a matter of stuffing it full of fresh herbs, garlic, and lemon (to keep it supermoist!), and roasting. The branzino will be light, tender, and flaky, and scented through with all our little additions. If your dinner guests aren't squeamish (and I hope they're not—this is what fish looks like! And you cooked it from scratch!), go ahead and serve with the head and tail still on.

MAKES 4 SERVINGS

4 tablespoons extra-virgin olive oil
4 fresh oregano sprigs
5 medium garlic cloves, smashed
2 whole branzino (about 1 pound each) or sea bass, head and tail on, cleaned
1 teaspoon sea salt
8 fresh thyme sprigs
4 fresh mint sprigs
1 bunch fresh chives or 4 scallions, cleaned and halved
2 lemons—1 thinly sliced, 1 cut into wedges for serving
Freshly cracked black pepper

In a small bowl, combine 2 tablespoons of the olive oil, half the oregano, and 1 clove of the smashed garlic. Let sit until the fish is ready.

Preheat the oven to 375°F. Line a rimmed baking sheet with parchment paper.

Pat the outside of the fish dry with paper towels and place the fish on the parchment, then drizzle each with 1 tablespoon of the oil. Sprinkle the insides and both sides of the fish with the salt.

Open the fish like a book and generously rub the inside with garlic. Divide the garlic, thyme, mint, the remaining oregano, the chives, and lemon slices between the fish, then close the fish and crack pepper over the top. Roast it 15 to 20 minutes, until the flesh is opaque and flakes delicately with a fork.

Either serve the fish whole on a platter with the oregano oil and lemon wedges on the side or remove and discard the herbs, garlic, and lemon slices from the fish, fillet it, divide the fish among 4 plates, and serve each drizzled with a spoonful of the oregano oil and a lemon wedge.

PAN-FRIED CALAMARI WITH CHARRED JALAPEÑO CHIMICHURRI

Before we had kids, John and I took a trip to Capri where we spent most of our days bobbing in the salty, cobalt waves or stretching out under the welcome shade of an umbrella on the craggy beach to people-watch chic Italians. We would peel ourselves away from this routine at lunch, when we feasted on cold rosé and terrifyingly hot plates of fritto misto: a mix of fresh squid, shrimp with the shell on, lemon wheels, and a few rosemary sprigs, all dusted with flour and salt, then dropped into hot oil until deeply golden brown. There is something particularly satisfying about eating salty, crunchy seafood when your own skin is crusted with sea salt and you can still hear lapping water all around. Maybe it's my Little Mermaid complex kicking in again. . . .

At home, I am obviously missing a few of the items that make this memory so charming: seaside environs, chic Italians, leisure time . . . but Hubby and rosé are here to stay! And simply fried calamari is fairly transporting when battered using my mother's technique with cornmeal—the mild sweetness goes great with delicate seafood—and served with a charred jalapeño chimichurri (or a generous sprinkle of salt and squeeze of lemon, if you prefer the more traditional rendition).

The trick is to make sure not to overcrowd the pan. If you do, not only will there be hot oil spitting at you, but the squid will steam and become rubbery rather than light and crispy. And make sure your family or guests are nearby when you start making these, because they should be enjoyed fresh from the pan, as hot as you can handle—it's a very festive way to start the meal.

MAKES 4 SERVINGS

CHARRED JALAPEÑO CHIMICHURRI

1 medium jalapeño pepper, left whole

3 medium garlic cloves, unpeeled

1 cup loosely packed fresh parsley leaves

1/4 cup loosely packed fresh mint leaves

1 scallion, roughly chopped

Zest and juice of 1/2 lemon

1 tablespoon white wine vinegar

1/3 cup extra-virgin olive oil

1/2 teaspoon kosher salt

(Ingredients continue on the next page.)

To make the chimichurri, adjust the oven rack to the uppermost position and preheat the broiler to high. Place the jalapeño and garlic cloves on a rimmed baking sheet and turn intermittently to char on all sides, 6 to 10 minutes total, depending on how hot your oven gets. You want the pepper skin to blister and char, but be careful not to let the inside of the pepper burn or the taste will be off. When cool enough to handle, peel the garlic and transfer to a food processor or blender. Remove and discard the stem from the jalapeño before adding it to the food processor (seed the jalapeño for less heat).

Add the parsley, mint, scallion, lemon zest, lemon juice, vinegar, olive oil, and salt to the food processor. Process until well combined, about six 1-second pulses. Scrape the chimichurri into a small bowl and set aside.

To make the calamari, in a medium bowl, stir together the flour, cornmeal, sugar, salt, and pepper to taste. Add the squid and toss to combine.

CALAMARI

- 3/4 cup cake or pastry flour (all-purpose flour or 00 flour works great, too)
- 3 tablespoons cornmeal (or corn flour—masa harina—for a less crunchy, more even coating)
- 1 teaspoon sugar
- 1 teaspoon kosher salt
- Freshly cracked black pepper
- 1 pound squid, cleaned, bodies cut into 1/4- to 1/3-inch rings, and tentacles left whole, patted dry
- 6 tablespoons extra-virgin olive oil
- Flaky sea salt

- Lemon for serving

In a large skillet, heat 3 tablespoons of the olive oil over medium-high heat. When the oil shimmers, grab a small handful of the squid and shake off the excess flour through your fingers. Drop the squid into the pan, reduce the heat to medium, and cook until browned, 1 1/2 to 2 minutes. Use a spatula to flip the squid and brown it on the other side, 1 to 1 1/2 minutes, then transfer it to a paper-towel-lined plate. Repeat with the remaining squid. Discard the oil if it darkens and replace with the remaining 3 tablespoons oil; let it heat to a shimmer before adding more squid.

Sprinkle the calamari with flaky salt, and serve with lemon and/or the chimichurri.

TROUT WITH ORANGE AND HERBS

I love the combination of orange and fresh herbs in this (almost) effortless dish. Fish is one of the fastest proteins to make for a light but filling dinner, and the trout is mild, flaky, and the perfect vehicle to soak up all that delicious citrus butter. The fried shallots on top add a nice pop of flavor and crunch.

MAKES 4 SERVINGS

- **3 tablespoons extra-virgin olive oil**
- **3 large shallots, halved and thinly sliced**
- **3 teaspoons kosher salt**
- **4 medium trout, gutted and cleaned**
- **Freshly cracked black pepper**
- **1/2 cup all-purpose flour**
- **1/2 cup fresh orange juice (2 to 3 oranges)**
- **3 tablespoons unsalted butter**
- **1/2 cup roughly chopped fresh herbs: chives, tarragon, basil, parsley, or mint**

In a large nonstick skillet, heat 2 tablespoons of the olive oil over medium-high heat. Add the shallots and 1/2 teaspoon of the salt and cook, stirring occasionally, until they start to brown, 2 to 3 minutes. Reduce the heat to medium and continue to cook until they are deeply browned, 4 to 5 minutes more. Transfer the shallots to a small bowl.

Season the inside and outside of each fish with 1 teaspoon of the salt and pepper to taste. Add the flour to a shallow dish and season it with the remaining 1 1/2 teaspoons salt and more pepper. Dredge the fish through the flour to coat each evenly (just on the outside).

Add the remaining 1 tablespoon olive oil to the pan and set it over medium-high heat. Place 2 trout in the pan and cook until browned, 4 to 6 minutes on each side. Transfer the trout to a platter and repeat with the remaining fish.

Add the orange juice to the pan and bring it to a simmer. Reduce the heat to low and swirl in the butter and most of the herbs. Spoon the sauce over the trout. Top with fried shallots and the rest of the fresh herbs.

TIP: *Trout is very mild and its texture is quite delicate, making it a good "starter" fish if you have picky palates around. Trout tends to be a sustainable option, and it's pretty affordable as well. To be sure you're getting the best fish available, check out the Monterey Bay Aquarium app and website for information on the most sustainable fish in your area.*

meat and poultry

CHUCK SKIRT
UNIT PRICE

KITCHEN SINK CHICKEN SALAD

I am really big on chicken salad. We'll typically roast or get a rotisserie chicken or two on Sunday nights. I pull off any meat that's left and reserve it in a glass bowl until the next day when I'm getting lunch together. I've tried a bajillion combinations—curried chicken salad with plump golden raisins; Asian chicken salad with a little sesame oil, sliced snow peas, and mint; Jamaican chicken salad (by the way, the Jerk Chicken on page 236 works amazingly well for this!) with ginger, green apple, and a little BBQ sauce. I love them all.

This is the version I come back to over and over because the unexpected combo of hot sauce, soy sauce, and maple syrup always hits the spot; and the cashews, apple, and celery bulk up even a small amount of chicken into a filling meal. People always hover when I make a big bowl, so that's a good sign I'm not crazy.

MAKES 4 SERVINGS

- 1/3 cup mayonnaise
- 1 tablespoon Dijon mustard
- 1 teaspoon apple cider vinegar
- 1 teaspoon hot sauce (I love Frank's RedHot or Cholula)
- 2 teaspoons soy sauce
- 1 teaspoon maple syrup
- 1/4 teaspoon kosher salt
- Freshly cracked black pepper
- 2 cups bite-size pieces cooked chicken
- 2 scallions, finely chopped
- 2 celery stalks, diced, plus 1/4 cup roughly chopped celery leaves
- 1/2 Granny Smith, Gala, or Pink Lady apple, halved, cored, and diced
- 1/2 cup salted roasted cashews or peanuts, optional
- 1 tablespoon of any fresh herbs you have around, chopped—I often throw in a little basil and parsley, but chives work great, and peppermint is an interesting take
- 8 Bibb lettuce leaves, crackers, or the bread of your choice for serving

In a large bowl, whisk together the mayonnaise, mustard, vinegar, hot sauce, soy sauce, maple syrup, salt, and pepper to taste.

Add the chicken, scallions, celery and celery leaves, apple, roasted cashews, and herbs to the dressing and stir to combine. Taste and season with additional salt and pepper as desired.

Serve in the lettuce leaves, on crackers, or on a sandwich.

GRILLED CHICKEN PAILLARDS WITH MELON SALSA FRESCA

I first had a version of the "salsa" that makes this dish so unbelievably delicious on a family trip to the islands. Every day for lunch we would get a beautiful piece of fresh-caught fish, drizzled with olive oil and grilled to tender perfection. But the accompanying bowl of finely chopped local fruits, flecked with chiles, ginger, scallions, fresh herbs, and lime juice, made everything else pale in comparison. We heaped the salsa on top, drinking up any leftovers like soup.

When we got back home, I started making my version of the mix and found that it was equally delicious over shrimp or chicken. It's a lot of chopping, but I promise it's well worth the effort and is bound to be your new favorite accoutrement. I went for chicken breasts because they're a little bit lighter, so the salsa really shines, and also because they cook so quickly, but you could totally sub in boneless skinless chicken thighs if you prefer.

MAKES 4 SERVINGS

- Four 6-ounce boneless, skinless chicken breasts
- 4 tablespoons extra-virgin olive oil
- 1½ teaspoons kosher salt
- 2 cups cubed (½ inch) cantaloupe or watermelon
- 4 scallions, thinly sliced
- ½ cup diced mango
- 1 inch fresh ginger, peeled and minced
- ¼ habanero (hottest), jalapeño (medium), or Fresno (mild) chile, minced (optional)
- ¼ cup finely chopped fresh parsley or cilantro, including stems
- Juice of 2 limes or 1 lemon
- 1 avocado, pitted, peeled, and diced
- 2 tablespoons vegetable oil (optional; needed only if grilling)

Place a chicken breast between 2 sheets of plastic wrap and use a meat pounder or heavy skillet to flatten it into a ½-inch-thick paillard. Place the pounded chicken on a large plate or platter and repeat with the remaining chicken breasts. Drizzle the chicken with 1 tablespoon of the olive oil, turning to coat the breasts on both sides, then sprinkle the chicken on all sides with 1 teaspoon of the salt.

In a medium bowl, combine the melon, scallions, mango, ginger, chile (if using), parsley, citrus juice, and remaining 3 tablespoons olive oil and ½ teaspoon salt. Gently stir in the avocado.

Prepare a gas or charcoal grill to high heat. Dip a folded paper towel into the vegetable oil and use tongs to grease the grill grates. Place the chicken on the grill and cook until it has grill marks, 2 to 3 minutes. Turn the chicken over and grill the other side until the chicken is cooked through, about 2 minutes longer. Transfer to a platter. (If cooking indoors, just replicate this process in a skillet. The chicken will be deeply golden brown on both sides and no longer pink or translucent in the center.)

Serve the salsa over the chicken.

TIP: *Any kind of seasonal fruit works in the salsa—you can use pineapple, peaches, plums, or nectarines in place of the mango or melon if you like.*

CIDER-BRAISED BRISKET WITH RED CABBAGE AND APPLES

Passive cooking is my dream. Inevitably, the meals that result when you cook something low (heat) and slow (timing) are intensely flavorful, even though you really only had to add a bunch of things to a pot and then let the ingredients work their own magic (with a few stirs now and then).

This is one of my favorite dishes to make when my family goes apple picking in late September. It's hearty and filling, and the smell of it cooking for a few hours in the oven makes my mouth water even as I write this. Season the brisket the night before so you have plenty of time to let it sit and flavor overnight in the fridge. This is a great dish to start on Friday when you get home from work and plan on cooking throughout the afternoon Saturday for an amazing dinner. Oh, and any leftovers will go very nicely on a crispy baguette dunked in some of the remaining juices for an autumnal take on the classic French dip—the perfect Sunday lunch. There, you have your whole weekend covered.

MAKES 6 SERVINGS

8 garlic cloves, minced

3 tablespoons dark brown sugar

2 tablespoons kosher salt

Freshly cracked black pepper

One 4-pound beef brisket

2 tablespoons olive or grapeseed oil

2 large white onions, halved and thinly sliced

2 bay leaves

1½ cups apple cider

¼ cup fresh orange juice

6 fresh thyme sprigs

5 cups thinly sliced red cabbage (about ¾ pound)

2 McIntosh, Pink Lady, or other cooking apples (not Granny Smith), halved, cored, and thinly sliced

1 heaping tablespoon Dijon mustard

Crusty baguette or other bread for serving

In a small bowl, mix together the garlic, brown sugar, salt, and pepper to taste. Pat the mixture all over the brisket, then wrap the brisket tightly in plastic wrap and refrigerate for at least 8 hours or up to 2 days.

Unwrap the brisket and blot it dry on paper towels. Let it come to room temperature while you preheat the oven to 325°F.

In a heavy-bottomed Dutch oven, heat the oil over medium-high heat for 2 minutes. Add the brisket and brown on both sides, about 8 minutes total. Transfer the brisket to a plate.

Reduce the heat to medium and add the onions. Cook, stirring often, just until the onions start to soften, 3 to 4 minutes. Add the bay leaves, ¼ cup of the apple cider, and the orange juice and stir and scrape up any browned bits from the bottom of the pan. Add the remaining 1¼ cups cider and the thyme sprigs to the pot, increase the heat to high, and bring to a simmer. Add the cabbage and apples, then nestle the brisket in the middle, fatty side up. Cover the pot with a sheet of foil and place the lid on top (this will create an extra tight seal).

Place the pot in the oven and cook the brisket for 1½ hours. Scoop some of the onions and cabbage up from the bottom of the pot over the top of the brisket. Re-cover the pot with the foil and place the lid on. Continue to braise the brisket another 2 to 2½ hours, until a paring knife easily slips into the center of the meat without any resistance. Remove from the oven and set the brisket on a cutting board to rest for 10 minutes. Slice it against the grain into thin pieces. Stir the mustard into the sauce in the Dutch oven and adjust the salt and pepper if needed. Serve brisket slices covered with the sauce. Crusty bread on the side is always a nice addition to help scoop up lost bits of meat and juicy apples and onions.

TIP: *Cabbage can be a hard flavor for kids to embrace, but the apples in the mix here help to mellow and sweeten the flavor a bit, so it's a good recipe to help introduce them. Chop the brisket finely and let them try it with a bit of the sauce over buttered egg noodles or whole wheat pasta.*

ASSOULINE

HONEY-LIME CHICKEN WINGS

If you're in this section of the book, you're likely not a vegetarian, and if you're not a vegetarian, you probably love chicken wings. They're the perfect ratio of meat to delicious, sticky sauce and crispy skin perfection, and so much fun to eat. We have this debate on *The Chew* all the time: Is it okay to eat messy finger foods like chicken wings on a first date? I maintain it is a thousand percent okay, not only because I think eating with your hands loosens people up, but because many dates end up not being the magic you were waiting for, and you might as well enjoy your food.

Then again, I might just make this argument because I love chicken wings (and luckily, so does my husband, though they were sadly missing from our first date). This particular sauce is sweet with honey and flecked with chile flakes, and then spritzed with lime at the end. If the date doesn't go well, you won't be able to blame the chicken.

MAKES 4 TO 8 SERVINGS

1/2 tablespoon ground cumin

2 teaspoons kosher salt

Freshly cracked black pepper

2 pounds chicken wings, wing tips removed (save for chicken stock), drumette separated from the wing

4 tablespoons extra-virgin olive oil

2 teaspoons cornstarch

2 garlic cloves, minced

3 scallions, thinly sliced, whites and green tops kept separate

1/4 teaspoon crushed chile flakes

1/4 cup honey

Juice of 2 limes, plus 1 lime halved for serving

Preheat the oven to 350°F.

In a large bowl, combine the cumin, salt, and pepper to taste. Pat the chicken wings dry with paper towels, add them to the spices, and toss to combine.

Arrange the chicken in a single layer on a rimmed baking sheet or baking dish and drizzle with 2 tablespoons of the olive oil, shaking the pan to evenly distribute the oil and wings. Bake for 20 minutes.

Meanwhile, make the glaze. In a small bowl, mix the cornstarch with 1 tablespoon water. In a medium skillet, heat the remaining 2 tablespoons olive oil over medium heat. Add the garlic and cook until fragrant, about 2 minutes. Stir in the scallion whites and chile flakes and cook 1 minute more. Stir in the honey, lime juice, and cornstarch mixture. Bring the sauce to a boil, reduce the heat to medium-low, and simmer until the sauce is slightly thickened, 2 to 4 minutes.

Pour the glaze over the chicken wings, stirring the wings around to coat them evenly. Return the baking sheet to the oven, and cook 15 to 20 minutes longer, until the wings are cooked through and the sauce is sticky. (For extracrispy wings, place them under a broiler for the last minute.)

Remove the wings from the oven and sprinkle with the scallion greens and a squeeze of lime. Serve hot.

JERK CHICKEN AND SWEET POTATOES

My senior year in college, a bunch of friends and I visited Jamaica. On the drive home after a trip we'd taken to hike up the side of a breathtaking waterfall, we discovered a little locals-only restaurant serving up the most insane jerk chicken and stinging cold beers. I've been trying to replicate the experience ever since.

Now, I don't have an outdoor pit, or the local wood that creates just the right smoke, or the expert hands of the Jamaican masters who make this stuff day in and day out. But I do have a good mouth for replicating meals that I love. Jerk seasoning is heady with flavors you typically find in pumpkin pie—allspice, cinnamon, nutmeg, ginger, and brown sugar—but tempered with cumin, thyme, and garlic. You can take the spiciness up or down a notch, depending on what you love—the hellfire-hot Scotch bonnet pepper is traditional, but that is for expert heat-eaters only. Any leftovers make for delicious chicken salad if you're going light, or stuffed into incredible empanadas if you want to fry up a golden delight as a party appetizer or just to treat yourself.

MAKES 4 SERVINGS

2 tablespoons plus 1 teaspoon grapeseed oil

2 large sweet potatoes, halved lengthwise, each half quartered into 4 wedges

8 scallions, ends trimmed but whole

3 teaspoons kosher salt

1 tablespoon light brown sugar

2 teaspoons ground allspice

1 teaspoon ground cinnamon

1 teaspoon dried thyme

1/2 teaspoon ground cumin

1/2 teaspoon ground ginger

1/2 teaspoon sweet paprika

1/2 teaspoon garlic powder

1/4 teaspoon freshly grated nutmeg

1/4 teaspoon cayenne (optional)

8 chicken pieces (drumsticks and thighs, separated)

Flaky sea salt

Preheat the oven to 400°F. Lightly coat a rimmed baking sheet with 1 teaspoon of the oil.

In a large bowl, combine the sweet potatoes and scallions. Drizzle with 1 tablespoon of the oil, and sprinkle with 1 teaspoon of the salt. Toss to combine, then turn the mixture out onto the baking sheet, leaving room on one side for the chicken.

In the same bowl, combine the brown sugar, allspice, cinnamon, thyme, cumin, ginger, paprika, garlic powder, nutmeg, cayenne (if using), and the remaining 1 tablespoon oil and 2 teaspoons salt. Stir to combine, then add the chicken and toss to coat well.

Arrange the chicken skin side up on the baking sheet with the veggies. Roast for 20 minutes. Reduce the oven temperature to 375°F and continue to roast about 20 minutes longer, until the thickest part of a chicken thigh reads 160°F on an instant-read thermometer and the sweet potatoes are tender.

Transfer everything to a platter for serving. Sprinkle with flaky sea salt and serve.

ALMOST MONGOLIAN BEEF SATAY

Mongolian beef, with its sweet-savory, slightly spicy crunchy exterior and tender beef inside, was my inspiration for these babies. I wanted to make them at home, and just a little bit healthier if I could. This recipe appropriately honors my lifelong fascination with ketchup. Together with a few other odds and ends, it makes the perfect, slightly sticky glaze that crisps around the edges to deliver delicious beef candy every time.

MAKES 12 SKEWERS (4 SERVINGS)

SPECIAL EQUIPMENT

12 wooden or metal skewers

SATAY

1/2 pound flank steak

3 tablespoons low-sodium soy sauce

2 teaspoons cornstarch

1 tablespoon dark brown sugar

3 garlic cloves, minced

1 teaspoon toasted sesame oil

1 lime, cut into small wedges for serving

SATAY SAUCE

1/4 cup ketchup

1 tablespoon honey

1 teaspoon Sriracha sauce

1/2 teaspoon kosher salt

Freshly cracked black pepper

If using wooden skewers, place them in a pan and cover with water. Let soak for 20 minutes while you make the recipe.

To make the satay, place the steak on a cutting board. Holding a chef's knife at a 45-degree angle to the cutting board, slice the steak against the grain so you end up with twelve 1/4-inch-thick and 1 1/4-inch-wide strips. Don't fuss too much; you just want meat that is thin enough to thread easily on the skewers and cook quickly.

In a medium bowl, mix 1 tablespoon of the soy sauce with the cornstarch until it is completely dissolved. Add the remaining 2 tablespoons soy sauce, the brown sugar, garlic, and sesame oil. Add the beef slices, turn to coat, cover, and refrigerate for at least 20 minutes or overnight.

To make the satay sauce, in a small bowl, whisk together the ketchup, honey, Sriracha, salt, and pepper to taste.

Line a baking sheet with foil. Remove the steak from the marinade and blot it dry with paper towels. Thread 1 piece of meat onto each skewer and set them on the prepared baking sheet.

Adjust an oven rack so it is 3 inches from the heat source and preheat the broiler to high. Brush both sides of the skewers with the satay sauce and broil the satay for about 3 minutes, or until browned. Turn the skewers and broil 2 to 3 minutes to brown the other side.

Serve the satay with lime wedges.

TIP: *This recipe works great with chicken breast or pork cutlets.*

Facts

NUTTY CHICKEN FINGERS WITH HONEY-MUSTARD BARBECUE DIP

The nutty coating on these gluten-free chicken fingers gets toasted and golden brown, giving them a buttery crunch that's much more nutritious than traditional breading. They're protein-packed, and sometimes I workout just so I can justify needing to eat these as an awesome recovery meal (they're great baked, too; see the Variation). Give them a try: I have no doubt they'll soon be requested by all the mouths in your home.

MAKES 4 SERVINGS

HONEY-MUSTARD BARBECUE DIP

- 1/4 cup mayonnaise
- 2 tablespoons barbecue sauce
- 1 tablespoon Dijon mustard
- 1 tablespoon honey
- 1/4 teaspoon kosher salt

CHICKEN FINGERS

- 1 teaspoon sweet paprika
- 1 teaspoon garlic powder
- 2 teaspoons kosher salt
- Freshly cracked black pepper
- Four 6- to 8-ounce boneless, skinless chicken breasts, cut crosswise into 1-inch-thick strips
- 1/3 cup blanched almonds
- 1/4 cup pumpkin seeds (pepitas)
- 3 tablespoons sesame seeds
- 2 large eggs
- 1 tablespoon tamari sauce (gluten-free) or soy sauce
- 4 tablespoons extra-virgin olive oil

To make the barbecue sauce, in a small bowl, whisk together the mayonnaise, barbecue sauce, mustard, honey, and salt.

To make the chicken fingers, in a medium bowl, whisk together the paprika, garlic powder, 1 teaspoon of the salt, and pepper to taste. Add the chicken strips and turn to coat them in the spices.

In a food processor, pulse the almonds 5 times. Add the pumpkin seeds and sesame seeds and pulse until the mixture is semifine. Transfer the mixture to a medium bowl.

Whisk the eggs and tamari sauce in a small bowl, then pour them over the chicken. Turn the chicken to coat, then dredge each piece through the almond mixture, taking care to coat all sides.

In a large nonstick skillet, heat 2 tablespoons of the olive oil over medium-high heat. Add about half of the chicken pieces, spreading them out evenly, then reduce the heat to medium. Cook without moving the chicken until it's browned, about 3 minutes, then carefully turn it over and brown on the other sides, 2 to 3 minutes longer to cook through. Transfer the chicken to a paper-towel-lined plate. Add the remaining 2 tablespoons oil to the skillet and cook the remaining chicken.

Serve the chicken with the sauce on the side.

VARIATION: *If you prefer to bake the chicken, it won't be as crispy but it will still be delicious. Spray the tenders and a rimmed baking sheet with an olive oil mister. Arrange the tenders on the sheet and bake for 12 to 15 minutes at 375°F, until they are cooked through, turning them after 8 minutes.*

LAMB-STUFFED PEPPERS

My father's family is Turkish, and they love to stuff peppers with just about anything. It's the veggie equivalent of a bread bowl—a delicious vessel to carry and present the food that also adds its own flavor, and of course it's edible! This aromatic blend of bulgur wheat, lamb, spices, dried fruit, nuts—and the unexpected hit of lime zest—is totally customizable. You can leave out the meat altogether and substitute finely chopped mushrooms, eggplant, or squash. I sometimes throw in some cooked brown lentils to bulk up the mix and add a little extra fiber and protein. The best part is, they're an excellent way to clean out your fridge and still look gourmet. Sunday-night perfection.

MAKES 4 SERVINGS

1/2 cup bulgur wheat

1 1/4 cups vegetable broth (made from Vegetable Broth Concentrate, page 69), chicken broth, or water

1/4 cup dried currants, raisins, chopped dried apricots, or chopped dried cherries

1/2 cup pine nuts

4 tablespoons extra-virgin olive oil

1 medium red onion, finely chopped

2 1/2 teaspoons kosher salt

2 teaspoons ground cumin

1/2 teaspoon crushed chile flakes

Freshly cracked black pepper

1/2 pound ground lamb

3 scallions, finely chopped

1 medium tomato, finely chopped

Zest and juice of 1 lime

1/2 cup finely chopped fresh mint leaves

Handful of fresh parsley, roughly chopped

Place the bulgur in a heatproof medium bowl. In a small saucepan, bring the broth to a boil. Pour 3/4 cup of the hot broth over the bulgur, cover the bowl with plastic wrap, and set aside for 1 hour.

Preheat the oven to 375°F.

Meanwhile, soak the dried fruit in just enough hot water to cover for 10 minutes. Drain and discard the soaking water.

In a large, dry skillet, toast the pine nuts over medium heat, shaking the pan often, until they are golden brown, for 2 to 3 minutes. Transfer the nuts to a small plate for later.

Heat 2 tablespoons of the olive oil over medium-high heat. Add the onion and 1/2 teaspoon of the salt and cook, stirring often, until the onion starts to brown around the edges, 2 to 3 minutes. Reduce the heat to medium and add the drained dried fruit, cumin, chile flakes, and pepper to taste and continue to cook until the onions are deeply browned, 5 to 6 minutes more. Transfer to a medium bowl and set aside.

Add 1 tablespoon of the olive oil to the skillet and set it over medium-high heat. Add the lamb and 1 teaspoon of the salt and cook, stirring often to crumble, until the lamb is browned and cooked through, 6 to 8 minutes. Transfer the lamb to the bowl with the onion.

To the lamb and onion, add the scallions, tomato, lime zest, lime juice, bulgur, mint, parsley, and pine nuts. Stir to combine. Taste and add more salt if needed.

- 2 red bell peppers, tops removed and seeded, with the bottom intact but shaved to lie flat
- 2 yellow bell peppers, tops removed and seeded, with the bottom intact but shaved to lie flat

Rub the peppers inside and out with the remaining 1 tablespoon olive oil and season with the remaining 1 teaspoon salt. Stuff the peppers with the bulgur mixture and arrange the peppers in a 9 x 13-inch baking dish. Pour the remaining 1/2 cup broth into the bottom of the dish and tightly cover the dish with foil.

Bake for 45 minutes, or until the peppers are tender and juicy and the lamb-bulgur mixture is hot throughout. Remove the foil and broil the peppers for 2 to 3 minutes to brown the tops if desired.

CARNITAS WITH FRESH CORN SALSA AND SPICED CHIPS

Don't be frightened by the cooking time on this dish. Most of the cooking is just a few stirs every now and then while you let the wonderfully spiced, slightly sweet (hello, sweetened condensed milk!) citrus-tomatillo sauce work its magic, giving you tender, succulent pork. Make extra so you can freeze and save it to stretch the fruits of your labor—it's great in tacos or sandwiches, over rice, or under an egg.

MAKES 4 SERVINGS

CARNITAS

- **2 poblano peppers (if they are very spicy, use 1)**
- **1 orange, peeled with some pith left on and quartered**
- **4 garlic cloves**
- **4 tomatillos, husked, rinsed, and halved (or 1 large green tomato, roughly chopped)**
- **1 jalapeño pepper, halved (seeds and ribs removed if you want it less spicy)**
- **1/2 medium yellow onion, halved**
- **1 teaspoon finely chopped fresh oregano or 1/2 teaspoon dried**
- **1 tablespoon plus 1/2 teaspoon kosher salt**
- **1 teaspoon ground coriander**
- **1 teaspoon ground cumin**
- **4 pounds boneless pork shoulder (butt), cut into 3-inch pieces**
- **2 tablespoons extra-virgin olive oil**
- **2 bay leaves**
- **1/4 cup canned sweetened condensed milk**

(Ingredients continue on the next page.)

To make the carnitas, char the poblano peppers either over the flame of a gas stove about 8 minutes, or on a baking sheet under the broiler for 6 to 10 minutes, using tongs to turn periodically to char all sides. Transfer the peppers to a heatproof bowl and cover the bowl with plastic wrap. Set aside for 15 minutes. When the peppers are cool enough to handle, peel away the charred skin. Trim off the stems, slice the peppers open, and scrape away the seeds.

In a blender, combine the peppers, orange, garlic, tomatillos, jalapeño, onion, oregano, and 1/2 teaspoon of the salt. Blend until smooth.

In a large bowl, combine the remaining 1 tablespoon salt with the coriander and cumin. Add the pork pieces and toss to evenly coat them with the spices.

In a Dutch oven, heat the olive oil over medium-high heat until it shimmers, 2 minutes. Working in batches if necessary (so you don't overcrowd the pot and steam the meat), add the pork to the pan in an even layer and cook, turning the pork with tongs occasionally, until the pork is a deep golden brown on all sides, 8 to 10 minutes.

Add the poblano puree and bay leaves to the pork and bring the sauce to a simmer. Cook for 5 minutes. Stir in the sweetened condensed milk, reduce the heat to low, cover, and cook, stirring occasionally, for about 1 1/2 hours. Uncover and cook, stirring occasionally, until the liquid is thick and juicy and the pork is totally tender and easily shreds with 2 forks, 1 to 1 1/2 hours more. If the pot bottom is dry, add the broth or water and stir to keep the meat from sticking.

1/4 cup chicken broth, vegetable broth (made with Vegetable Broth Concentrate, page 69), or water, if needed

1/4 cup sour cream for serving (optional)

SPICED CHIPS

Vegetable oil, for frying

1 teaspoon kosher salt

1/2 teaspoon chipotle chile powder

1/2 teaspoon smoked paprika

1/4 teaspoon ground cumin

1/8 teaspoon ground cinnamon

1/8 teaspoon cayenne pepper

Eight 6-inch corn tortillas, cut into 1-inch-wide strips

SALSA

1 orange

Kernels from 4 ears of corn (sweet white corn is best)

1 Fresno chile or jalapeño pepper, thinly sliced crosswise (optional)

Juice of 1 lime

2 tablespoons roughly chopped fresh mint

2 tablespoons roughly chopped fresh parsley

1/2 teaspoon fine sea salt

Freshly cracked black pepper

To make the spiced chips, pour about 2 inches of oil (you need enough to completely submerge the chips) into a large heavy-bottomed pot and heat until an instant-read thermometer reaches 350°F.

In a small bowl, combine the salt, chile powder, smoked paprika, cumin, cinnamon, and cayenne.

Working in batches, fry the tortillas strips until both sides are golden brown and the chips are crisp, 2 to 3 minutes total. Use a slotted spoon to transfer them to a paper-towel-lined plate to drain. Sprinkle the spices over the chips immediately and continue frying the remaining tortilla strips.

To make the salsa, segment the orange (see Segmenting Citrus on page 27), working over a medium bowl to capture as much juice as possible. Add the corn, chile (if using), lime juice, mint, parsley, salt, and pepper to taste to the orange, toss to combine.

Remove the pork from the pot and place it on a large platter. Use 2 forks to shred it. Ladle a few spoonfuls of the broth over the pork. Serve the pork with the corn salsa, spiced chips, and sour cream (if using) on the side.

VARIATION: *For an extra smoky note, broil or grill the corn on the cob before removing the kernels. The little bit of char adds a nice, earthy taste to the salsa.*

TIP: *The crispiest chips come from slightly stale tortillas, so either cut the chips and leave them out overnight or dry them for 5 to 10 minutes in a 200ºF oven. And if you don't feel like making tortilla chips, toss store-bought ones with the spice blend for a quick fix.*

TIP: *You can make this dish perfectly in a slow cooker! If you have a slow cooker that can brown meat, excellent. If not, do the browning on the stovetop, then transfer to the slow cooker. Then combine the poblano blend and condensed milk, and pour it over the top. Cook it low and slow, 6 to 8 hours, until the meat is totally tender and pulls apart with two forks.*

STICKY, SPICY BABY BACK RIBS

Here's a confession: I had never tried making my own ribs until I met my mother-in-law, Nada, when John and I started dating in college. One of my first trips out to meet his family in Chicago, she made her famous basted baby backs and I was hooked. Slathered in sticky, smoky-sweet sauce with a hit of spice that's just right, the smell coming off these as they bake away hour after hour is too much to resist. With meat that falls right off the bone—perfect for picking at when you're "helping" in the kitchen—the only thing that could possibly make her recipe better is finding out how easy it is to make. I've included her set-it-and-forget-it technique as a sidebar here in case you want to give it a try, and you should!

Her version is still my favorite, but I concocted the following recipe as a riff on her gold standard to shave off a little cooking time, and with homemade sauce that you can make in bulk one weekend and store or freeze to always have on hand. To shave even more time, you can definitely use a favorite store-bought sauce. It may not be the original, but plates are licked clean around here when I make these!

MAKES 4 SERVINGS

RIBS

Oil or cooking spray

Two 8-rib slabs baby back pork ribs

1 tablespoon extra-virgin olive oil

2 teaspoons kosher salt

1 teaspoon garlic powder

1 teaspoon onion powder

1 teaspoon mustard powder

1 teaspoon smoked paprika

Freshly cracked black pepper

BARBECUE SAUCE

3 tablespoons extra-virgin olive oil

1 medium yellow onion, diced

2 medium garlic cloves, minced or pressed

3 tablespoons tomato paste

1½ cups tomato puree

¼ cup molasses

3 tablespoons apple cider vinegar

To make the ribs, adjust one oven rack to the middle position and another rack to the upper-middle position and preheat the oven to 300°F. Line a rimmed baking sheet with foil and set a wire rack on top of the baking sheet. Lightly coat the rack with oil or cooking spray.

Rub the ribs with the olive oil. In a small bowl, mix together the salt, garlic powder, onion powder, mustard, smoked paprika, and black pepper to taste. Sprinkle the seasoning all over both sides of each rack of ribs. Set the ribs on the wire rack and cover the entire baking sheet with foil.

Bake the ribs for 1½ hours, or until they're golden brown. When you insert a knife between the ribs, it should slip in easily at first and then get a bit stuck in the center.

While the ribs bake, make the barbecue sauce. In a medium saucepan, heat the olive oil over medium-high heat. Add the onion and cook, stirring occasionally, until it is golden brown, 3 to 4 minutes. Add the garlic and cook until fragrant, about 1 minute. Stir in the tomato paste and cook 3 minutes more.

Stir in the tomato puree, molasses, vinegar, honey, smoked paprika, cayenne, bay leaf, chili seasoning, salt, and black pepper to taste. Bring to a simmer over medium-high heat, reduce the heat to

- **2 tablespoons honey**
- **1 teaspoon smoked paprika**
- **1/4 teaspoon cayenne pepper (less if you're not into heat)**
- **1 bay leaf**
- **3/4 teaspoon chili seasoning (or 1/4 teaspoon chipotle chile powder)**
- **1 teaspoon kosher salt**
- **Freshly cracked black pepper**

medium-low, and cook, stirring occasionally to keep the sauce from sticking to the bottom of the pan, until the color of the sauce deepens and it reduces by about one-fourth, 30 to 45 minutes. Remove the bay leaf. Taste the sauce and add additional salt and cracked pepper as desired. You can now puree the sauce with an immersion blender if desired. Divide the sauce in half.

Remove the foil from the top of the ribs. Liberally brush half the barbecue sauce over both racks. Bake uncovered for about 30 minutes, or until the ribs are completely tender and a knife easily slips into the center of one.

Preheat the broiler to high. Brush the ribs with half the remaining barbecue sauce and set the ribs on the upper-middle rack. Broil for 2 to 3 minutes, until the sauce sizzles. Cut each rack in half and serve with the remaining barbecue sauce on the side(.

NADA'S BABY BACK RIBS

In case you want to make my mother-in-law, Nada's, version, which is still my favorite and uses store-bought BBQ sauce (making the process even easier): In her words, "Get some choice ribs, cut them into strips of four, and season generously with salt and fresh cracked pepper. Pour some of your favorite store-bought BBQ sauce (I like Stubb's Smokey Mesquite Bar-B-Q Sauce) down in a double-layered disposable foil roasting pan—you have to double-layer the pan because it will be heavy once all the sauce and meat goes in, and it makes cleanup easy—then arrange the ribs layer by layer, adding enough sauce to completely smother them. Cover the whole thing with aluminum foil and bake at 350°F for 3 1/2 to 4 hours, removing the tin foil for the final 15 minutes so the meat tenderizes and the sauce bakes thickly onto each rib. You'll know they're ready when you can pull a bone away with almost no resistance. They're the best when you put them in the oven and completely forget about them." She knows what she's talking about!

HOISIN-GLAZED PORK AND TURKEY MEATLOAF

Meatloaf needs no introduction, but this one gets kicked up a notch with the Asian flair of fresh ginger, scallions, and a hoisin sauce glaze. It's familiar but exotic at the same time, and so simple to make. Leftovers also make a sick and twisted sandwich the next day—I like mine open-faced: Layer a piece of whole-grain bread with a slick of mayo and spicy Chinese mustard if you have it (if not, Dijon works fine) and a thick slice of meatloaf. Pop it in the oven at 350°F to heat through. Top with a mix of fresh mint, basil, and parsley or cilantro, thinly sliced jalapeño, shredded carrots, and a healthy squeeze of lime. Oh, baby.

MAKES 8 SERVINGS

- Cooking spray
- 1¼ cups whole wheat panko breadcrumbs
- ½ cup whole milk
- 3 large eggs
- ½ cup minced fresh parsley leaves or cilantro
- ¼ cup minced fresh basil leaves
- 4 scallions, minced
- 6 garlic cloves, finely minced
- ½ medium white onion, grated on a box grater
- 1 tablespoon finely grated fresh ginger
- 2 teaspoons toasted sesame oil
- 2 teaspoons kosher salt
- Freshly cracked black pepper
- 1 pound ground pork
- 1 pound ground turkey
- ⅓ cup hoisin sauce
- 2 tablespoons ketchup

Preheat the oven to 350°F. Line a broiler pan rack or wire rack with foil and set it on top of a rimmed baking sheet. Lightly coat the foil with cooking spray, then use a sharp knife to make a few slits in the foil (this will allow the fat from the meatloaf to drip down onto the baking sheet).

In a large bowl, whisk together the panko, milk, eggs, parsley, basil, scallions, garlic, onion, ginger, sesame oil, salt, and pepper to taste. Add the ground pork and turkey and stir or use your hands to gently combine, being careful not to overwork the meat.

Shape the meat mixture into a 12-inch long loaf and place it on the foil-lined rack. Flatten the top slightly and square off the ends. In a small bowl, whisk together the hoisin sauce and ketchup. Pour about half the sauce over the meatloaf and use a brush or spoon to generously coat the sides and top.

Bake for 1 hour to 1 hour 10 minutes, until the internal temperature reads 160°F on an instant-read thermometer, brushing with glaze every 20 minutes or so. Let the meatloaf cool for 10 to 15 minutes, then transfer to a platter, slice, and serve.

TIP: *You can make a double batch of meatloaf mixture and place one half of the mixture in a disposable loaf pan to freeze. To bake, thaw overnight in the refrigerator, remove from the loaf pan onto a lined baking sheet, and glaze and bake as instructed.*

VARIATION: *For an extra decadent loaf, melt 1 tablespoon unsalted butter in a large skillet over medium-high heat. Add the panko and toast until golden brown, stirring often, 2 to 3 minutes. Continue with the rest of the recipe.*

ITALIAN-STYLE TURKEY MEATBALLS

Because I have a daughter who loves meat, I often find myself looking for ways to combine it with the vegetables I want to be plentiful in her diet. I came up with this riff on a turkey meatball when Philo decided she no longer liked broccoli—gotta love that stubborn toddler phase!—but I still wanted her to eat it. I minced the broccoli and tossed it right into the meatball mix, seasoning the whole blend up with pizza spices and Parmesan. The result was stupendous for two reasons: (1) Philo loves them—plain or crumbled with red sauce over pasta for a fast and healthy Bolognese, and (2) I cannot get enough of these things. They're light but so filling, the perfect low-carb afternoon snack that's protein-packed if you're looking for a quick, postworkout treat.

MAKES ABOUT 18 MEATBALLS (4 SERVINGS)

1 tablespoon olive oil, plus more for the baking sheet

1/2 teaspoon garlic powder or granulated garlic

1/4 teaspoon onion powder

1/4 teaspoon dried oregano

1 teaspoon kosher salt

Freshly cracked black pepper

1/4 cup finely chopped fresh flat-leaf parsley

1/2 cup grated Parmigiano-Reggiano

1 pound ground turkey (light and dark meat) or chicken

1/2 sweet yellow onion, grated on a box grater

2 garlic cloves, minced

3/4 cup whole wheat panko breadcrumbs

1 large egg, lightly beaten

1 teaspoon Worcestershire sauce

1 cup chopped broccoli stem and florets

Preheat the oven to 375°F. Line a baking sheet with foil and lightly rub it with a little olive oil.

In a large bowl, combine the garlic powder, onion powder, oregano, salt, pepper to taste, parsley, and Parmigiano and stir to combine. Add the turkey, onion, minced garlic, panko, egg, and Worcestershire sauce and combine gently. Add the broccoli and the remaining 1 tablespoon olive oil and use your hands or a wooden spoon to just incorporate.

Wet your hands, shape the mixture into balls the size of golf balls, and place them on the prepared baking sheet. Bake for 15 to 20 minutes, until cooked through.

TIP: *If you can't find whole wheat or regular panko breadcrumbs, use about 1 cup whole wheat Italian-style breadcrumbs and skip the garlic powder, onion powder, and salt.*

TIP: *You can freeze cooked and cooled meatballs for easy weeknight meals! Just reheat them in the oven or with a little olive oil in a skillet over medium heat to serve.*

SKIRT STEAK WITH BROWN SUGAR-SPICE RUB

We make this steak over and over again all summer long because it is the perfect meal to grill: simple, fast, and delicious. The spice rub is extremely efficient—15 minutes with it will do the trick, but overnight is ideal to help the steak get a deep, golden brown crust as it cooks. While you have the grill fired up, throw on a few spicy peppers to serve with the steaks.

MAKES 4 SERVINGS

1 tablespoon light brown sugar

1 tablespoon garlic powder

1/2 teaspoon chipotle chile powder

1 teaspoon ground cumin

1 teaspoon dried oregano

1 1/4 pounds skirt steak, cut crosswise into 4 pieces

4 tablespoons extra-virgin olive oil

Kosher salt

Flaky sea salt and freshly cracked black pepper for serving

In a medium bowl, combine the brown sugar, garlic powder, chipotle powder, cumin, and oregano. Rub the mixture all over the steak pieces, place the meat in the bowl, and set aside for 30 minutes (the meat can rest with the spices for up to 24 hours; if preparing more than 30 minutes ahead of cooking, refrigerate).

Prepare a gas or charcoal grill to high heat, or set a grill pan over high heat for 3 minutes. Use a few folded paper towels or a dishrag and long grilling tongs to grease the grill grate with 1 tablespoon of the oil.

Drizzle the steaks with 1 tablespoon of the oil and season with salt on all sides, then set them on the grill. Cook until the steaks have defined and deeply caramelized grill marks and release easily from the grill, 3 to 4 minutes. Flip and repeat on the opposite side to finish cooking to desired doneness, 2 to 3 minutes more for medium rare (the steak will continue to cook while it rests). Remove the steak to a cutting board and let rest for 10 minutes.

Season one section of the cutting board with 1 tablespoon of the oil and a sprinkle of salt. Set 2 of the steak pieces on top of the seasoning and slice into thin strips against the grain. Add the remaining 1 tablespoon of oil and a pinch more salt to the board and slice the remaining 2 steak pieces. This is a Michael Symon trick that allows each piece to get a little extra seasoning from the oil and salt. Transfer the steak and any accumulated juices to a platter and serve sprinkled with sea salt and pepper.

CHICKEN WITH PRESERVED LEMONS, APRICOTS, AND WHOLE WHEAT COUSCOUS

This is one of those dishes that looks like it took a long time to make, but I won't tell anyone you got it all done in under thirty. Couscous is basically just tiny pasta, and it cooks in no time flat. You could totally make the chicken on its own and serve it over cooked quinoa, lentils, or even brown rice if you prefer, but I love the way the couscous soaks up all the flavor of the browning chicken and the broth infused with apricots, chiles, and a touch of that salty preserved lemon.

MAKES 4 SERVINGS

- 2 tablespoons extra-virgin olive oil
- 4 bone-in, skin-on chicken thighs
- 1½ teaspoons kosher salt
- ¾ pound fresh or cooked chicken sausage (if using cooked, slice the sausage on the bias into ½-inch-thick pieces)
- 2 medium yellow onions, halved and thinly sliced
- 1 preserved lemon, seeded and finely chopped
- ½ cup chopped dried apricots
- 1 bay leaf
- 2 dried red chiles
- Freshly cracked black pepper
- 3 cups low-sodium chicken broth
- 1½ cups whole wheat couscous
- 2 tablespoons finely chopped fresh flat-leaf parsley

In a Dutch oven, heat the olive oil over medium heat. Season the chicken with 1 teaspoon of the salt and add it to the pan skin side down. Cook until the skin is golden brown and releases easily from the pan bottom, about 8 minutes. Turn the chicken over and cook until the other side is browned, 8 minutes more. Transfer the chicken to a plate.

Add the chicken sausage to the pan (if using fresh chicken sausage, squeeze it from the casing into the pan in small chunks). Cook the sausage, stirring often, until it is golden brown and cooked through, 4 to 5 minutes. Use the slotted spoon to transfer the sausage to the plate with the thighs.

Add the onions to the pan with the remaining ½ teaspoon salt and cook, stirring often, until the onions are deeply browned, 7 to 8 minutes. Add the preserved lemon, apricots, bay leaf, chiles, and pepper to taste and stir to combine.

Add 1 cup of the broth and bring to a boil. Add the chicken thighs, skin side up, reduce the heat to low, and cover the pot. Cook for 5 minutes. Stir in the sausage and couscous along with the remaining 2 cups broth. Cover and cook until the chicken is cooked through and the couscous is plump, 6 to 8 minutes. Serve sprinkled with the parsley.

TIP: *If you don't have preserved lemons, garnish the finished dish with the zest of ½ lemon for a similarly bright citrus note.*

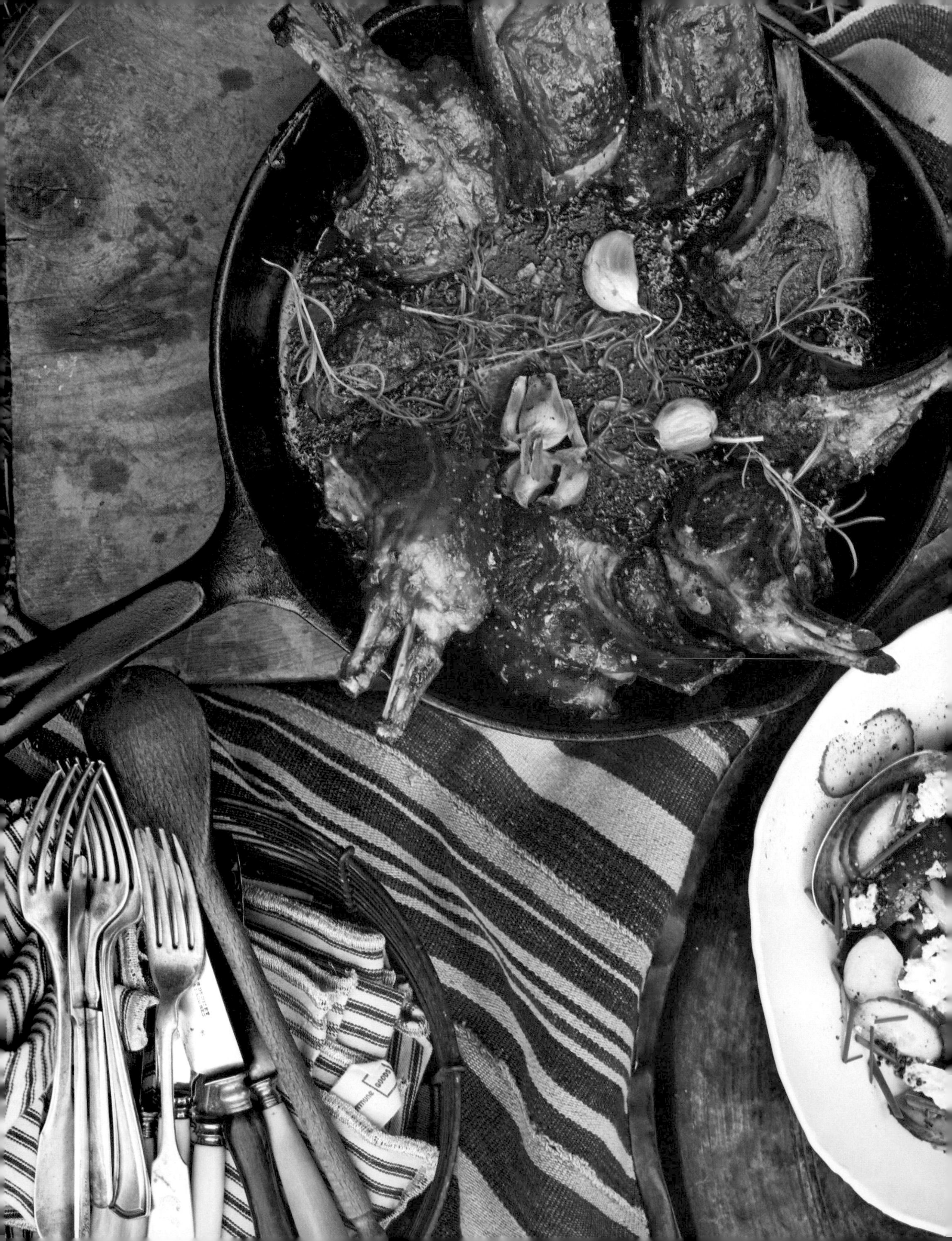

APRICOT-ROSEMARY GLAZED LAMB CHOPS

My husband, dad, and brother are all major fans of lamb chops. They'll happily eat them simply grilled with a little olive oil and salt, but when I decided to make this quick glaze out of some leftover apricot jam and a few sprigs of rosemary and garlic, it was game over. Though it's a little more cleanup, it's worth the added step of finishing in the oven to get a sticky glaze on the golden brown chops. Perfect for cozy family dinners, summer grilling, and feeding party people.

MAKES 4 SERVINGS

Eight 1½-inch-thick lamb rib chops (if you like lamb cooked to medium and more surface area for the glaze, get single ribs about 1 inch thick rather than double cuts), "frenched" optional

1 tablespoon plus ¼ teaspoon kosher salt

Freshly cracked black pepper

2 tablespoons extra-virgin olive oil, plus more if needed

3 garlic cloves, finely minced

1 tablespoon minced fresh rosemary

½ cup apricot jam (you can sub peach, plum, or any stone fruit)

¼ teaspoon crushed chile flakes (optional)

Preheat the oven to 400°F.

Place the lamb chops on a cutting board. In a small bowl, mix together 1 tablespoon of the salt and pepper to taste. Season both sides of the chops with the salt and pepper mixture and set aside.

In a medium skillet, heat 1 tablespoon of the olive oil over medium heat. Add the garlic and rosemary and cook until fragrant, about 1 minute. Stir in the apricot jam, remaining ¼ teaspoon salt, and 2 tablespoons water and bring to a simmer. Cook, stirring occasionally, until the jam is slightly thickened, about 2 minutes.

Heat a large skillet over high heat for 3 minutes. Add the remaining 1 tablespoon olive oil. When it's shimmering hot, add about half of the lamb chops to the pan. Brown the chops on one side for 3 minutes. Flip and cook another 2 minutes, until a golden brown crust forms (they will still be very rare at the center). Transfer the chops to a rimmed baking sheet and repeat with the remaining chops, adding more olive oil to the skillet if needed.

Brush both sides of the chops with the apricot glaze. Place the baking sheet in the oven and bake the chops until the center of a chop reads 120°F on an instant-read thermometer, 3 to 4 minutes for medium-rare (cook to 125°F, about 1 to 2 minutes longer, for medium chops). Transfer the chops to a platter, brush with more glaze, let rest for 5 minutes, and serve.

VARIATION: *To grill, cook for about 3 minutes on each side over medium-high heat. Brush the cooked side with the glaze after turning the chops, then brush with more glaze before serving.*

BRAISED CHICKEN THIGHS WITH ALMONDS AND OLIVES

You know what I love about braises? They smell great while they're cooking, they look great when you put them down on a table and do the big reveal (cue angels singing), and they taste *grrrrreat*. But you know what I really love about braises? They are (almost) impossible to mess up. Because by creating a superflavorful broth that gently caresses and flavors the meat and vegetables as they cook, everything stays exceptionally moist and juicy. It's like a spa day for the meat—it gets bathed and coaxed to tender perfection . . . and then it gets eaten.

This combo with the meaty olives and tender bite of the almonds yields a particularly comforting chicken dinner. The wine and butter sauce doesn't hurt, either.

MAKES 4 SERVINGS

- **1 tablespoon unsalted butter**
- **1 tablespoon extra-virgin olive oil**
- **8 bone-in, skin-on chicken thighs**
- **1½ teaspoons kosher salt**
- **Freshly cracked black pepper**
- **Leaves from 3 fresh thyme sprigs**
- **2 shallots, halved and thinly sliced**
- **2 garlic cloves, minced**
- **½ cup pitted Castelvetrano olives**
- **¼ cup Marcona almonds, chopped**
- **¼ cup dry white wine**
- **2½ cups low-sodium chicken broth or homemade vegetable broth (made from Vegetable Broth Concentrate, page 69)**
- **½ cup finely chopped fresh flat-leaf parsley and stems**

In a Dutch oven, melt the butter in the olive oil over medium heat. Season the chicken thighs with 1 teaspoon of the salt and pepper to taste. When the butter is melted, add the chicken skin side down to the pan. Cook the chicken until the skin is golden brown and it releases easily from the pan, about 6 minutes. Turn the chicken over and cook until the other side is browned, 4 to 5 minutes more. Transfer the chicken to a plate.

Reduce the heat to medium-low and add the thyme leaves to the pan. When they start to sizzle, add the shallots and the remaining ½ teaspoon salt. Cook, stirring often, until the shallots soften, 3 to 4 minutes. Add the garlic and cook another minute. Stir in the olives and almonds.

Increase the heat to medium and add the wine, stirring and scraping up the browned bits from the bottom of the pan. When the wine comes to a simmer, return the chicken to the pan skin side up along with any accumulated juices, then pour in 2 cups of the chicken broth. Increase the heat to high and bring the broth to a boil.

Reduce the heat to medium-low and simmer, uncovered, until the chicken is cooked through and the sauce thinly coats the back of a spoon, about 15 minutes. Check on the chicken after 8 minutes and if the pan looks dry, add the remaining ½ cup broth.

Serve the chicken with a ladle of the sauce with olives and almonds and a shower of fresh parsley.

CRISPY CHICKEN WITH ZUCCHINI

I came up with this combo because I was craving chicken fried rice but wanted to avoid eating a giant bowl of simple carbs (basically, just a sugar shot to your body). The chicken gets unbelievably crisp in the pan as long as you don't try to move it around too much—one of the great times in life when less work yields better results! The zucchini and onion double your pleasure by soaking up all the tasty soy sauce and butter (no, I'm not afraid of butter or oil, even when I'm trying to eat healthfully, and you shouldn't be, either—fat is brain food! And it helps everything taste better, and you stay full for longer. The trick is to use just enough of it and in the right place to make it count).

If you really want rice, go ahead and sauté some more minced onion with a little more butter and soy sauce and toss in leftover brown rice to reheat with a splash of water, then add this chicken mix on top for a bountiful bowl.

MAKES 2 SERVINGS

- **3 tablespoons butter, coconut oil, or extra-virgin olive oil**
- **1/2 large yellow onion, finely chopped**
- **1 medium zucchini, sliced into 1/4-inch-thick rounds**
- **2 teaspoons soy sauce**
- **2 cups shredded cooked chicken (about half a chicken; a rotisserie chicken works well)**

In a large skillet, heat 1 1/2 tablespoons of the butter or oil over medium-high heat. Add the onion and cook, stirring often, until it's slightly browned, about 3 minutes.

Add the zucchini and cook, stirring often, until it softens and portions start to darken, 2 to 3 minutes.

Add the remaining 1 1/2 tablespoons butter or oil, the soy sauce, and chicken and toss to combine. Arrange the chicken in a single layer in the pan and cook, without stirring or moving the chicken, until it's browned and portions are crisp, about 3 minutes. Use a spatula to flip the chicken over and let the other side brown, about 2 minutes more. Serve on its own in a bowl (delightful!), or over any cooked grain for an even more filling meal.

TRUFFLE SALT ROAST CHICKEN WITH LENTILS AND SQUASH

So you may be looking at the truffle salt in this dish and shaking your head. But don't judge!! A jar of the stuff delivers $500 worth of truffle flavor for the price of a couple fancy lattes. And it's just one of the things that makes this dish so special.

I love veggies and lentils cooked in the drippings of a roasting chicken, because it gives this otherwise very healthy combination a decadent feel. The salt under and on the skin of the chicken creates a deeply golden, supercrisp skin and juicy, flavorful meat. This is definitely a dish worth showing off, so call some friends over, open a bottle of wine, and bask in the compliments.

MAKES 4 SERVINGS

SPECIAL EQUIPMENT

twine, for tying the chicken

ROAST CHICKEN

- Extra-virgin olive oil
- 1 tablespoon coarse truffle salt (I knowwww . . . but it's so good!! Do it!!)
- 1 tablespoon finely chopped fresh thyme leaves plus 6 fresh thyme sprigs
- Freshly cracked black pepper
- 2 large garlic cloves, peeled but whole
- 1 whole chicken (3½ to 4 pounds)
- 1 tablespoon unsalted butter, melted
- 1 onion, quartered

(Ingredients continue on the next page.)

To roast the chicken, preheat the oven to 425°F. Place a roasting rack on a rimmed baking sheet and lightly coat the rack with olive oil.

In a small bowl, mix the truffle salt, chopped thyme, and pepper to taste. Use a Microplane-style rasp (or a garlic press) to grate the garlic into the salt, then use your fingers to rub it into the salt.

Set the chicken on a cutting board and use your fingers to gently separate the skin over the breast from the breast meat, creating a pocket. Don't be afraid to get in there, but take care not to tear the skin. Grab about half the herbed truffle salt and massage it into the meat and under the skin. Repeat at the thigh joint, using your fingers to separate the meat from the skin and rubbing half the remaining salt in the pocket. Brush the chicken all over with the melted butter, then rub the last bit of salt over the skin. Stuff the cavity with the onion quarters.

Tuck the wings behind the backbone and tie the ends of the drumsticks together using kitchen twine. Turn the chicken breast side down and set it on the roasting rack. Add ⅓ cup water to the bottom of the pan—this will help to steam the chicken and keep it moist as it cooks—and roast for 40 minutes.

Meanwhile, to start the lentils, bring a large pot of water to a boil. Add the lentils and cook until they are al dente, about 20 minutes. Drain and set aside.

LENTILS AND SQUASH

- 1 cup Puy lentils (French green lentils)
- 2 pounds kabocha squash, halved, seeded, and cut into 1/2-inch-thick wedges (butternut squash or pumpkin works great, too)
- 2 tablespoons extra-virgin olive oil
- 1 teaspoon kosher salt
- 2 tablespoons sherry vinegar
- 1/4 cup finely chopped fresh scallions
- 1/2 cup roughly chopped fresh parsley leaves

Transfer the rack with the chicken on it to a cutting board. Add the squash to the baking sheet, drizzle with 1 tablespoon of the olive oil and sprinkle with 1/2 teaspoon of the salt. Replace the chicken (on the rack) over the vegetables and use tongs or a long-handled wooden spoon to turn the chicken over, breast side up. Roast the chicken and vegetables for 20 minutes.

Remove the pan setup from the oven and add the lentils to the bottom of the pan. Roast again until the juices run clear and the temperature at the thickest part of the thigh is about 160°F, about 40 minutes more.

Use tongs to transfer the chicken to a platter, and let sit for 10 minutes.

In a small bowl, whisk together the vinegar, scallions, parsley, and the remaining 1 tablespoon olive oil and 1/2 teaspoon salt. Pour the vinaigrette over the lentils and squash, stirring to coat them, and taste for salt and pepper and adjust if necessary. Carve the chicken, and arrange pieces on a platter. Surround the chicken with the squash and lentils and serve family style.

VARIATION: *You can parboil wheat berries, brown rice, barley, or farro to stand in for the lentils if you like. Toss a few cups of spinach in with the lentils and squash for a warm salad-y side.*

TURKEY VEGGIE BOLOGNESE

Bolognese sauce is the workhorse of our week. I love to make a big batch on the weekend, then freeze individual portion sizes to reheat in the moment. I started adding tons of veggies to my Bolognese when I realized that I could get my daughter to eat almost anything if it's simmered with rich meat and her all-time favorite: red sauce. She would bathe in the stuff if I let her. I know this, because I would have bathed in the stuff if my mother had let me. Our Italian roots are strong.

The veggies cook down and sweeten the sauce, making it much more complex and varied than traditional Bolognese. I do sometimes add milk to make it a little creamy, but you can definitely use tomato puree instead and keep the dish light but still very filling. I love using turkey rather than beef, because it is flavorful but gives you a little less of that thick layer of fat on top (lean ground beef feels like a waste to me), but you can totally use ground beef, or a combo of the two. The longer this mixture sits and simmers, the better, so don't be afraid to make it an hour ahead and let it mellow until you're ready to dig in. This strategy also gives you more time to squirrel a few more spoonfuls into your mouth to taste test . . . chef's perks.

MAKES 4 SERVINGS
(WITH LEFTOVERS FOR ANOTHER PASTA DINNER)

3 medium carrots, peeled and roughly chopped

2 medium celery stalks, roughly chopped

1 large yellow onion, roughly chopped

1 small beet, peeled and roughly chopped

5 garlic cloves, roughly chopped

2 tablespoons extra-virgin olive oil

Kosher salt

1 pound ground turkey (preferably dark meat)

2 teaspoons fresh oregano leaves or 1 teaspoon dried

3 tablespoons tomato paste

1½ cups dry white wine, chicken broth, homemade vegetable broth (made from Vegetable Broth Concentrate, page 69), or water

In a food processor, combine the carrots, celery, onion, beet, and garlic. Pulse to roughly chop, then let the machine run until the mixture is fine, about 5 seconds.

In a Dutch oven, heat the oil over medium-high heat. Add the vegetable mixture and 1 teaspoon of the salt, reduce the heat to medium, and cook, stirring often, until all the moisture is evaporated and vegetables are fragrant and sweet, 15 to 20 minutes.

Increase the heat to medium-high. Crumble in the turkey and add the oregano and the remaining 1 teaspoon salt. Cook, stirring often to crumble, until the turkey is cooked, 6 to 8 minutes.

Add the tomato paste and cook for 3 minutes, then add the wine and bay leaf and bring to a simmer over medium-high heat. Reduce the heat to medium-low and gently simmer until the sauce is reduced by half, 3 to 4 minutes.

Add the milk or tomato puree and canned tomatoes and cook until the sauce thickens slightly, about 30 minutes. Season with fresh cracked pepper. Taste and adjust the seasoning with more salt and pepper if needed. Leave half the sauce (about 4 cups) in the pot and save the rest for another time (cool and freeze in a 1-quart-size

- 1 bay leaf
- 3/4 cup whole milk or tomato puree
- 1 1/2 cups canned diced or crushed tomatoes
- Freshly cracked black pepper
- 1 pound spaghettini or spaghetti
- 2 tablespoons finely chopped fresh parsley leaves
- 1/2 cup finely grated Parmigiano-Reggiano cheese

resealable freezer bag for up to 3 months). Let the sauce sit and all the flavors blend and distribute while you cook the pasta.

Bring a large pot of salted water to a boil. Add the pasta and cook it 1 minute less than the package instructs. Reserving 1/2 cup of the pasta water, drain the pasta and add to the sauce with a splash of the pasta water. Use tongs to toss and combine. Serve sprinkled with the parsley and Parmigiano.

TIP: *If you buy organic and give your vegetables and fruit a good scrub—bonus if you have an all-natural or homemade produce wash to really get them clean—there's little need to peel your produce. Save yourself time, and get the added bonus of all the nutrients in the skin and peel you'd otherwise be throwing away!*

HARVEST

desserts

And here we are at dessert.

In this chapter, you'll find the treats that satisfy my sweet tooth and make it count. There are many I've tried to make a little bit lighter without losing any hedonism, like the Baked Cider Doughnuts and Better Brownies (fudgy chocolate morsels so healthy you can basically eat them for breakfast). The Blueberry Tea Cake is one of my favorites for everyday tea parties with my two-year-old, and she's also a big fan of the Chocolate Truffle Animal Cookies (if her mother hasn't eaten them all first). The Outlaw Carrot Cake with Brown Sugar Buttercream is pretty magical—I've done away with the raisins and cream cheese and it's so much better!—and for an easy dinner-party dessert, the freeform Peach and Almond Galette is a friend to messy bakers—and happy mouths—everywhere. And for all out indulgent madness, you must make my Vanilla Pots de Crème with candied pecans . . . and toast to an evening well lived!

BAKED CIDER DOUGHNUTS

One of my favorite traditions growing up in New Jersey was our annual trek to go apple picking at Ochs Orchard in Warwick, New York, every September. After fifty minutes on the road, winding through forests and sleepy towns, you finally arrive at the orchard. Rows and rows of trees await, bearing crisp, ripe apples in every possible variety. We beelined straight for the Golden Delicious and Honeycrisps, loading up bag after bag of fresh-picked apples that would soon become apple pies and crisps and roasts in our all-night-long bake fest.

Sounds totally delightful, right? Well, I haven't even told you the best part. As you're leaving the orchard, the rich perfume of frying dough awaits you. My friends, if you have never had a hot apple cider doughnut straight from the fryer, you have not lived. Rich, buttery, dense, and coated in cinnamon sugar, this is the kind of thing that's worth burning fingers and tongue (and diet plans) to eat with glee after an afternoon of healthy apple eating. I find myself pining for them the rest of the year, so I finally decided to make my own, riffing on a yeasted potato doughnut recipe to give these guys the rich, moist but fluffy texture I so love. I bake them in this recipe just to make them a smidge healthier, but I've included frying directions as a variation option in case you want the full orchard experience. Don't say I never did anything for you.

MAKES 12 DOUGHNUTS

DOUGHNUTS

- 1 small russet potato (about 6 ounces), peeled
- 2 teaspoons kosher salt
- 1/4 cup apple cider
- 1 large egg plus 1 large egg yolk
- 2 tablespoons grapeseed oil
- 1/4 cup packed dark brown sugar
- 2 cups all-purpose flour, sifted, plus extra for rolling and shaping
- 3/4 teaspoon ground cinnamon
- 1 1/2 teaspoons instant yeast (Fleischmann's RapidRise or Red Star Quick-Rise)
- 3 tablespoons unsalted butter, at room temperature

(Ingredients continue on the next page.)

To make the doughnuts, bring a medium saucepan of water to a boil. Add the potato and 1 teaspoon of the salt and cook until the potato is tender when pierced by a fork, 15 to 18 minutes. Drain and set aside to cool, then press it through a potato ricer or food mill, or grate it on the small holes of a box grater.

In a stand mixer fitted with the whisk attachment, whisk the apple cider, whole egg, egg yolk, and grapeseed oil until combined. Add the brown sugar and remaining 1 teaspoon salt and whisk to combine. Switch to the dough hook and add the potato, sifted flour, cinnamon, and yeast and mix on low speed until the dough comes together, stopping occasionally to scrape the bottom and sides of the bowl.

When the dough comes together in a mass, increase the mixer speed to medium-low and add the butter a pinch at a time until it is all added. Continue to mix on medium speed until the butter is worked in, 1 to 2 minutes.

Turn the dough out onto a lightly floured surface. Gently knead it into a ball, return it to the mixer bowl, and cover the bowl with

CINNAMON SUGAR

1/3 cup granulated sugar

2 teaspoons ground cinnamon

plastic wrap. Set aside in a warm, draft-free spot until the dough doubles in volume, 1 to 1 1/2 hours (depending on the temperature of the room).

Line a rimmed baking sheet with parchment paper. Lightly flour a work surface and place the dough on top. Divide the dough in half and return one piece to the mixer bowl and cover. Sprinkle the other piece with more flour and gently roll it out into a 1/2-inch-thick sheet. Use a 2 3/4-inch biscuit cutter to stamp out as many rounds as possible. Use another 7/8-inch cutter to stamp out the center. Place the doughnuts on the lined baking sheet. Set the scraps aside and repeat the rolling and cutting with the other piece of dough. Then press all of the scraps together, roll out the dough, and punch out as many additional doughnuts as possible. Toss any remaining scraps but save the doughnut holes for homemade munchkins. Cover the baking sheet with a kitchen towel and set aside for 20 minutes.

While the doughnuts rise again, preheat the oven to 350°F.

To make the cinnamon sugar, in a wide bowl, whisk together the sugar and cinnamon.

Bake the doughnuts for 12 to 15 minutes (doughnut holes are done in 10 to 12 minutes), until they are puffy and golden. Toss them straight from the oven into the cinnamon sugar. Serve doughnuts warm or at room temperature.

TIP: *If you don't have a stand mixer, you can use a large bowl and hand whisk in place of the whisk attachment, and switch to a wooden spoon in place of the dough hook to cream and blend the mixture. Once the dough comes together and becomes too hard to stir with the spoon, you can then knead the butter in a few pinches at a time on a floured surface until just combined. Gather dough into a ball and place it in a large bowl, cover with plastic wrap, and let the dough rise as specified before continuing with the rest of the steps.*

VARIATION: *Although baking yields very good results, to make these doughnuts extra indulgent and authentic to the orchard experience, they should be fried. Pour 3 inches of neutral oil (such as peanut) into a large shaallow pot (the amount will depend on the size of the pot, but probably at least 2 quarts) and heat it over medium-high heat until an instant-read thermometer reads 360°F. Working in batches and being careful not to overfill, add the doughnuts and fry, turning them a few times, until golden brown on both sides and puffed, about 3 minutes total. Dunk from the oil into the cinnamon sugar, then transfer to a wire rack to cool slightly. Doughnut holes will fry in 1 to 2 minutes total. Serve the doughnuts warm or at room temperature.*

CANDIED PECAN AND ROASTED STRAWBERRY SUNDAES

When I entertain, dessert is a must, but more than once I've forgotten it in the oven during dinner, only to find a lovely charcoal lump lying where a crumble had once been. If you're prone, as I am, to living in the moment perhaps a bit too much, it's a good idea to always have the fixings for a quick sundae on hand. All you'll need are these easy "fancy" toppings and some ice cream in the freezer (which I know you have, don't play) for a festively easy dessert. P.S. If you're having a lighter moment, this juicy-crunchy duo is pretty great over some yogurt, too.

MAKES 4 SERVINGS

- 3 cups strawberries, hulled and halved
- 2 tablespoons honey
- 1 pint of your favorite ice cream (vanilla is always a charmer)
- Candied Pecans (recipe follows)

Preheat the oven to 350°F. Line a rimmed baking sheet with parchment paper.

In a medium bowl, toss the strawberries with the honey, then arrange them cut side up on the baking sheet. Roast the strawberries for 20 minutes, or until they are soft and juicy. Transfer the strawberries to a bowl to cool. (They can be refrigerated in an airtight container for up to 1 week.)

Break the pecans into bite-size pieces. Add a scoop of ice cream to each of 4 bowls. Top with a spoonful of strawberries. Add another scoop of ice cream, more strawberries, and some pecans.

CANDIED PECANS

Nuts made into candy. You need them for salads, oatmeal, and of course dessert.

MAKES ABOUT 1¼ CUPS

- 1 cup roughly chopped pecans
- ⅓ cup maple syrup
- ⅓ cup packed dark brown sugar
- ½ teaspoon kosher salt
- ½ teaspoon chipotle chili powder (optional, if you like smoky with your sweet)

To make the candied pecans, cook the pecans in a large nonstick skillet over medium heat, shaking the pan often, until toasted, 2 to 3 minutes. Add the maple syrup, brown sugar, salt, and chili powder (if using) and stir to combine. When the sugar is dissolved, remove from the heat and transfer the pecans to a parchment-paper-lined plate to cool. They can be stored in an airtight container for up to 3 days.

SOUR APPLE POPS

I'm the girl who wants lemonade with double lemon and half the sugar, and this is my kind of ice pop—more tart than sweet, and so refreshing on a hot summer afternoon. You can add a little honey or simply syrup—equal parts sugar and water, heated together so the sugar dissolves—if you find the juice too sour for your liking. Or, if you want even more of a pucker, go for Granny Smith apples!

If you have kids, ice pops always seem to be in high demand, so let them mix and match their own blends. It's an easy way to cut back on extra or artificial sugars that are rampant in packaged pops, and will probably save you some dolla dolla bills, too.

MAKES ABOUT 6 POPS
(DEPENDING ON THE SIZE OF THE MOLDS)

- 4 Gala or Pink Lady apples, peeled and quartered
- 1 English (seedless) cucumber, quartered, or 2 Persian (mini) or Kirby cucumbers, halved
- 3 limes, peel removed, fruit quartered

In a juicer, juice the apples, cucumber(s), and lime.

Divide the mixture among ice pop molds, then refrigerate at least 2 hours; getting the pop blend as cold as possible before freezing helps ensure the pops aren't icy. Freeze until hard, at least 4 hours or preferably overnight.

TROPICAL FRUIT POPS

This intoxicating mix of sweet tropical fruit, creamy coconut milk, and just a hint of fresh lime juice is basically the cheapest vacation you'll ever take.

MAKES 8 TO 10 POPS
(DEPENDING ON THE SIZE OF THE MOLDS)

- 2¾ cups chopped fresh or thawed frozen mango, papaya, pineapple, guava, or melon
- 3 tablespoons honey
- Juice of 2 limes
- 1 cup coconut milk

Combine all the ingredients in a blender and blend until smooth. Refrigerate at least 2 hours.

Divide the mixture into ice pop molds and freeze until hard, at least 4 hours or preferably overnight.

BETTER BROWNIES

If I could eat only one dessert for the rest of my life, it would probably be an extra fudgy brownie, warm from the oven, with a scoop of homemade vanilla ice cream on top. If only I could eat this dessert as often as I would like (every day . . . maybe every meal). Sadly, this cannot be. So I came up with my version of a brownie that lets me celebrate my love of this decadent chocolate beast and feel good every bite of the way.

Black bean flour is the unsung hero of extra fudgy brownies, and it happens to be insanely good for you while replacing the need for all-purpose flour entirely. Sweet potato here might also seem a little strange—but get to know her; she'll help make these sweet and seductively moist while loading you up on healthy vitamins and minerals. I hesitate to call these "brownies you could eat for breakfast" . . . but I sometimes do (it's kind of the best part if you're cleaning up after a dinner party the next morning before anyone else is awake—just you, a frothy cappuccino, and the last leftover brownie bite!). So you know I won't judge you.

MAKES 18 MINI-BROWNIES

- 1 large sweet potato
- 2 tablespoons unsalted butter, melted
- 2 large eggs
- 1/2 cup packed dark brown sugar
- 1 teaspoon pure vanilla extract
- 1/2 cup semisweet chocolate chips
- 1/3 cup hot coffee
- 3/4 cup unsweetened cocoa powder
- 1/2 cup black bean flour
- 1/2 teaspoon baking soda
- 1 teaspoon kosher salt

Preheat the oven to 350°F. Lightly coat 12 to 18 cups of a mini-muffin tin with cooking spray.

Prick the sweet potato a few times with a fork and microwave until it is completely soft and tender, about 7 minutes. Scoop out the flesh and set 1 cup in a large bowl (save the rest of the flesh and the skin for a snack!). Whisk in the melted butter, eggs, brown sugar, and vanilla.

Add the chocolate chips to a small bowl and pour the hot coffee on top. Stir until melted, then add it to the sweet potato mixture.

In another bowl, combine the cocoa powder, black bean flour, baking soda, and salt. Add the cocoa mixture to the sweet potato mixture and stir just until combined.

Use a spoon to fill the muffin cups three-quarters full (you'll have enough batter for 18 mini-muffins). Bake for about 8 minutes, or until a cake tester inserted into the center of a brownie comes out with a few moist crumbs attached and the brownies resist light pressure. Let the brownies cool in the pan for 5 minutes, then turn them out onto a wire rack to cool. Repeat with any remaining batter. The brownies will keep in an airtight container for up to 3 days.

TIP: *If you prefer cakey brownies, use teff flour in place of black bean flour and only 1/4 teaspoon baking soda plus 1/4 teaspoon baking powder.*

PEACH AND ALMOND GALETTE

Galettes are a gift to beginner bakers everywhere, because they're meant to be freeform and a little rough around the edges. I also happen to prefer them to traditional pies, because you get the right amount of crisp crust to tender, juicy fruit filling. And while tarts take lots of fancy laying into a pan and pinching fluted edges, a galette is essentially just a delicious dough, rolled flat and then folded like gift wrapping around the most delicious fruit you can find—in this case, a collection of tart-sweet stone fruits tossed with just a bit of lemon juice and turbinado sugar that caramelizes and glistens hot from the oven. It's a pretty sensational—and sensationally easy—dessert.

MAKES ONE 10-INCH GALETTE

DOUGH

1 1/2 sticks (6 ounces) cold unsalted butter, cut into 1/2-inch cubes

1/2 cup sliced almonds

1 cup all-purpose flour

1 cup white whole wheat flour

3 heaping tablespoons light brown sugar

1/2 teaspoon baking powder

1/2 teaspoon kosher salt

3/4 cup ice water

1 tablespoon fresh lemon juice

PEACH FILLING

1 1/2 pounds (6 small or 3 large) peaches (see Tip for alternatives)

Juice of 1 lemon

1/2 cup granulated sugar

Kosher salt

1 tablespoon cornstarch

1 large egg

2 tablespoons turbinado sugar

To make the dough, place the butter cubes on a small plate and set it in the freezer.

In a food processor, process the almonds until they are fine. Add the flours, brown sugar, baking powder, and salt and pulse to combine. Add the frozen butter cubes and pulse until there aren't any pieces larger than a small pea, about twenty 1-second pulses.

Transfer the mixture to a medium bowl. In a small liquid measuring cup, combine the ice water and lemon juice. While raking the dry ingredients with a fork, drizzle in the liquid, just until there aren't any dry bits in the bottom of the bowl and when you pinch some of the dough together, it holds firm and doesn't crumble apart. Depending on how dry the flour is and the humidity of the room, you will use 10 to 12 tablespoons of liquid (up to 3/4 cup).

Place a large sheet of plastic wrap on the counter and transfer the dough to the plastic wrap, pressing and shaping it into a 1/2-inch-thick disc. Wrap tightly in plastic and refrigerate for at least 30 minutes or up to 2 days.

To make the peach filling, halve the peaches, remove the pits, slice each half into quarters, and place in a large bowl.

Add the lemon juice, granulated sugar, and a pinch of salt to the peaches and toss to combine. Set aside for 5 minutes, then pour some of the juices into a small bowl and whisk the cornstarch into the juices. Pour the cornstarch mixture over the fruit and toss to combine. Line a rimmed baking sheet with parchment paper.

On a lightly floured work surface, roll the dough into an 1/8-inch-thick round. Drape the dough over a rolling pin and transfer it to the prepared baking sheet. Place the peaches in the middle of the dough, leaving a 3-inch border of dough uncovered. Fold the edges over the peaches, loosely pleating the dough and leaving the galette open in the middle. Refrigerate the galette for at least 30 minutes or up to 2 hours, until the dough is chilled through.

Preheat the oven to 375°F.

In a small bowl, whisk the egg with 1 teaspoon water and a pinch of salt. Brush the dough with the egg wash and sprinkle the turbinado sugar over the top. Bake for 40 minutes, or until the dough is browned and the peaches have deepened in color. Let the galette cool 10 minutes, then slice and serve warm or at room temperature.

TIP: *Any combination of stone fruits work in this galette, including plums, cherries, apricots, and nectarines. Fresh figs, apples, and pears work well, too!*

VARIATION: *Instead of an egg wash, try brushing the dough with a slightly watered-down apricot jam before sprinkling with turbinado sugar for an extra fruity golden brown bite.*

PEELING STONE FRUIT

I don't mind leaving the skin of my fruit intact for rustic desserts like crostatas, but in case you're wondering how to get rid of the pesky peel, a vegetable peeler will work well for ripe fruit. If your fruit is still pretty hard, you can use this French technique (called concasse) to quickly slip it out of its skin. Bring a large saucepan of water to a boil. Use a paring knife to make a small X in the bottom of each peach. Gently drop the peaches into the boiling water for 10 to 45 seconds, just until the skin at the X starts to curl. Transfer the peaches to a bowl of ice water. Peel them when cool.

BASIL AND BERRIES LEMONADE SORBET

Every August, my family heads to Maine for a week in the wilderness. My grandparents have six children, and each of them has multiple children of their own, so when we gather the herd of roughly thirty-five people, it's a pretty epic sight. Kids of all ages run rampant, and I can never decide whether my favorite memories are the ones in the kitchen, whipping up batch after batch of blueberry pancakes for weekend breakfasts, or our late-night games of capture the flag, played (dangerously) by the light of the moon and the occasional flashlight.

This recipe is inspired by the drink my grandmother has out all summer long: her delightfully refreshing basil lemonade—extra tart! I went ahead and added some berries and froze it into sorbet. And I will let you in on a little secret: Though this makes for a wonderful family-friendly dessert, it also happens to pair perfectly with a pour of vodka, tequila, or a simple splash of bubbly Prosecco (or Cava, or Lambrusco, or Champers, duh) if you're looking to put your guests in an especially festive mood.

MAKES 1 QUART

1 cup granulated sugar

1 cup lightly packed fresh basil leaves

6 cups frozen berries (blueberries, strawberries, blackberries, raspberries)

3/4 cup fresh lemon juice (about 4 lemons)—taste yours before adding this whole quantity; we really like it tart!

In a medium saucepan, combine the sugar and 1 cup water and bring to a boil over medium-high heat. Stir occasionally until the sugar is dissolved, then add the basil, remove from the heat, cover the pan, and set aside to steep for 15 minutes. Strain the syrup (discard the basil leaves) and refrigerate until well chilled.

In a blender, combine the frozen blueberries, lemon juice, and chilled basil syrup. Blend until smooth, then pour the mixture into a flat-bottomed freezer-safe pan or container. Cover the pan and freeze until the sorbet is firm enough to scoop, about 2 hours.

VARIATION: *To make granita, pour the mixture into a 9 x 13-inch pan and freeze until the mixture starts to crystallize, 45 minutes to 1 hour. Use a fork to rake the mixture every 30 minutes until it's completely icy and frozen, about 3 hours.*

CRISP GINGERSNAPS

My grandmother is part Swedish, and any dessert with ginger makes me think of her. She's a huge fan of warm gingerbread, hot from the oven with a spoon of gently whipped cream. But gingersnaps are her real weakness. Every winter, I look forward to sitting by the fire in her kitchen, with a little pile of these wonderfully warming, spiced cookies and a mug of tea to dunk them into so they soften up just a little. They're perfect to have on hand in the cookie jar for a little after-dinner digestive that's not too sweet—the ginger is so soothing. And any broken bits at the bottom of the jar are amazing crumbled over ice cream (try it with coffee flavor, stoppp.).

MAKES 2½ DOZEN COOKIES

- 2½ cups all-purpose flour
- 2 teaspoons ground ginger
- 2 teaspoons ground cardamom
- 1 teaspoon ground cinnamon
- ¼ teaspoon freshly grated nutmeg
- ½ teaspoon kosher salt
- Freshly cracked black pepper (optional)
- ½ teaspoon baking soda
- ¾ cup packed dark brown sugar
- ¼ cup molasses
- 2 tablespoons heavy cream
- 1½ sticks (6 ounces) unsalted butter, melted
- 2-inch piece fresh ginger, peeled and finely grated
- ½ cup turbinado sugar for garnish (optional)

In a medium bowl, whisk together the flour, ground ginger, cardamom, cinnamon, nutmeg, salt, pepper to taste (if using), and baking soda.

In a large bowl, whisk together the dark brown sugar, molasses, and cream until well combined. Add the melted butter and fresh ginger and whisk to combine, then add the flour mixture and stir with a wooden spoon until the dough is well mixed.

Divide the dough into 3 equal pieces and wrap each in plastic wrap. Refrigerate until completely hard and cold, at least 2 hours or preferably overnight.

Preheat the oven to 350°F. Line a baking sheet with parchment paper.

Roll a piece of dough between 2 sheets of parchment paper to an ⅛-inch thickness. Transfer the dough (still in the parchment) to the refrigerator to chill while you repeat with the other two pieces of dough.

Remove the first sheet of dough and peel away the top sheet of parchment. Use a 2-inch cookie cutter to stamp out rounds (or any shape you like), then carefully transfer the cookies to the prepared baking sheet, leaving 1 inch between cookies. Set the scraps aside. Sprinkle the turbinado sugar (if using) onto the cookies before baking.

Bake the cookies for 10 to 12 minutes, until they are firm and evenly browned. Slide the parchment onto a wire rack and cool completely. Line the baking sheet with a new piece of parchment paper, and continue with the remaining sheets of dough. Gather the scraps and lightly roll them out. Stamp out as many cookies as possible, discarding any leftover scraps. Store the cooled cookies in an airtight container for up to 1 week.

GLASS-PRESSED COOKIES

A fun way to make these cookies with kids, especially if you don't feel like rolling and cutting out cookies, is to scoop out about 1 tablespoon of dough and roll it to make a 1-inch diameter ball (a great place to put tiny hands to work!). Roll the ball in turbinado sugar and set it on a baking sheet lined with parchment paper. Repeat until you have 12 cookies to a sheet, leaving 2 inches between the cookies. Dip the bottom of a juice glass in flour (choose a glass with a decorative bottom for pretty designs on your cookies), then use it to flatten out each dough ball until it is 1/4 inch thick. Move the parchment paper with the pressed cookie dough to a baking sheet and place in the refrigerator. Continue forming cookies on a new piece of parchment. Stack the layers of parchment paper on top of each other and refrigerate the sheets of cookies for 30 minutes or overnight, then bake 1 sheet of cookies at a time using another baking sheet. (Taking the one from the fridge straight to the oven might warp your pan.)

BLUEBERRY-CHAMOMILE COMPOTE

This compote is supereasy to make, and yields a surprising flavor combination that goes beautifully spooned over toast or yogurt in the morning, a slice of pie or cake (try the Blueberry Tea Cake on page 298), with cheese for an appetizer, or added to a simple scoop of ice cream to immediately make something store-bought look homemade and *arteeeeesanal*—which means better.

MAKES 2 CUPS

- **1/4 cup granulated sugar**
- **2 tablespoons honey**
- **3 chamomile tea bags**
- **2 1/2 cups fresh or frozen blueberries**
- **1 teaspoon cornstarch**
- **1 tablespoon fresh lemon or lime juice**
- **1/4 teaspoon kosher salt**

In a large skillet, bring 1/2 cup water to a boil over medium-high heat. Add the sugar, stir to dissolve, then stir in the honey. Remove from the heat and add the tea bags. Cover the skillet and set aside for 10 minutes to steep. Remove the tea bags, pressing on them with a spoon to extract as much liquid as possible.

Return the chamomile syrup to a simmer over medium-high heat and add the blueberries. Cook until the blueberries start to pop, about 3 minutes. Stir the cornstarch into the lemon juice and add to the blueberries with the salt. Cook 1 minute more, then remove from heat. The mixture will thicken further as it cools. When the compote cools completely, store in an airtight container in the fridge for up to 1 week.

BLUEBERRY TEA CAKE

I have fantasies about living in London one day, but the closest I'll come for now is having tea time with my daughter on the regular. She'll pour me fake tea from her plastic tea set all day long, and she goes bananas when I set up the real thing (warm milk and sugar for Philo; creamy Earl Grey for Mommy) and let her help me make a batch of this light, moist vanilla cake, dotted with blueberries that explode in your mouth and topped with a crisp brown-sugar streusel.

I've used this batter to make muffins, a loaf, and a single layer cake, and I love that it's a delectable dessert or afternoon delight that requires no fancy frosting or special technique to make perfectly every time. And when your whole house is perfumed with caramelizing sugar and fruit, you may be well on your way to a weekly tradition. It's not the healthiest, nor the least healthy, cake out there. It's just right for everyday celebrations, which is what this book is all about.

MAKES ONE 9-INCH SQUARE CAKE

- **2 sticks (8 ounces) plus 1 tablespoon unsalted butter, at room temperature**
- **2 1/2 cups all-purpose flour**
- **2/3 cup packed light brown sugar**
- **Kosher salt**
- **1/2 teaspoon baking powder**
- **1/4 teaspoon baking soda**
- **3/4 cup sour cream**
- **2 tablespoons fresh lemon juice**
- **3/4 cup granulated sugar**
- **3 large eggs**
- **2 teaspoons pure vanilla extract**
- **2 cups fresh or frozen blueberries**

Preheat the oven to 350°F. Grease a 9-inch square cake pan with 1/2 tablespoon of the butter, lay down two sheets of parchment paper perpendicular to each other, leaving overhang to use as tabs to lift the cake out when it is cooked, and grease again with another 1/2 tablespoon butter.

To make the streusel, in a medium bowl, whisk together 1 1/4 cups of the flour, 1/3 cup of the brown sugar, and a pinch of salt. Melt 6 tablespoons of the butter in the microwave. Drizzle in the melted butter and use a fork to stir the mixture together until large streusel-like crumbs form. Set the streusel aside.

To make the batter, in a large bowl, whisk together the remaining 1 1/4 cups of the flour, the baking powder, baking soda, and 1 teaspoon salt. Set aside.

In a small bowl, stir together the sour cream and lemon juice. Set aside.

In a stand mixer fitted with the paddle attachment, combine the granulated sugar and the remaining 1/3 cup brown sugar and 10 tablespoons butter and cream on low speed until the mixture is combined. Increase the speed to medium-high and cream until the butter is airy, about 2 minutes. Reduce the speed to medium and add the eggs one at a time, beating well and scraping the sides and bottom of the bowl as needed between each addition. Add the vanilla and beat to combine.

Reduce the speed to medium-low and add half the reserved flour mixture, then the sour cream mixture, then the rest of the flour mixture, mixing until combined and scraping down the bowl as needed. Remove the bowl from the stand and fold in the blueberries.

Scrape the mixture into the prepared baking dish. Top evenly with the streusel and bake for 1 hour to 1 hour 15 minutes, until a cake tester inserted into the center of the cake comes out with just a crumb or two attached. The top will be a rich golden brown under the streusel, and the cake will give springy resistance to pressure.

Use the parchment paper to remove the cake from the pan, then discard and cool the cake completely on a wire rack. Cut into squares and serve, or cover with a dome or plastic wrap for up to 3 days (though there's no chance it lasts that long in your kitchen).

TIP: *This batter works very nicely in a muffin tin, a loaf pan, or practically any baking dish. The cook time will vary depending on whether you use a dark coated pan, cast iron, or glass dish, so just keep an eye out for the golden brown top and springy texture to make sure you don't overcook.*

PORT-BRAISED APPLE AND PEAR CRISP

Everyone knows and loves apple pie. But when you're looking for a riff that takes about one-tenth the work for all the payoff, this is your girl. I combine apples and pears to get a little variety from bite to bite, and the addition of port makes this a distinctly grown-up dessert—with the bonus thrill of turning the fruit a glowing garnet red. The streusel topping is my lazy-girl's life hack for when I have zero interest in making a real crust. And really, it's not much of a trade-off when the result is luscious, juicy fruit topped with a crisp, sugary, almost cookie-like coating.

MAKES 6 SERVINGS

2 Granny Smith apples, peeled, halved, cored, and thinly sliced
1 Bosc pear, peeled, halved, cored, and thinly sliced
1 cup packed light brown sugar
2-inch piece fresh ginger, peeled and grated
1½ teaspoons cornstarch
½ teaspoon ground cinnamon
½ teaspoon kosher salt
1¼ cups ruby port wine or apple cider
1½ cups white whole wheat flour
½ cup roughly chopped pecans
1 teaspoon ground ginger
1 stick (4 ounces) unsalted butter, melted
Vanilla ice cream for serving
Honey for serving

Preheat the oven to 375°F.

In an 8- or 9-inch square baking dish, toss the apples, pear, ½ cup of the brown sugar, the fresh ginger, cornstarch, cinnamon, and ¼ teaspoon of the salt. Add the port and stir to combine.

In a medium bowl, combine the flour, pecans, ground ginger, and remaining ½ cup brown sugar and ¼ teaspoon salt. Pour the melted butter around the sides of the bowl and use a fork to stir and rake the mixture together into large streusel-type crumbs.

Sprinkle the crumbs over the fruit and bake the crisp 35 to 40 minutes, until the juices bubble around the edges in thick, slow bubbles. (If the streusel topping starts to get dark too quickly, tent it with a sheet of foil.)

Serve the crisp warm with a scoop of vanilla ice cream and a drizzle of honey.

CHOCOLATE TRUFFLE ANIMAL COOKIES

I made these thinking they would be a nice treat to have around the house for kidlets rather than the boxed animal crackers we all grew up with—delicious, but often full of processed fats and corn syrup. Of course, I also thought it would be fun to make them chocolate, too. They baked up and were cute, if a little rougher around the edges than the traditional forms. And then I tried one. Holy moly.

The chocolate is deep and rich, and the cookies are crisp but tender. They basically melt in your mouth. They're like a chocolate truffle made babies with an animal cracker, hence the name. I think the kids liked them, too, but to be honest, the adults ate so many I'm not even sure if they got any.

MAKES 2 TO 3 DOZEN COOKIES (DEPENDING ON THE SIZE OF THE CUTTER)

- 1/2 cup all-purpose flour
- 1/2 cup whole wheat flour
- 1/2 cup Dutch process cocoa powder
- 1/2 teaspoon baking soda
- 1/2 teaspoon kosher salt
- 1 stick (4 ounces) unsalted butter, at room temperature
- 2/3 cup packed light brown sugar
- 2 tablespoons honey
- Milk for serving

In a medium bowl, whisk together the flours, cocoa, baking soda, and salt.

In a stand mixer fitted with the paddle attachment, cream the butter with the brown sugar on low speed until combined. Increase the speed to medium, add the honey, and cream until the mixture is airy, 3 to 4 minutes, scraping down the sides and bottom of the bowl as needed.

Reduce the speed to medium-low and add the flour mixture, mixing until there aren't any butter streaks left in the dough, about 30 seconds. The dough will look a bit dry and sandy.

Place a large sheet of parchment paper on a work surface and set the dough on top. With another piece of parchment, press the dough into a disc about 1/2 inch thick. Use a rolling pin to roll the dough between the two sheets of parchment to a rectangle that is 1/8 inch thick. Slide the parchment onto a rimmed baking sheet and refrigerate for 30 minutes or up to 3 days.

Preheat the oven to 350°F.

Remove the top layer of parchment and use it to line a rimmed baking sheet (trim to the size of the baking sheet so it fits in nicely). Use fun cookie cutters to stamp out as many cookies as possible—animal shapes are great, but any theme is fun, and you can use an upside-down glass with a thin rim if needed. Stamp them out close together so you don't have a whole lot of dough scraps.

Use an offset spatula to transfer the stamped out shapes to the lined baking sheet. Gather the scraps and gently press them together (if the dough gets difficult to work with, refrigerate it for 10 to 20 minutes before proceeding), then re-roll and stamp out a few more cookies; discard the remaining scraps.

Bake for 12 minutes, or until the cookies are dry and firm around the edges and the centers still give slightly to light pressure. Slide the parchment onto a wire rack to cool the cookies. Serve with milk. Store any leftovers in an airtight container for up to 5 days.

PISTACHIO CAKES WITH ROSE-CARDAMOM ICING

This dessert is an homage to my family in Turkey, where nearly every dessert will include pistachios in some way. You rarely find these divine little green nuts used in the United States except as oversalted snack food at the airport. But they're delightfully rich and buttery, adding a mellow sweetness and a densely moist texture to these cakes.

I'm also obsessed with cardamom, another ingredient that's not used very often in the States but is awesome in everything from tea to rice to pudding. It's a flavor all its own—but it's usually in chai tea, so you've probably tasted it before.

I've made these bad boys gluten-free with a combo of pistachios, almonds, and coconut and tapioca flour, which gives you a very dense and moist cake as opposed to the lighter crumb you might get with all-purpose flour. The technique is basically a lot of blending in the food processor, so don't be overwhelmed by the long ingredient list. You bake them in a muffin tin and turn them out upside down, giving you the elegant cone-shaped cakes that look oh-so-fancy when you glaze them with a simple royal icing scented with rose water. Pinkies up!

Putting rose or cornflower petals on top is totally optional, but they're worth grabbing from a local Middle Eastern food store or online if you want an extra-high-impact dessert. These cakes end up so dainty and beautiful, it's (almost) a shame to eat them.

MAKES 12 MINI-CAKES

CAKES

- Cooking spray
- 1 cup raw pistachios
- 3/4 cup slivered almonds
- 1/3 cup coconut flour
- 3 tablespoons tapioca flour
- 1 1/4 teaspoons baking powder
- 1 teaspoon ground cardamom
- 1/4 teaspoon baking soda
- 1 teaspoon kosher salt
- 2 large eggs
- 2/3 cup granulated sugar
- 3/4 cup 2% Greek yogurt
- 2 teaspoons pure vanilla extract
- 1/4 cup extra-virgin olive oil

(Ingredients continue on the next page.)

To make the cakes, preheat the oven to 350°F. Line 12 cups of a muffin tin with paper liners or lightly coat with cooking spray.

In a food processor, process the pistachios and almonds until finely ground, about 15 seconds.

Sift the coconut flour, tapioca flour, baking powder, cardamom, baking soda, and salt into a large bowl. Whisk in the nut mixture.

In a stand mixer fitted with the whisk attachment, whip the eggs and sugar until the mixture is thick, creamy, and pale, about 2 minutes.

In a small bowl, whisk together the yogurt and vanilla, then, with the mixer on medium-low speed, add the pistachio mixture in three additions, alternating with the yogurt mixture. Drizzle in the olive oil, then increase the speed to medium-high and mix for 15 seconds.

Divide the batter among the muffin cups and bake for 20 to 22 minutes, until a cake tester inserted into the center of a mini-cake comes out clean. Remove the cakes from the oven (but leave the oven on). Let the cakes cool completely in the pan, then turn

GLAZE AND GARNISH

1/4 cup pistachios

1 1/4 cups powdered sugar

3/4 cup heavy cream

1 teaspoon rose water

Dried flower petals: rose, cornflower, or lavender are beautiful (optional)

them out of the pan onto a wire rack set over a baking sheet and leave them upside down (flat bottom facing up).

For the garnish, place the pistachios on a rimmed baking sheet and toast them in the oven until fragrant, about 6 minutes, shaking to redistribute halfway through. Transfer the pistachios to a cutting board to cool, then roughly chop them.

Meanwhile, to make the glaze, in a medium bowl, whisk together the powdered sugar and cream, then add the rose water and 1 tablespoon water, whisking until well combined.

If you used paper liners, carefully remove them from the mini-cakes and discard. Spoon glaze over each cake. (If the glaze doesn't spill over the sides of the cupcake in long, slow drips, mix in 1 to 2 more teaspoons of water.) Place about 1 teaspoon of chopped toasted pistachios over each mini-cake and add a few rose petals (if using). Let the glaze set up for about 20 minutes before serving. These are best if eaten within 2 days of baking.

VARIATION: *Orange flower water is also a beautiful and exotic flavor—try using it in place of the rose water.*

VEGAN PBJ PAW PRINTS

These delicious peanut butter and jelly cookies are shaped like adorable bear claws—fun for kids and delicious for adults. They're rich yet relatively healthy, given the flaxseeds and oats that replace any all-purpose flour, plus only 1 cup of sugar in the dough.

MAKES 2½ DOZEN COOKIES

- **½ cup quick-cooking oats**
- **1 heaping tablespoon flaxseeds or flaxmeal**
- **½ teaspoon baking soda**
- **1 teaspoon pure vanilla extract**
- **½ cup granulated sugar**
- **½ cup packed light brown sugar**
- **½ teaspoon kosher salt**
- **1 cup creamy peanut butter or sunflower butter**
- **½ cup of your favorite jam or jelly**
- **⅓ cup peanuts (optional, for the toes)**

Using a small food processor, pulverize the oats (and flaxseeds, if using) to a fine powder. Transfer the mixture to a medium bowl (if using flaxmeal, add it now) along with ⅓ cup water, the baking soda, and vanilla. Use a wooden spoon to combine.

Stir in the sugars and salt, then stir in the peanut butter until the dough is well combined.

Line two rimmed baking sheets with parchment paper. Form the dough into about thirty 1-inch balls and divide them between the prepared baking sheets, setting the cookies about 2 inches apart. Use your finger to make an indention in the center of each ball and fill each with ½ teaspoon of the jam. Stick 3 peanut halves (if using) into the top of the ball to make "toes." Place the baking sheets in the refrigerator and chill for 20 minutes.

Preheat the oven to 350°F.

Bake each sheet of the paw prints for 15 minutes total, or until they are firm. Remove the cookies from the oven and let them cool on the baking sheet for 5 minutes, then transfer to a wire rack to cool completely. The cookies can be stored in an airtight container for up to 1 week.

TIP: *Roll up some dough—if it crumbles apart easily, mix in 1 more tablespoon of water. The dough should just hold together—a lot of this depends on the kind of peanut butter you use. Try buying freshly ground at the store, or a natural no-sugar-added peanut butter without stabilizers.*

OUTLAW CARROT CAKE WITH BROWN SUGAR BUTTERCREAM

Ooooh, carrot cake. You make me crazy. I love you so much, you rich, sultry combo of carrots, nuts, sugar and spice. But why must you always have raisins to ruin you?

I've gone totally rogue, and this is my outlaw carrot cake. I'm taking the raisins out, and the cream cheese frosting, too. Whipped brown sugar buttercream gently coats my dense, spiced, fruitless, not-too-sweet cake. Don't start yelling at me about how this isn't like any carrot cake you've ever had before. It's not, you're right! It's better. And (slightly) better for you. Except, maybe, the frosting . . . I bet we're about even there. But wait, I'm sorry—we're talking about BROWN SUGAR BUTTERCREAM, so there is just no comparison.

I've added carrots two ways—some blended together with the wet ingredients and some shredded and folded in at the end, so you get maximum flavor and texture. It's so good to be bad.

MAKES 1 LOAF CAKE

CAKE

1/3 cup melted butter, plus extra to grease the pan

1 cup whole wheat flour (white whole wheat flour will yield a lighter texture)

3/4 cups all-purpose flour

2 teaspoons baking powder

3/4 teaspoon baking soda

1 teaspoon ground cinnamon

1 1/2 teaspoons ground cardamom

1/2 teaspoon kosher salt

1/4 cup molasses

3/4 cup packed dark brown sugar

2 large eggs

1 teaspoon pure vanilla extract

1 cup pureed cooked carrots (see Tip)

3 carrots, scrubbed, trimmed and coarsely grated on the medium holes of a box grater

3/4 cup walnuts and/or pecans, toasted (see Toasting Nuts, page 14) and chopped

(Ingredients continue on the next page.)

To make the cake, preheat the oven to 350°F. Lightly coat an 8 1/2 x 4 1/2-inch loaf pan with butter. Line with parchment paper, leaving enough overhang to use as handles, then coat with more butter. This will make removing your cake a breeze.

In a large bowl, whisk together the flours, baking powder, baking soda, cinnamon, cardamom, and salt.

In a large bowl, use a hand mixer or whisk to combine the molasses, brown sugar, eggs, and vanilla. Add the carrot puree and mix to combine. With the hand mixer on medium speed or whisking vigorously, slowly pour the melted butter into the carrot blend to emulsify (it helps to put your bowl on a nonslip surface, like a damp kitchen towel).

Pour the carrot mixture into the flour mixture and stir, using a wooden spoon, until just combined. Fold in the grated carrots and chopped nuts.

Scrape the batter into the prepared loaf pan and bake the cake for 40 minutes, or until the center bounces back to light pressure and a cake tester inserted into the center comes out clean. Let the cake cool for 10 minutes in the pan, then gently lift the cake from the pan using the parchment paper overhang. Remove and discard the paper and let the cake cool completely on a wire rack lined with parchment paper.

VANILLA BROWN SUGAR BUTTERCREAM

2/3 cup unsalted butter, at room temperature

1 vanilla bean, halved lengthwise (see Vanilla Bean 101, page 48)

1 teaspoon pure vanilla extract

1 3/4 cups powdered sugar, sifted

1/3 cup packed dark brown sugar

3 tablespoons heavy cream

Flaky sea salt, to finish

While the cake cools, make the buttercream. Place the butter in a large bowl. Scrape the seeds from the vanilla bean into the bowl and add the vanilla extract. Using a hand mixer, beat on medium speed until the mixture is light and airy, 1 to 2 minutes, scraping down the sides and bottom of the bowl as needed.

Add the sugars and mix on low speed to combine. Increase the speed to medium for 30 seconds. Stop the mixer, add the cream, and change to the whisk attachment. Beat on medium speed until combined, then increase the speed to medium-high and beat until airy, 1 to 2 minutes. This yields a beautiful, very light and fluffy buttercream. (If you don't have the whisk attachment and want to use the regular hand mixer to complete the frosting, it will yield less fluffy—but still delicious—results.)

Frost the cooled cake with the buttercream, sprinkle it lightly with flaky sea salt, slice, and serve.

TIP: *I will often buy organic carrot baby food when making this recipe (butternut squash or pumpkin baby food works too, or canned pumpkin puree), but if you would like to make pureed carrots from scratch, start with 1 pound carrots, scrubbed, trimmed, and cut into chunks. In a medium saucepan, combine the carrots with water to cover. Bring to a boil over medium heat and cook until soft and easily smashed with a fork, about 20 minutes. Drain them well (or the cake will be too wet!), cool, and puree in a food processor. You can do this well in advance and freeze.*

VARIATION: *Bake the cake in two lightly greased 9-inch round cake pans and double the frosting recipe for a pretty layer cake. Or bake it as cupcakes. Different cake and muffin tin sizes will affect baking time, so just watch for doneness. A toothpick inserted into the center of the finished cake should come out clean with just a few moist crumbs attached.*

NUTTY BANANA "ICE CREAM"

This is one of my favorite all-pleasure, no-guilt desserts because it tastes like the creamiest ice cream, but the only sugar comes from ripe bananas. You can make the entire thing vegan if you use a splash of dairy alternative milk to blend (almond, hemp, and coconut milks are all nice). Plus the protein from the nut butter . . . pull up a spoon!

MAKES 1 PINT

- **2 large very ripe bananas, peeled and cut into thirds, then frozen**
- **2 tablespoons nut butter (almond, cashew, or peanut)**
- **1 teaspoon pure vanilla extract**
- **1/4 cup nut milk, or whole or reduced-fat (2%) dairy milk**
- **1/4 teaspoon kosher salt**
- **1 1/2 teaspoons Frangelico, amaretto, or vodka (optional)**

In a blender, combine the frozen bananas, nut butter, vanilla, milk, salt, and liquor (if using). Blend until smooth.

Transfer the mixture to an airtight container and freeze until it is a scoopable consistency, about 3 hours.

TIP: *Adding a little bit of alcohol to ice cream helps it stay smooth and creamy rather than become very icy, because alcohol has such a low freezing temperature. But too much alcohol will make it so the ice cream never sets up, not necessarily a bad thing if you're in the mood for a boozy milkshake!*

VANILLA POTS DE CRÈME

Every time I go to a fancy restaurant and they have chocolate pots de crème on the menu, I curse them. Why not vanilla?! Vanilla, thick and creamy, with hints of caramel and flecks of vanilla bean, why won't they show you any love? I will. I will show you lots of love. I will show you this insanely easy (if not superhealthy) take on a thicker vanilla pudding or custard, and then we're going to top it with insanely easy candied pecans (which, as an aside, should always be in your cupboard to throw on salads or yogurt or an ice cream sundae with roasted strawberries, as seen on page 278—anywhere that needs a little pop of sweet, buttery, candied goodness), and then we're going eat our little hearts out and think about how much better this is than eating chocolate pots de crème at a fancy restaurant.

MAKES 6 SERVINGS

2 large eggs plus 5 large egg yolks

1/2 cup sugar

1/2 teaspoon kosher salt

1 vanilla bean, split lengthwise (see Vanilla Bean 101, page 48)

2 2/3 cups heavy cream

Flaky sea salt for serving

Candied Pecans (page 278)

In a medium saucepan, whisk the whole eggs, egg yolks, sugar, and salt. Scrape in the vanilla seeds. Whisk in the cream, then set the pan over medium heat and whisk constantly until the mixture is thick enough to coat the back of a wooden spoon, 5 to 6 minutes (don't let the mixture boil or the yolks will scramble—if you let a little scrambling happen by accident, don't worry: We're going to strain the whole thing out to make it smooth, but too much scrambling will affect the taste).

Strain the mixture through a fine-mesh sieve and into a large measuring cup, then divide it among six 6-ounce ramekins. Arrange the ramekins on a baking sheet, then wrap the sheet with plastic wrap and refrigerate for at least 2 hours or up to 3 days. If you need the space, you can just wrap and refrigerate individual ramekins.

Serve the chilled pots de crème sprinkled with flaky sea salt and the candied pecans sprinkled on top.

TIP: *Save the vanilla bean! Grind it to a fine powder with sugar to make vanilla sugar for baking or drop it into a bottle of vodka or bourbon to make vanilla-infused spirits.*

LILLET
1872
LILLET

CHEWY COCONUT-CHOCOLATE CHIP COOKIES

Baking is the best babysitter. I can't tell you the number of times Philo has been on the verge of an epic meltdown and getting her into the kitchen to crack eggs, mix, measure, and mess around has been the only—and perfect—antidote.

For these ultra-chewy and tender cookies, I started with the traditional chocolate chip cookie, took out some sugar and half the butter (but left enough to keep it delicious!), swapped the flours, and added oats and shredded coconut, which toast and caramelize to give the cookies an extra chewy texture.

The most important step in the whole process is one I learned from a friend of my grandmother's named Mona Lisa—her smile is great, but her cookie trick is a national treasure that will guarantee you cookies with perfectly crisp edges and soft, chewy centers. Here's what you need to do: take the baking sheet out of the oven halfway through baking and bang it hard on the open oven door before rotating the pan and returning it to finish baking.

The other trick is to let the dough rest in the fridge for 30 minutes or (preferably) overnight, which allows for more even cooking (the ingredients will all be the same temperature), and a rested dough will give you richer, more intensely delicious flavors.

MAKES 2 DOZEN COOKIES

1/2 cup whole wheat flour
1 cup quick-cooking rolled oats
1 cup unsweetened shredded coconut
1 teaspoon baking soda
1 teaspoon kosher salt
1 stick (4 ounces) unsalted butter, at room temperature
1/2 cup packed light brown sugar
1/4 cup granulated sugar
1 teaspoon pure vanilla extract
1 large egg, at room temperature, plus 1 egg yolk
1/2 cup semisweet chocolate chips

In a medium bowl, whisk together the flour, oats, coconut, baking soda, and salt.

In a stand mixer fitted with the paddle attachment, cream the butter, brown sugar, and granulated sugar on medium-high speed fluffy and yellow.

Add the vanilla and the eggs, one at a time, beating after each addition for 30 seconds.

Reduce the speed to medium-low and add the flour mixture in three parts, beating for about 10 seconds after each addition. Add the chocolate chips and mix until just combined.

Cover the bowl with plastic wrap and refrigerate for at least 30 minutes or overnight.

Preheat the oven to 350°F. Line a rimmed baking sheet with parchment paper.

Scoop out portions of dough the size of golf balls, roll them between your palms loosely, and place them 2 inches apart on the baking sheet (you'll need to bake the cookies in several batches). Bake for

14 minutes, or until the cookies are set around the edges. Halfway through baking, remove the pan from the oven and drop it onto a heat-safe flat surface, such as the open oven door (this deflates the cookies, creating a deliciously chewy center and crisp edges—in other words . . . perfect!). Immediately return the cookies to the oven, rotating the pan 180 degrees, and complete baking, until the center resists light pressure but is still somewhat soft.

Let the cookies cool on the baking sheet for 5 minutes, then transfer them to a wire rack to cool completely. Repeat to make the rest of the cookies.

TIP: *When you're measuring flour, don't scoop it from the bag or jar with your measuring cup, as this can pack the flour and overfill, meaning your cookies will be too dry. Instead, spoon flour into your measuring cup until it's mounded, then use the flat side of a knife to scrape off the excess and make level.*

TIP: *To store extra dough and make future cookie baking a breeze, roll out balls and freeze them on a cookie sheet. Once they're set, transfer them to a resealable freezer bag or airtight container and keep them frozen for up to 3 months. Let the dough balls sit out at room temperature for 15 minutes before baking as usual.*

TIP: *Make these into ice cream sandwiches! Let your favorite ice cream soften for 10 to 15 minutes, then scoop a dollop onto an upside-down cookie. Top with another cookie and press down to seal, then freeze for 20 minutes before serving.*

CHOCOLATE-DULCE DE LECHE LAYER CAKE

I feel like this recipe's title should be all the incentive you need to rush into the kitchen and start preparing to enjoy chocolate cake lavished with dulce de leche . . . cream cheese . . . freaking frosting!!! But just in case you are unsure of how ridiculous this combo is, let me tell you that chocolate cake is chocolate cake (this one is extra chocolatey, and made with whole wheat pastry flour, almond flour, and sour cream) and dulce de leche is truly one of the great gifts to sweet tooths (teeth?) everywhere. The sticky-sweet, buttery-rich sauce that comes from slowly cooking sweetened condensed milk is an earthy caramel, perfect for topping sundaes, sandwiching between cookies, drizzling over warm brownies, and now blending with cream cheese to make a topping unlike any other.

My advice is to make a double batch of frosting, because somehow a large amount always goes missing.

MAKES ONE 2-LAYER CAKE

DULCE DE LECHE FROSTING

One 14-ounce can sweetened condensed milk

7 tablespoons cream cheese, at room temperature

1/3 cup plus 2 tablespoons powdered sugar

1 3/4 sticks (7 ounces) unsalted butter, at room temperature

Flaky sea salt

CHOCOLATE CAKE

2 sticks (8 ounces) unsalted butter, at room temperature, plus 1 tablespoon for greasing the pans

1/2 cup Dutch process cocoa powder

1/4 cup boiling water

1 1/2 cups packed light brown sugar

4 large eggs

2 teaspoons pure vanilla extract

(Ingredients continue on the next page.)

To make the dulce de leche, set the can of sweetened condensed milk on its side in a large, high saucepan and cover with water so it is completely submerged. Bring the water to a simmer over medium-high heat, then reduce the heat to medium and gently simmer for 2 hours, adding water as needed to keep the can covered. It's important to keep it covered with water the entire cooking time so that the temperature inside the can stays at an even 212°F—otherwise, you risk it exploding! (scared emoji face) Use tongs to transfer the can to a kitchen towel and set aside to cool.

To make the chocolate cake, use 1 tablespoon of the butter to grease two 9-inch round cake pans. To make it extra easy to remove the cooked cakes from their pans, cut out two circles of parchment paper to fit into the bottom of your cake pans. Line the bottom of each pan with a paper circle, then flip the paper over so both sides are greased. In a small bowl, whisk the cocoa powder with the boiling water until smooth. Set aside.

In a stand mixer fitted with the paddle attachment, cream the remaining 2 sticks butter and the brown sugar on medium speed until light and airy, about 2 minutes. Reduce the speed to medium-low and add the eggs, one at a time, scraping the bowl between additions. Add the vanilla, increase the speed to medium, and beat for 1 minute.

Add the cocoa mixture and beat until just combined.

2 cups whole wheat pastry flour
1/2 cup almond flour
2 1/4 teaspoons baking powder
3/4 teaspoon baking soda
1 1/4 teaspoons kosher salt
1 cup semisweet chocolate chips
1 cup sour cream

In a large bowl, whisk together the flour, almond flour, baking powder, baking soda, salt, and chocolate chips.

With the mixer on low speed, add half the flour mixture to the butter mixture, then the sour cream, then the rest of the flour mixture, scraping down the sides and bottom of the bowl as needed.

Divide the batter between the 2 prepared cake pans, shaking each pan gently to distribute evenly. Bake for 25 minutes, or until the center of the cake layers resists light pressure and a cake tester inserted into the center comes out with just a few moist crumbs attached. Let the cakes cool for 10 minutes in the pans, then run a knife around the edges of the cakes to separate them from the pan, and carefully invert the layers onto a wire rack lined with parchment paper. Set aside to cool completely.

To make the frosting, in a stand mixer fitted with the whisk attachment, beat the cream cheese on medium speed until smooth. Open the sweetened condensed milk can and pour all but 2 tablespoons into the bowl with the cream cheese (save the 2 tablespoons for later). Whip until smooth, then add the powdered sugar and whip on low speed to combine. Increase the speed to medium-high and whip until smooth. Add the butter and whip on medium-high speed until smooth.

Place a cake layer on a cake plate. Add half of the dulce de leche frosting and spread evenly, then place the other cake layer on top. Frost the top and sides of the cake with the remaining frosting. Drizzle the reserved dulce de leche over the top and use a toothpick to swirl it around. Sprinkle flaky sea salt over the top. Slice and serve. (The cake will keep in a covered container for 2 days. If the temperature in your kitchen is very warm, refrigerate the cake, then let it sit out at room temperature for 20 minutes before serving.)

ACKNOWLEDGMENTS

To my family and friends, you have been my willing guinea pigs, stewards, and playmates in the creation of this piece of my heart (and stomach) on paper. Thank you for showing me that dining together should always be a celebration, and for making me the happiest cook! And a special thanks to my *Chew* crew: Mario, Michael, Carla, and Clinton. Together we have consumed more delicious food and had more fun than any humans should be allowed!

Amy Neunsinger, thank you for the handiwork of your sunlit lens, which adorns this book with visual gems. You are obscenely talented, a brilliant mind, and a generous friend, and I am so lucky to know all these things firsthand. Andrew Mitchell, digital guru, thank you for making perfect images even more perfect, and also for being just the Zen Buddha we needed to tame our estrogen fest.

Frances Boswell, I don't know what I loved/needed more: your parenting advice, Chinese herbal remedies, essential four p.m. chocolate, or glorious leftover feasts. To you and your attending kitchen vixens, Christine Buckley, Denise Ginley, and Judy Mancini, thank you for wielding your culinary magic, yielding everyday opulence on plate after festive plate.

Kaitlyn DuRoss, your wonderful, whimsical eye made sure every scene in this book is memorable. Thank you and Sophia Pappas for both indulging and reining in my love of your enviable supply of copper bowls, matte black china, and lace.

Raquel Pelzel, thank you for lending your culinary and mama wisdom to making sure the recipes in this book will be winners at every table, and for being such a dream with whom to cook, chat, and of course, taste all the bites!

David Larabell, book agent extraordinaire, thank you for wanting to own this book as badly as I wanted to write it. And to Mark Mullett, Stephanie Paciullo, Zachary Nadler, Eric Wattenberg, and the rest of my CAA family, you are all a billion bomb emojis and I am so grateful to have you.

To my William Morrow beauties! Cassie Jones, brave editor of my stream-of-consciousness food memories. I have loved every second we get to collaborate. Thank you for having so much fun with me and being into (most of) my weirdness. Kara Zauberman, thank you for being the unbelievably organized brain that kept every ball seamlessly in the air at all times, and even more miraculously, always with a smile! Liate Stehlik and Lynn Grady, thank you for continuing to let me make good on my plans to woo America's taste buds with foods that are decadently healthy and healthily decadent. Anwesha Basu, Michelle Podberezniak, and Tavia Kowalchuk, thank you for letting people know this book exists and is not, in fact, just a several-hundred-page diary I keep on my computer. Mumtaz Mustafa, thanks to you and your beautiful cover—I feel like this book is finally ready for the ball! Suet Chong, considering I read cookbooks like novels, the simplicity, organization, and beauty of the interior of this cookbook were paramount to me. You have outdone yourself! Rachel Meyers and Anna Brower, thank you for bringing it all to life and on to bookshelves!

And finally thank you, John, tireless champion of this and every other project. You are my favorite person with whom to enjoy all my meals—and every moment in between. And thank you to our children, Philomena and John Jr., for being my everyday fireworks, kitchen sidekicks, and the crazy cutests! May we have a million more happy meals together. I love you!

menu inspiration

spring dinner party

Zucchini Ribbons with Mint and Pomegranate 109

Wheat Berries with Sweet Potato and Charred Chile Vinaigrette 181

Apricot-Rosemary Glazed Lamb Chops 259

Outlaw Carrot Cake with Brown Sugar Buttercream 305

summer dinner party

Watermelon-Goat Cheese Salad 98

Cauliflower and Zucchini Orecchiette 187

Whole Roasted Branzino 219

Chocolate–Dulce de Leche Layer Cake 313

fall dinner party

Roasted Plums with Tahini Dressing 97

Truffle Salt Roast Chicken with Lentils and Squash 265

Baked Cider Donuts 275

winter dinner party

Burst Grape and Radicchio Salad 102

Shredded Root Vegetable Pancakes 164

Hoisin-Glazed Pork and Turkey Meatloaf 250

Vanilla Pots de Crème 308

brunch with the girls

Shirred Eggs with Bacon and Kale 19

Sunshine Citrus Muffins 26

Spinach Salad with Crispy Chickpeas and Apples 92

date night

Shaved Brussels Sprout Salad with Pecorino and Capers 94

Mussels Provençal with Toasts 213

Port-Braised Apple and Pear Crisp 295

easy weeknight

Kale and Plum Salad with Miso Vinaigrette 91

Rigatoni with Green Monster Pesto and Kale Chips 179

Jerk Chicken and Sweet Potatoes 236

Sour Apple Pops 281

or Crisp Gingersnaps 289

playdate

Herby Falafel (kids *love* these, and adults do, too) 141

Italian-Style Turkey Meatballs 252

Chocolate Truffle Animal Cookies 297

Vegan PBJ Paw Prints 303

boss coming over

Saint's Salad with Ginger-Maple Vinaigrette 103

Cider-Braised Brisket with Red Cabbage and Apples 232

Peach and Almond Galette 285

picnic

Seared Garlic-Lime Shrimp Banh Mi 117

Philly Cheesesteak Quesadillas 128

Thai Niçoise Salad 106

Sweet Potatoes with Fresh Cherries and Pecans 148

Blueberry Tea Cake 293

summer luncheon

Avocado Toast with Lemon-Chile Oil 127

Grilled Chicken Paillards with Melon Salsa Fresca 230

Basil and Berries Lemonade Sorbet 287

grill out

Cucumber, Peach, and Feta Salad 105

Skirt Steak with Brown Sugar–Spice Rub 254

Chewy Coconut-Chocolate Chip Cookies 311

fiesta

Pozole Verde 79

Millet "Burrito Bowl" 196

Carnitas with Fresh Corn Salsa and Spiced Chips 245

Candied Pecan and Roasted Strawberry Sundaes (try the variation on the nuts with a dash of chipotle chile powder to amp up the Latin flair!) 278

middle eastern feast

Feta and Dill Sigara Boreks 122

Harissa-Roasted Carrots with Crispy Caper Gremolata 171

Lamb-Stuffed Peppers 242

Pistachio Cakes with Rose-Cardamom Icing 301

vegan delight brunch

Vegan Veggie Love Muffins 24

White Bean Salad with Celery 93

Zucchini and Delicata Squash Panini with Muhammara 133

Cashew Soba Noodles with Fried Shallots 188

Nutty Banana "Ice Cream" (made with nut or coconut milk) 307

feel-good comfort foods

Oatmeal Banana Nut Bread 13

Warrior Waffles 40

Kale, Sausage, and White Bean Soup 75

Roasted Tomato Soup with Giant Cheesy Herb Croutons 82

Smoky Salmon and Avocado Wedge Salad 216

Curried Egg Salad Sandwich with Dressed Greens 119

Butternut Squash and Ricotta Toast 135

Crispy Brown Rice Pilaf with Merguez and Dates 191

Cauliflower Alfredo Mac 'n' Cheese 194

Almost Mongolian Beef Satay 238

Crispy Chicken with Zucchini 263

Better Brownies 282

clean eats

Frittata with Spinach, Olives, and Chicken Sausage 34

Chocolate-Almond Breakfast Bars 23

Oatmeal Frittata with Cinnamon-Apple Compote 36

Chilled Cucumber-Yogurt Soup 70

Carrot Salad with Parsley and Golden Raisins 110

Warm Spring Pea Soup 85

Warm Lentil-Citrus Salad 100

Quinoa Salad with Lemon, Herbs, and Feta 193

Poached Salmon with Dill Tzatziki 215

Whole Roasted Branzino 219

Grilled Chicken Paillards with Melon Salsa Fresca 230

UNIVERSAL CONVERSION CHART

oven temperature equivalents

250°F = 120°C
275°F = 135°C
300°F = 150°C
325°F = 160°C
350°F = 180°C
375°F = 190°C
400°F = 200°C
425°F = 220°C
450°F = 230°C
475°F = 240°C
500°F = 260°C

measurement equivalents

Measurements should always be level unless directed otherwise.

1/8 teaspoon = 0.5 mL
1/4 teaspoon = 1 mL
1/2 teaspoon = 2 mL
1 teaspoon = 5 mL
1 tablespoon = 3 teaspoons = 1/2 fluid ounce = 15 mL
2 tablespoons = 1/8 cup = 1 fluid ounce = 30 mL
4 tablespoons = 1/4 cup = 2 fluid ounces = 60 mL
5 1/3 tablespoons = 1/3 cup = 3 fluid ounces = 80 mL
8 tablespoons = 1/2 cup = 4 fluid ounces = 120 mL
10 2/3 tablespoons = 2/3 cup = 5 fluid ounces = 160 mL
12 tablespoons = 3/4 cup = 6 fluid ounces = 180 mL
16 tablespoons = 1 cup = 8 fluid ounces = 240 mL

INDEX

Note: Page references in *italics* indicate photographs.

D

Q

R

S

T

V

W

Y

Z